International Law

LAW OF PEACE

N.A. MARYAN GREEN
M.A., LL.B. (Cantab.)

Of the Middle Temple, Barrister
Avocat, Paris Court of Appeal
Former Lecturer in Law, Sheffield University
Former Member of the Secretariat, Council of Europe
Diploma of the Hague Academy of International Law

MACDONALD AND EVANS

Macdonald & Evans Ltd.
Estover, Plymouth PL6 7PZ

First published 1973
Second edition 1982

©

Macdonald & Evans 1982

0 7121 0956 0

Printed in Great Britain by
Butler and Tanner Ltd,
London and Frome

Foreword

From fifty to thirty years ago one would have concluded that there had been reached some grand climacteric in the Anglo-American literature of international law: some watershed's edge comparable to that which the completion of Viner's work marked in the history of the literature of the common law. One would have said, that is, that the whole subject had become too vast to be comprehended any more by single-handed authors. For no comprehensive textbook seemed to have appeared in America since Hyde's work (1922) and none in England since Westlake (1908), excepting always, but still excepting Brierly's brilliant essay on the *Law of Nations* (1928) as no more than an essay. In future, one would have said, the law would be written about in its several departments — treaties, claims, protection and so forth — in books more comparable to *Lewin on Trusts* and *Williston on Contract* than to either the old abridgments or even the institutes which succeeded them.

It has been a striking feature of the last few years, however, that the single-handed textbook has reappeared. Mr Starke, Professor O'Connell, Dr Brownlie, Professor Gregg, Mr Fawcett and Mr Brown have each in turn presented us with their individual, and be it said all most valuable, individual accounts of the whole law — or at least the whole law of peace. All these gentlemen, it is to be remarked, are primarily teachers (at least if Mr Fawcett will accept that title also among the many to which he is entitled). Now Mr Maryan Green, who is primarily an international civil servant, joins this courageous and competent company.

These epithets are used advisedly and with a due deference. For it takes a deal of courage to attempt the exposition of the whole law, and a kind of competence which is distinctive. Sweeping glances are possibly only from an elevated viewpoint selected and attained — and here Mr Maryan Green's confession of a European bias is to be noted. Sweeping glances, too, must be to a degree indifferent to detail. The new abridgments, however, if in consequence they are not devoid of statements with which one can disagree, have by

iii

virtue of their panoramic character a refreshing quality, and a value all of their own, and another is to be greatly welcomed. Mr Maryan Green promises a further volume on the use of force and war. His attention is respectfully directed to his own exposition of the maxim *pacta sunt servanda*.

Clive Parry, LL.D.,
Professor of International Law
at the University of Cambridge

Preface to the First Edition

This volume contains a short exposition of the main rules of the contemporary law of peace. It is hoped, in due course, to produce a second volume which will deal with the use of force short of war, armed conflicts (war) and neutrality.

In a work having the title *Law of Peace*, and particularly one laying claim to contemporaneity, it would not be unreasonable to expect to find sections dealing with international criminal law, international economic law, and perhaps disarmament law. However, their omission is partly a question of arrangement of materials and partly a question of selection. I have preferred a more traditional presentation. The table of contents is taken from the *Model Plan for the Classification of Documents in the field of Public International Law*, which is appended to Resolution (68) 17 of the Committee of Ministers of the Council of Europe (a copy of which may be obtained on request from the Directorate of Information, Council of Europe, Strasbourg). This *Model Plan* is the work of a committee of experts from the member states of the Council of Europe which included some very distinguished international lawyers. It may be said to represent a commonly agreed European view of the content of public international law today.

The statement of the law with regard to treaties, diplomats and consuls, and the sea, is based on the multilateral conventions on these topics, since I believe that the rules set out in these conventions represent a more accurate expression of contemporary international law than any other. The judgment of the majority of the court in the *North Sea Continental Shelf Case* (I.C.J., 1969) does certainly indicate that this view cannot be pressed too far, but a combination of special factors was in evidence in that case.

A special word must be said about the section on international organisations. I consider that the time has come when the treatment of this topic must be something other than an exposition of the law of the United Nations, together with occasional references to other organisations. An attempt has therefore been made to set out a series of rules which may be taken to apply to all international organisations of which there are now more than 200 — unless their constituent instrument provides otherwise. This development will bear some parallel with the early attempts to formulate a company law or law of corporations. As such, it is of course experimental and is offered more in the hope of provoking discussion than as a definitive statement. An adequate presentation of the law of particular organisations, and principally that of the United Nations, would require a separate book; so this part of the *Model Plan* has been omitted. Nor is there any systematic treatment of the specialised agencies and of their complicated interlocking structure with the United Nations (called occasionally "the legal organisation of the international community" or, more accurately, "institutionalised co-operation in economic, social and cultural fields"), although descriptions are given of the International Telecommunications Union and the International Civil Aviation Organisation in the section on the law of the air. The reader is referred to the Appendix to Volume 1 of *Oppenheim's International Law*, seventh edition by Sir Hersch Lauterpacht, for information about specialised and other agencies of the United Nations as they existed in 1957, and to the Carnegie *Manual of International Law* edited by Max Sǿrensen, Chapter 10, for a more up-to-date account.

So far as the presentation of the material is concerned, I have tried as far as possible to divorce myself from any specifically national context (by reaction against some writers who seem too much influenced by the practice of their own state, their own courts, and writers of their own legal tradition). I admit, on the other hand, to an undoubted European bias. I have for example, in some cases, consciously set forth rules which may apply only as a European regional variant of international law. Nor can I be sure that in other places I have not done the same thing unconsciously.

Footnotes have been dispensed with, references to cases and treaties being set out in tables, the latter containing some additional information about treaties, such as if or when they have entered into force, how many states are party to them, where the text may be consulted and so forth. References to other legal writings have, in general, been omitted: in the few places where a work is cited, the name and author are given in the text. Examples taken from state practice illustrating rules set out in the body of the text have been reduced to a minimum. Where examples are given, they have been incorporated in the text. Finally, matters generally to be found in footnotes, subsidiary rules or comment on rules set out in the text, have been either eliminated or incorporated.

Over the four years during which this work has been in preparation,

I have received the constant support and encouragement of Professor Clive Parry, of Cambridge University. I wish to express here my deep sense of gratitude for this, as also for all the help and criticism I received from him during the preparation of the manuscript.

Not being a specialist in every branch of the law of peace, I have sought advice of acknowledged authorities on certain topics. My good fortune and their own generosity have enabled me to consult: Professor Iain MacGibbon, of Edinburgh University, for the parts on sources and the law of the sea; Professor Atle Grahl-Madsen, of the Norwegian School of Economics, Bergen, Norway, for the section on refugees; M. Karel Vasak, Secretary General of the International Institute of Human Rights, for the section on human rights; a friend in the Foreign and Commonwealth Office for the section on consuls; M. Alex-Charles Kiss, distinguished author of the *Répertoire Français de Droit International* for reading the sections on nationality and aliens (more particularly the French version, now under preparation); Mr Francis Jacobs and Mr Andreas Khol, of the Secretariat of the European Commission of Human Rights for much valuable comment on various matters, and the section on international organisations in particular. I am very grateful to each of these friends for the time and trouble they have taken in commenting on and suggesting revision of my drafts, and for their interest and support in the bringing to press of this work. As tradition requires, I am obliged to state that I nevertheless assume sole responsibility for the version now presented.

N.A.M G.

Strasbourg, France
August 1972

Preface to the Second Edition

In the eight years since the Preface to the First Edition was written, the principal development in international law has been in respect to the Law of the Sea. This may be taken as a direct reflection of the fact that technological advances have made it possible to exploit the resources of the bed of the sea at considerable depths, chiefly, of course, for the extraction of petrol and gas. Indeed, in the North Sea is to be found the hub and centre of the single largest new industrial development in Europe, and similarly oil-drilling rigs and platforms and floating hotels for the work force are changing the nature of all those parts of the seas and oceans having a continental shelf. For this reason the whole of the section on seas and waterways has been rewritten. The reader is, however, warned that the law of the sea is in a far from settled state.

The remainder of this edition contains far fewer amendments than the author feared would be necessary when he first presented the work to public appraisal. Account has been taken of a criticism in the British Yearbook of International Law, Vol. 47, concerning the treatment of the International Court of Justice and the question of jurisdiction before that Court. The remainder of the changes concern the bringing up to date of various statistical information, and considerable revision of presentation to make for more palatable reading. Due account has been taken also of the Vienna Convention on the Succession of States in respect of Treaties.

One area which does not seem to require much revision is the section on international organisations. The somewhat revolutionary treatment in the First Edition seems to have met with general approval. The parallel drawn with the "early attempts to formulate a company law" has been reinforced by the insertion of a new sub-section on the "Merger of international organisations" to reflect the new practice in this area.

The author must beg forgiveness that the companion volume on the "Law of War" is not yet ready; and also, rather sadly, that the translation of this volume into French has not yet been achieved. With patience, professional life and work permitting, these omissions will be put right in the coming years.

N.A.M G.

Paris, 1982

Contents

Table of Cases

This is a table of the names of cases cited in this volume in alphabetical order, including some diplomatic incidents which were not subject to judicial appraisal, together with references to the court, the date, and an indication of where the full text of the decision can be found.

Table of Treaties

This is a table of treaties cited in this volume in chronological order of the date of their conclusion, with information as to the parties or the number of parties as at 31st December 1977, and accompanied by references to the treaty series or other works where the complete text of the treaty may be consulted.

Abbreviations

A.C.	*Appeal Cases* (United Kingdom)
A/CONF.	Series for United Nations documents concerning conferences organised by the General Assembly
A.D.	*Annual Digest of Public International Law Cases,* 1919-49
A.J.I.L.	*American Journal of International Law,* 1907-
All E.R.	*All England Law Reports,* 1936- (United Kingdom)
Annuaire Français	*Annuaire Français de Droit International,* 1955-
B.F.S.P.	*British and Foreign State Papers,* 1806-
B.I.L.C.	*British International Law Cases*
B.Y.I.L.	*British Yearbook of International Law*
Clunet	Chancery Reports from the Chancery Division of the High Court of Justice (United Kingdom); *see* "Q.B." for companion set of cases.
Cmnd.	Papers presented to Parliament by command of His/Her Majesty (United Kingdom)
Cranch	*United States Supreme Court Reports,* 1805-15
Doc.	Document
ECOSOC	Economic and Social Council of the United Nations
ELDO	European Space-Vehicle Launcher Development Organisation.
ESA	European Space Agency
ESRO	European Space Research Organisation
E.T.S.	*European Treaty Series,* Council of Europe publications

F. Supp.	*Federal Supplement,* containing decisions of United States District Courts
G.A.	General Assembly of the United Nations
G.B.	Great Britain
H.M.S.O.	His/Her Majesty's Stationery Office, London
Hudson, *Cases*	Hudson, *Cases and other Materials on International Law,* third edition (1951)
Hudson, *Legislation*	Hudson, *International Legislation.* A collection of texts of multipartite international instruments of general interest, 9 vols. covering the period 1919-45.
I.C.A.O.	International Civil Aviation Organisation
I.C.J.	International Court of Justice
I.C.J. Reports	*International Court of Justice, Reports of Judgments, Advisory Opinions and Orders*
I.L.C.	International Law Commission of the United Nations
I.L.M.	*International Legal Materials*
I.L.O.	International Labour Organisation
I.L.R.	*International Law Reports,* 1950-
I.O.I.	*International Organisation and Integration,* Ed. Van Panhuys, Brinkhorst and Maas, 1968
I.T.U.	International Telecommunications Union
J.O.	*Journal Officiel* of the French Republic
L.N.T.S.	*League of Nations Treaty Series*
Malloy's Treaties	*Malloy's Treaties, Conventions, etc., between the United States of America and other Powers.*
Manual of Military Law, Pt III	*The Law of War on Land,* being Part III of the *Manual of Military Law,* United Kingdom War Office, H.M.S.O. 1958
Martens	Martens, *Recueil des Traités*
Martens, *N.R.*	Martens, *Nouveau Recueil*
Martens, *N.R.G.*	Martens, *Nouveau Recueil Général*
Martens, *Causes Célebres*	Martens, *Causes Célebres du Droit de Gens,* second edition, 5 vols. (1858-61)
M.L.R.	*Malayan Law Reports*
Moore, *International Arbitrations*	Moore, *History and Digest of the International Arbitrations to which the United States has been a Party,* 6 vols. (1898)

NATO	North Atlantic Treaty Organisation
O.A.S.	Organisation of American States
Off. J.	*Official Journal*
Peaselee	Peaselee, *Constitutions of Nations*, 3 vols. (1950)
P.C.A.	Permanent Court of Arbitration
P.C.I.J.	Permanent Court of International Justice, or, according to the context, *Publications of the Permanent Court of International Justice*
	Ser. A — Judgments
	Ser. B — Advisory Opinions
	Ser. A/B — Cumulative collections of judgments and Advisory Opinions given since 1931
	Ser. C — Acts and documents relating to judgments and Advisory Opinions
Q.B.	Queen's Bench Reports from the Queen's Bench Division of the High Court of Justice (United Kingdom)
Res.	Resolution
R.I.A.A.	*Reports of International Arbitral Awards,* United Nations Publication
S.A.L.R.	*South African Law Reports*
S.C.	Security Council of the United Nations
S.L.R.	*Scottish Law Reports*
Stat. at L.	United States *Statutes at Large*
T.I.A.S.	*United States Treaties and Other International Acts Series*
U.K.T.S.	*United Kingdom Treaty Series,* 1892-
U.N.T.S.	*United Nations Treaty Series*
U.P.U.	Universal Postal Union
U.S.	*United States Supreme Court Reports*
U.S.T.	*Unites States Treaties in Force*
U.S.S.R.	Union of Soviet Socialist Republics

CHAPTER 1

International Law in General

I. NATURE, PURPOSE AND BASIS

INTERNATIONAL LAW AS LAW

Those who approach international law after having studied a national legal system (municipal law) may feel the need either to revise their conception of "law" or to take the view as many do, that "international law is not law." Those who take the latter view may be surprised to learn that every state in the world, that is to say their statesmen and governments, acts on the assumption that inter-state relations are governed by law. The reader may thus be advised to do likewise.

International law appears to differ in at least two significant respects from law as it is reflected in municipal legal systems. There is no legislature or law-making authority; and there is no police force or army to enforce obedience to the law or sanction breaches of it. To affirm the legal nature of international law, it is thus necessary to establish that neither of these elements is indispensable to the existence of a legal system.

Since, however, the nature, purpose and basis of international law are only adaptations to the field of inter-state relations of the nature, purpose and basis of law itself, the method adopted in the following paragraphs is to proceed from the general (law itself) to the particular (international law as a species of law). This chapter terminates with some remarks about the value in a legal system of a legislature, the enforcement of the law, and the use of force in inter-state relations.

The nature of law and of international law

Law is utilitarian and dynamic: it is the servant of Man, not his master. The law does not exist in some perfect conceptual form — but only in relation to Man's behaviour. Consequently, it will change to keep in step with the advancing sophistication of society and the needs of its members.

1

While the utilitarian and dynamic nature of the law deserves to be stressed, there are other influences which tend to introduce a static element. Justice is immutable, and reason itself seems to require, in the interests of justice, observance of certain rules and principles in spite of changes in time, space and circumstances. This perhaps explains the "general principles of law".

In the history of international law, the Naturalist School took the abstract concepts of justice and reason as their point of departure; the "law of Nature" in its pure form, was essentially an attempt to explain the nature of international law as the application of reason to the relations between states so as to obtain a just solution of their differences.

In opposition to the "Naturalists," the "Positivists" proclaimed the complete independence of law from any outside influence, such as abstract justice or the inherent needs of Man. To the extent that this school insisted upon the complete freedom of the community to prescribe its own laws, the influence of the Positivists was beneficial; but by insisting that "only that was law which had been made so by the express act of the community," they attempted to introduce into international law a harmful limitation which, moreover, did not reflect the facts. Inclusion of the "general principles of law" amongst the sources which the Permanent Court of International Justice was to apply marked the demise of this part of the positivist doctrine.

In our own day, the movement towards the international protection of human rights has involved recognition of the fact that the principal concern of the law is with the needs of Man.

The purpose of law
While speculation about the nature of law is perforce theoretical, the function of law is severely practical, for it is an instrument without which people would be unable to live together in society or in a community. For the purpose of law within a community is to introduce order into the relations of its members through the establishment of known and predictable barriers to conduct. The more sophisticated the society, the greater the need for law. The rule "What is not forbidden is allowed" is indicative of the function of law in society.

The basis of law and of international law
It is easier to say what is not the basis of international law than what is. According to one theory, it is the consent of states which provides this basis; according to another, the basis of international law lies in the "fundamental rights of states". It is not difficult to conclude that the first doctrine derives from the positivists, the

second from the naturalists (the latter being merely an adaptation to states of the natural rights of Man).

Neither is satisfactory. As Brierly has written: "A customary rule is observed not because it has been consented to, but because it is believed to be binding" (*The Law of Nations*, sixth edit., p. 52). Individual members of a legal system are not asked whether they accept the rules of law, and are not permitted to withdraw their consent. They either obey the law or find themselves punished by or excluded from the society or community whose rules they refuse to accept.

While it is no doubt true that it is the perpetual aspiration of those who live in a society to perfect it and to ensure that the fundamental rights of its members are respected, the difficulty of this theory is that one cannot ascribe "rights" of any kind, whether fundamental or not, to the members of the community until there is a legal system which can give them this character.

The problem of the basis of international law is no different from that of the basis of law in general. Logic itself excludes any purely legal answer to this question. For example, to assert that the rule *pacta sunt servanda* — agreements are to be observed — is the basis of law fails to explain *why* agreements are to be observed, the very object of the enquiry.

Laws, or legal systems, exist only in relation to societies or communities, and the basis of law must be found from an analysis of those concepts. Men live in societies, and states live in a community, because to do so meets certain of their needs, and yields certain advantages. On the other hand, life is possible in society only if the behaviour of the other members is subject to a reasonable degree of predictability and kept within certain limits. In exhange for the benefit to the individual of living in the society, the other members insist on his observance of these restraints. Wholesale non-observance means destruction of the society and this is the ultimate sanction, to prevent which all lesser sanctions are imposed and, theoretically, accepted.

What characterises each member of a given society is the assumption by the person concerned that he is a member of it, or, in the case of an outsider, that he is not. This sense of belonging suggests a possible sanction, namely the threat of exclusion or "banishment". In the eighteenth and nineteenth centuries admittance to the family of "civilised" nations was considered a privilege. Recognition by the existing members of the new member carried with it the advantage of being admitted to a community of states whose mutual relations were governed by rules of law and which were to that extent predictable and orderly.

WHO MAKES THE LAW?

Nascent societies, realising the advantages of restraining the behaviour of their members within bounds of predictability, began to exercise collective pressure on unwilling members to restrain their conduct within these bounds. From this, it was a short step to the punishment of those who transgressed them. To be and remain within the society meant submitting to its rules. The greater the number of rules, the more clearly defined and closely knit the society. The origin of those rules was never questioned, or, if it was, was answered by the simple assertion that it was the collectivity, "society itself", which made them. To insist, as some do, that before there can be a legal system there must be some person or body which "makes" the law is to be, historically speaking, myopic: for this is an assertion that runs in the face of the historical evolution of societies the world over. Of course the creation of a legislature is a land-mark in the evolution of a society, but the importance of this step will depend upon the number of its members. Where this is millions, it is difficult to see how laws could be made without confiding their making to a smaller body. But where the number of members is quite small (and the number of states in the world today is still only about 150) it is possible to get by without a legislature.

How are laws made in the international community?

Laws are made today within the international legal system in largely the same way that they were made in nascent societies, and are still made in primitive tribes, that is to say by the interaction of the conduct of each upon the others. Because this has been a continual process, the limits of some types of conduct are known in advance; but in other cases, these limits can be discovered only by acting first and then observing the reaction of the rest of the international community afterwards. The General Assembly of the United Nations now provides an opportunity for speeding up the process of formation of law through the practice of states, since it acts for the international community as a forum in which to register collective reaction to the individual acts of states and other significant contemporary developments.

One of the disadvantages of not having a legislature is that it becomes more difficult to discover the content of the law. If the laws are not written down and issued in the form of edicts by a legislature, where does one look for information about the content of the law? In the international community, this difficulty is partly met by the use of the treaty, for treaties play the role both of contracts, and, to some extent, of legislation. There are now, however, so many treaties that a government may very well not know itself what is the extent of its treaty obligations in respect of any particular matter. A work of classification is long overdue, and it is only by resorting to the storage and information retrieval possibilities of computers that states will be able to have ready access to that ever-growing part of international law which has its source in treaties.

Evidence of law formed by custom was in the past to be found only in government archives, and these were either secret, or, if accessible, hidden amongst a mass of state papers having nothing to do with international law. Such evidence is only now becoming available through publication in some states of *Digests of state practice in the field of international law.*

Why is the law obeyed?

People obey the law because they consider it to be in their own interest to do so. Since, however, people do not always obey the law, and sometimes obey it only out of fear of the consequences of breaking it, this statement needs some qualification. Each member of society has a personal and public motivation: in the case of the former, he pursues his own ends, generally in competition with, and at the expense of, the other members; in the case of the latter, he is prepared to accept the restraints placed by society on his behaviour, and to contribute towards the well-being of society (for example by the payment of taxes), and these things he will do in the general interest. For he recognises that what is in the general interest is in his interest as a member of society, although it may be against his interest as an individual. It is in this sense of the word "interest" that the statement in the first sentence of this paragraph is meant.

If this is true, it means that people obey the laws because, by and large, they agree with them. If the society is democratic, they have helped to make them, or at least silently acquiesced in their making. Only in totalitarian states are the laws likely to be resented by significant proportions of the population, which alone gives rise to the need to impose obedience by force.

No free society could exist for long if the reason that people obeyed the law was simply because they would be punished if they did not do so. The earliest examples of law enforcement involved the collective and spontaneous action of the other members of the society. The "hue and cry" in Anglo-Saxon England is an example. The introduction of police-forces in western societies was relatively late; legal systems had already existed for several countries before their arrival. The absence of a police-force in the service of the community is not therefore a relevant factor in understanding the nature of law, whether in a national or an international context.

Lawful and unlawful use of force

Of all aspects of Man's behaviour which need to be restrained if he is to live in society, it is his use of force which is the most important. On the other hand, the ability of the society to maintain an armed force greater than that of internal rebels and external aggressors alike is the measure of its ability to survive. These two different aspects of the use of force run together. For use of force by members of society in circumstances forbidden by law can be contained, and offenders punished, by employing the greater force upon which the survival of society depends.

What distinguishes societies of men from the community of states is that the latter, since it comprises all the states in the world, knows, as of yet, of no external force against which it must establish a force of its own if it is to survive. There is then in international law no force at the disposal of the whole community. The result has been that the international community has found it extremely difficult to circumscribe the behaviour of states in relation to their individual use of force; and its relative failure, even today, to prescribe binding rules in this area has set the limit to the contribution of international law towards the moulding of states into one community.

However, a rule of law must exist before it can be enforced, and the Charter of the United Nations, drafted by the victors of a bloody war, agreed upon two basic rules concerning the use of force by states:

(a) ". . . that all members shall refrain in their international relations from the threat or use of force against the territorial integrity or political independence of any state . . ." (Article 2(4)).

(b) "Nothing in the present Charter shall impair the inherent right of individual or collective self-defence [against] an armed attack . . ." (Article 51).

In international relations, force is thus used lawfully in self-defence, and unlawful in all other circumstances (unless by the United Nations itself or on its behalf).

The international community is at present unable to impose obedience to these rules, or to sanction their breach. This does not deprive them of their "legal" character, but every breach unpunished brings the law into disrepute. However, the law's enforcement can never be more effective than the means the community is prepared to assign to this purpose, so that the international legal system will be obliged to labour under this weakness for some time to come.

II. RELATIONSHIP BETWEEN
INTERNATIONAL LAW AND
MUNICIPAL LAW

IN GENERAL

Like many of the most disputed doctrinal questions, the problem
of the relationship between international law and municipal law is
of theoretical interest only, in the sense that no practical situation
can arise in which the matter can be put to the test. Any jurisdictional situation must be based on or be assigned to either the international or the national level, since there is nothing in between. If
an alien is mistreated, one of two jurisdictional situations might
arise, or both. If the alien brought proceedings before the national
courts of the state of his residence, the judge would apply the
national law, and, for him, that would be final. The authorities of
the alien's nationality might then intervene on the diplomatic level
and invoke the international responsibility of the other state. If the
matter came before a tribunal endowed with international jurisdiction, it would apply international law — and that also with final
effect. Before the national judge it would be idle to argue about
international law: equally before the international judge it would be
pointless to argue the national law. In other words the relationship
between international law and municipal law will depend upon the
jurisdiction before which the situation is brought for judgment; if
national, municipal law will prevail, if international, international
law. There is no intermediate situation.

We shall accordingly now confine our attention to considering
what is the status of municipal law in a case before an international
jurisdiction, and vice versa.

MUNICIPAL LAW BEFORE INTERNATIONAL COURTS

Before an international tribunal, municipal law is considered, if
relevant at all, as a *fact*. The fact should be verified as well as
circumstances allow, and a manifest error in the appreciation of a
rule of municipal law has been treated as sufficient to annul an
arbitral award, but neither more nor less so than would a material
error concerning any other relevant fact.

The case is slightly more complicated where the rule of international law itself refers to a criterion which is one of municipal
law. This frequently happens in relation to nationality. There is no
rule of international law which decides which individuals will have

which nationality. Each state is free to decide this matter for itself. Where an individual's nationality is relevant in an international case, it is the municipal law of the state of the alleged nationality which must be referred to. Where this is in doubt, the international tribunal will require the party alleging the fact to prove it in relation to the case in issue. It was thus possible for an international tribunal to decide for the purposes of the case before it that it was not satisfied that Mr Flegenheimer had United States nationality, although the State Department asserted that he did, on the basis of a United States judicial decision taken in respect of this very point! For, although Mr Flegenheimer was still a United States national according to the nationality law of the United States, the tribunal found it not sufficiently proven that he was included in the category of "United Nations nationals" — a phrase which included nationals of the United States — who alone were to be compensated, by virtue of the treaty of peace between the Allied Powers and Italy of 1947, for losses supported during the Second World War.

INTERNATIONAL LAW IN MUNICIPAL COURTS

In principle, municipal law may ignore international law: if a state incorporates rules of international law into its municipal law, it does so as a matter of free choice and convenience. Some states provide in their constitutions that their laws should be "in conformity with international law", and most states do ensure by one means or another that the rules of international law are resorted to for the resolution of appropriate disputes before their national courts. There are sound reasons for their doing so, since by the nature of the case such disputes may be taken up again on the international level once the municipal court has given final judgment. On this international level, it is no longer the judiciary, nor even the legislature, which is responsible, but the executive, which in the name of the state is answerable to the other state or states involved, and may be obliged to make reparation. The case of *Mortensen* v. *Peters* (High Court of Justiciary, Scotland, 1906) provides an illustration. An Act of Parliament had made it an offence for "any person" to trawl in the Moray Firth, even outside the three-mile limit. The Act applied to Mortensen, a Danish national, for whom it was argued that international law forbade the application of Scottish law to aliens outside the bounds of United Kingdom jurisdiction (the three-mile limit). The judges declaring that "for us an Act of Parliament is supreme, and we are bound to follow its terms" decided that "any person" included aliens. As a result of the fine levied in that case, the Danish Foreign Office lodged a diplomatic protest and the United Kingdom Government, disavowing the interpretation made by the court, was obliged to apologise and pay over a sum in reparation. It is to avoid this kind of conflict that states try to ensure that their municipal law reflects, and where necessary incorporates, rules of international law. The techniques for doing so differ as to whether the international law in question is of treaty or customary origin.

Treaties and municipal law

It is the government — the executive — which makes treaties and signifies on the international level the state's assent to be bound thereby. Now to be effective, many treaties need to be implemented not only on the international but also on the national plane, as part of municipal law. But the task of making the law falls to the legislature and not the executive.

The procedure by which treaties, or more exactly, the rights and obligations arising under treaties, are "transformed", "incorporated" or merely "take effect" in municipal law varies from state to state. In the United Kingdom, an "enabling" Bill is presented to Parliament, and only when once passed into law as an ordinary statute does the executive ratify the treaty. Frequently the treaty source is not even mentioned in the text of the statute, which is accordingly applied and interpreted by the courts just like any other law of purely national origin. In the United States, the Constitution provides that treaties constitute "the supreme law of the land", but the Senate, an organ of the legislature, aids the executive in deciding whether to ratify the treaty. Other states provide that treaties, once ratified, are to be applied by the national courts subject normally to some administrative act such as publication in an official gazette. In certain of these states, such as France, the treaty is by this method "incorporated" into French law: it is for example the French version of the treaty, published in the official gazette, which is authoritative, whether or not French was one of the official languages of the treaty. In other states (the Federal Republic of Germany, Austria) the treaty is not incorporated, but is received into their national law as a treaty. Even in states where the courts consider the treaty *qua* treaty, requiring neither transformation nor incorporation to become effective in municipal law, subsequent statutes modify treaty law. In other words, there is no theory of the supremacy of treaty law over laws of national origin.

Customary international law and municipal law

Since customary international law is reflected in, and has grown out of, the practice of states, and since state practice is reflected as much in the judgments of national courts and the enactment of laws as in the acts of the executive, it would be surprising if municipal law was often found to be in contradiction with customary international law. Some rules of customary origin, such as those on state immunity, have been based almost exclusively on the practice of municipal courts: in other cases the subject-matter falls outside the ordinary purview of municipal court supervision, with the result that, if ever a case does arise, there is no ready-made rule of municipal law to deal with the matter. Rather than admit a lacuna or indulge in open law-making, the courts will turn to any rule of international law which would provide a solution of the case while declaring, following a tradition of Anglo-American origin, that "international law is part of our law". In fact, however, that is true only where the municipal court needs to fill the gap. Given a statute, or a decision of a hierarchically superior court the court will follow the national law, even if contrary to international law.

Often confounded with this question is the case where a court needs proof of a fact or a status which would be beyond its jurisdiction to decide for itself, and which involves matters with which international law is concerned. For example, whether a state is at war or peace is not a matter which any municipal court can suitably decide. Again, whether some party to the proceedings is the government of a foreign state or a mere band of rebels is something which the government will decide as a matter of high policy: a national court is simply not competent to do so and can only ask the executive for the answer to the question. Similar considerations apply to whether a geographical location is within the boundaries of a foreign state. The treatment by the executive of aliens outside state territory (act of state) is, in the United Kingdom, also beyond the jurisdiction of national courts, but this is only an illustration of the fact that it is international law which settles the limits of national jurisdiction — and thus the jurisdiction of national courts.

CHAPTER 2

The Sources and Evidences of International Law

The difference between sources and evidences of international law is that the former actually make the law, while the latter merely purport to state it. Treaties, custom and the general principles of law are sources: judicial decisions and doctrine, described in Article 38 of the Statute of the International Court of Justice as "subsidiary means", are evidences.

I. THE SOURCES OF INTERNATIONAL LAW

How is the law made? There is no legislature to make laws for the members of the international community. The General Assembly of the United Nations comes closest to performing this function although its resolutions are not of binding legal effect except in the context of that organisation. Analogies with the sources of any municipal law (such as English law or French law) are therefore misleading.

There can be no authoritative and exhaustive statement of the sources of any legal system. Instead, reference may be made to what the International Court of Justice is directed to apply as international law. This is laid down in Article 38 of the Statute of the Court which, as an integral part of the Charter of the United Nations, has the same authority as that text. Article 38 reads as follows:

"1. The Court, whose function is to decide in accordance with international law such disputes as are submitted to it, shall apply:

(a) international conventions, whether general or particular, establishing rules expressly recognised by the contesting states,

(b) international custom, as evidence of a general practice accepted as law;

(c) the general principles of law recognised by civilised nations;

(d) subject to the provisions of Article 59, judicial decisions and the teachings of the most highly qualified publicists of the various nations, as subsidiary means for the determination of rules of law."

The remainder of this Chapter may be treated as a commentary upon the text of this Article.

TREATIES

Treaties, like contracts, create rights and obligations between the parties to them. "International conventions" is another name for treaties. "Whether general or particular" relates simply to whether the treaty is one to which many states are parties (general) or only some states, including the contesting states (particular). A treaty between two states is called bilateral; one between more than two states, multilateral. "Establishing rules expressly recognised by the contesting states": Treaties do not make law (of general application) but rules (as between the parties). They are "expressly recognised" when the state by a voluntary act becomes "party" to the treaty, i.e. when it ratifies the treaty or otherwise becomes bound by its provisions. Treaty rules become the "law" for the parties because of the existence of the law of treaties which gives them this effect, in the same way that under municipal law a contract may incorporate the law for the parties because of the effect of the law of contract.

Law-making treaties

Literally, there is no such thing as a law-making treaty, but since nearly all writers on the subject give this name to a series of treaties of a special category, the terminology is followed here. In the absence of a legislature, states frequently find it convenient to conclude a multilateral treaty, the object of which is not so much to accord mutual rights and obligations as to state in a comprehensive manner what in their view the law is, or ought to be. A better name would therefore be a "law-stating" treaty. The rules set out in a law-stating treaty bind the states party to it in the same way as any other treaty; but these states are also "bound" irrespective of the treaty, because in their opinion the treaty states the law. Whether a law-stating treaty does make the law will depend not upon any force inherent in the treaty but upon the subsequent practice of states, and in particular the attitude taken to the rules it contains by "third" states. If the latter accept the new statement of the law contained in the treaty, and align their own practice to it, because they too think this is what the law is or ought now to be, then that is what the law becomes. But any other statement of the law not in treaty form, such as one set out in a resolution of the

General Assembly of the United Nations, would be authoritative in much the same way if the contemporary and future practice of states demonstrated that it was a correct statement.

A "law-stating" treaty which became "law-making" was the International Convention concerning the Laws and Customs of War on Land of 1907 (Hague Convention No. IV): the preamble contained the words ". . . until a more complete *code of the laws of war* can be drawn up, the . . . Parties deem it expedient to declare. . . ." Other examples are: the Declaration of Paris, 1856 (on neutrality in maritime warfare); the Genocide Convention of 1948; and the United Nations Charter, particularly Articles 2(3) and (4).

Treaties constituting international organisations

The International Court of Justice has decided that the Charter created the United Nations with "an objective personality", viz. one binding upon non-members. In the *Reparation for Injuries Case* (I.C.J., 1949) the International Court of Justice advised that the United Nations had the capacity to bring an international claim against Israel, at that time not a member of the United Nations, for failure to protect adequately a United Nations official who was assassinated there by terrorists. Any international organisation created by a treaty between states probably has some "objective" existence.

CUSTOM

Definition

There is no definition of custom, but the description of it as a "general practice accepted as law" contains most of the constituent elements.

The practice of states

The practice of a state is shown by its acts and attitudes in its international relations with other states. When it becomes clear that each state acts in the same way, or takes up the same attitude to the acts or omissions of other states, the practice is uniform. When there is a repetition of such uniform practice over a period of time, the practice is constant. State practice which is both uniform and constant creates a "usage".

Custom requires a "general practice". No precise answer can be given to the question of how general the practice needs to be. So long as a group of states follow the practice, and accept it as law, there is a custom. All customs have begun in the same way, and become of increasingly universal application as more states align their practice to them.

A period of time

In the *North Sea Continental Shelf Case* (I.C.J., 1969), the court had this to say about the period of time necessary for the formation of a custom:

> "Although the passage of only a short period of time is not necessarily, or of itself, a bar to the formation of a new rule of customary international law, an indispensable requirement would be that within the period in question, short though it might be, state practice, including that of states whose interests are specially affected, should have been both extensive and virtually uniform in the sense of the provision invoked."

The time interval to which the court referred may be seen from the circumstance that the Convention on the Continental Shelf was opened for signature in 1958 and came into force in June 1964, while the proceedings were brought in February 1967.

Accepted as law – opinio juris

To become a rule of customary international law, a usage must be recognised, by the states which conform to it, as having now become of binding legal force. Usage which imposes a burden becomes a custom when states no longer feel able to act in a manner different from the usage, or in other words feel that they must, in law, follow this usage. The burden has then become an obligation.

Omission to act

State practice can be shown not only by acts but also by attitudes, including an omission to act. The legal significance of such passivity can be judged only by its motive. In *The Lotus Case* (P.C.I.J., 1927) the Permanent Court of International Justice said: "States have often abstained from instituting criminal proceedings . . . only if such abstention were based on their becoming conscious of a duty to abstain would it be possible to speak of an international custom."

Proof of custom

Because a practice may be regional or general, but need not be universal, a state party to a dispute before a court must "prove that the custom is established in such a manner that it has become binding on the other party." In the *Asylum Case* (I.C.J., 1950) the International Court of Justice said:

> "The party which relies on a custom . . . must prove that . . . the rule invoked by it is in accordance with a constant and uniform usage practised by the states in question, and that this usage is the expression of a right appertaining to the state grating asylum and a duty incumbent on the territorial state. The facts . . . disclose

so much uncertainty and contradiction . . . in the exercise of diplomatic asylum, and in the official views expressed . . . so much inconsistency in the rapid succession of conventions on asylum, ratified by some states and rejected by others, and the practice has been so much influenced by considerations of political expediency . . . that it is not possible to discern in all this any constant and uniform usage, accepted as law."

Legal effects of custom

Can a custom bind states which did not contribute to its creation? States do not agree upon this point. There are two theories.

(a) Yes. In particular it can bind newly-created states accepted as members of the international community on analogy with a newly born child in a national legal system. Most Western and traditional states support this theory.

(b) No. This would be contrary to the principle of the legal equality of states. According to this theory, the entry without reservation into official relations with other states signifies only that the new state accepts that group of principles and rules of international law which are the basis of relations between states, but not necessarily other rules. Communist states and recently created states support this theory.

A state may deliberately opt out of a custom in the process of formation, by consistently and unequivocally refusing to accept it. In the *Anglo-Norwegian Fisheries Case* (I.C.J., 1951) the International Court of Justice decided that Norway would not, for this reason, have been bound by the rules as to the method for the delimitation of base-lines from which to draw her territorial waters even if this method had become customary, which the court in fact decided it had not.

Special custom

A state may create a special rule for itself, if other states permit it to do so. For example it may, by a unilateral act, lay claim to the sea-bed beyond the limits of territorial waters. Other states then have a choice of response: to make a protest, which must be brought to the knowledge of the asserting state; or to acquiesce, if only by the absence of protest — but an acquiescing state must be proved to have had knowledge of the facts as to which it is alleged to have acquiesced. An example is the Truman Declaration in 1945 declaring the jurisdiction and control of the United States over the natural resources of the sea-bed and sub-soil of the continental shelf beyond the limits of the territorial waters, because oil had been discovered there which it was possible to exploit. Other states with a sea-coast not only acquiesced in the Truman Declaration, but rapidly made similar claims themselves. The evolution of the customary rule as to the continental shelf — the right to explore and exploit the sea-bed up to a certain distance from the sea-coast — therefore evolved from a special to a general custom very rapidly, and was "codified" in 1958.

Comity

The word "comity" means courtesy. As an act of courtesy states accord each other, and particularly their official representatives, special privileges over and above anything that may be required under international law. Historically speaking, most of the rules of diplomatic law started as rules of comity.

GENERAL PRINCIPLES OF LAW

The third source is "the general principles of law recognised by civilised nations". There is some confusion as to the meaning and scope of this expression. Are these principles of international law, of municipal law, or of all known legal systems whatever their qualification?

General principles of international law

Examples of these general principles are the equality of states, and the independence of states. These cannot be a source of international law. However, some states and writers do not agree that on any meaning of the term "law", "the general principles of law" are a source of international law (in particular communist states). They point out that Article 38 merely says: "The court whose function is to decide in accordance with international law such disputes as are submitted to it, shall apply." In their view it can hardly be in accordance with international law to apply general principles of municipal law, from which they conclude that the general principles are of international law.

General principles of municipal law

Those who support this theory do not consider that all general principles of municipal law are meant. And even those which are included but which in their muncipal setting have crystallised into legal institutions, are not incorporated in their entirety, i.e. together with all their subsidiary rules, for example estoppel in the Anglo-Saxon sense, and the trust in the trusteeship system: it is only the principle which is incorporated.

General principles of all legal systems

Before a principle could be said to be general, a further test must be satisfied: the principle must be applicable to international relations.

Thus principles drawn from the law of land would be excluded because the law of land is almost totally unsuited for application to state territory.

The word "civilised" in the expression "recognised by civilised nations" refers to states with a developed legal system.

Judicial recourse to general principles of law

In the absence of custom or treaty provisions, an international court may have recourse to general principles of law where and to the extent that this is necessary for the performance of the judicial function. This reference to the judicial function relates to the question whether a court can return a *non liquet*, i.e. refuse to give judgment on the merits because of the absence of applicable law. In other words, is international law a theoretically complete system of law capable of providing a legal answer to every dispute? Article 38 (1) (c) enlarged the court's function to enable it to settle the dispute, in the absence of other applicable law, by resort to general principles of law. In doing so, the court is not making new law, but is stating, with authority, that a principle which is to be found in all developed municipal legal systems is a general principle of law, and is therefore also present in international law (as it would be present in any other legal system). This is illustrated by the following statement by the Permanent Court of International Justice in the *Chorzow Factory (Merits) Case* (P.C.I.J., 1928): "It is a principle of international law, and even a general conception of law, that any breach of an engagement involves an obligation to make reparation.'

The Permanent Court of International Justice and the International Court of Justice have made most use of their power to enunciate general principles in the fields of evidence, procedure and jurisdiction, e.g. *nemo judex in re sua, res judicata,* litispendence, and the use of indirect or circumstantial evidence.

Constituent elements

We may now sum up: before a court can incorporate a general principle of law, it must be satisfied that it is:

(a) a principle, its surrounding subsidiary rules being ignored;
(b) general, i.e. present in all developed municipal legal systems;
(c) relevant to international relations; and
(d) necessary for the resolution of the dispute before the court.

Equity

Equity is sometimes considered as a separate source of international law: it seems better, however, to think of equity as a particularly fertile field for the enunciation of general principles of law. As Brierly has said, ". . . some principles may fairly be considered so reasonable as to be necessary to the maintenance of justice under any legal system" (*Law of Nations*, fifth edition, page 63). This is illustrated by the two following examples.

(a) "One party cannot avail himself of the fact that the other has not fulfilled some obligation, or has not had recourse to some means of redress, if the former party has, by some illegal act, prevented the latter from fulfilling the obligation" (*Chorzow Factory (Jurisdiction) Case* (P.C.I.J., 1927)).

(b) "It is an established rule of law that a plea of error cannot be allowed as an element vitiating consent if the party advancing it contributed by its own conduct to the error" (*Temple (Merits) Case* (I.C.J., 1962)).

Ex aequo et bono
Paragraph two of Article 38 reads: "This provision shall not prejudice the power of the court to decide a case *ex aequo et bono*, if the parties agree thereto." A case decided *ex aequo et bono* is not decided on the basis of law, and vice versa. To date, the International Court of Justice has not been asked so to decide.

II. THE EVIDENCES OF INTERNATIONAL LAW

JUDICIAL DECISIONS
Judicial decisions state, but do not make, the law: they should therefore be thought of as evidences rather than sources of law. However, some decisions acquire, with the passage of time, or because of the status of the court, an authority which decisively affects the future shaping of the law (*Reparations for Injuries Case* (I.C.J., 1949)). The decisions referred to are not only those of the Permanent Court of International Justice and the International Court of Justice: they include all international courts and municipal courts.

Decisions of international courts
Decisions of the International Court of Justice and the Permanent Court of International Justice are naturally accorded most weight (except where the court is almost equally divided, as in the *Lotus Case*).

The doctrine of precedent and judicial consistency
In international law there is no doctrine of precedent. Article 59 of the Statute of the International Court of Justice states that "the decision of the court has no binding force except between the parties and in respect of that particular case". However, legal

principles stated in one case are often re-stated in identical, or repeated in indistinguishable, terms in other cases. The case-law of the International Court of Justice and the Permanent Court of International Justice would not have been different in any significant respect if the doctrine of precedent had applied. In the one case (*Interpretation of the Peace Treaties Case* (I.C.J., 1950)) where the court might be thought to have employed a principle different from that which had been applied in an earlier case, the court took pains to distinguish the cases on their facts: "in the opinion of the court, the circumstances of the present case are profoundly different from those . . . in the *Eastern Carelia Case* (P.C.I.J., 1923)." The explanation for this is simple: in any legal system, it is part of the judicial function to be consistent.

International arbitration tribunals
International arbitration tribunals are set up by two or more states to judge disputes between them, generally on the basis of international law. The difference between such tribunals and international courts is that the former are *ad hoc* while the latter are permanently established. The Reports of International Arbitral Awards, given since 1922, run to no less than fifteen volumes. The best have had an undeniable influence on shaping the law, for example the award of Judge Huber in the *Palmas Island Arbitration* (1928), which contains a classic exposition of the process by which sovereignty is acquired over territory.

International military tribunals
Military tribunals such as those established for the trial of the major German and Japanese war criminals have made a significant contribution to the development of the law on the duties of the individual in international law, as well as on aspects of the laws of war. The present-day authority of these judgments, however, rests less on their formulation by a tribunal than on the acceptance of the legal principles underlying the judgments by the General Assembly of the United Nations.

Decisions of national courts
Constant and uniform decisions of the national courts of different states on a topic of international law, for example the exercise of criminal jurisdiction in territorial waters, diplomatic and consular privileges, state immunity, and prize law, are evidences of international law. Such decisions are also evidence of concordant state practice, since the practice of a state can be shown through the acts of its courts as well as through those of its government. They are, therefore, from another point of view indicative of the source of the rules of law of which they constitute evidence.

Some writers see a development by which national courts assume the role of courts of first instance, leaving international courts to play the role of courts of appeal. This is not the position. On the contrary national courts play a double role in international law.

National courts considered as courts
National courts apply "international law" only to the extent that the national legal system permits. Each state decides this differently: in some states it is a rule of the constitution that international law overrides national law. In the United Kingdom there is room for the application of "international law" only where there is no pre-existing municipal law (statute or case-law) constituting a binding precedent.

The national court considered as an organ of its own state
It is this fact which will normally suffice to deprive the judgment of recognition as international law by other states. To the extent that court decisions reflect the view of the government (for example, in the United Kingdom, by their acceptance of a Foreign Office Certificate) such decisions have evidentiary value not of international law itself, but of the state's view of the position in international law.

DOCTRINE
"Doctrine" means "the teaching of the most highly qualified publicists of the various nations." It is considered a subsidiary means for the determination of the law, resorted to only in the absence of treaty, custom or general principles of law. Because the processes by which the law is laid down in the international community are, by contrast to a developed municipal system, rudimentary, there is both more need and more scope for accurate exposition of the law. Only writers with an international reputation will be influential individually: Gidel (*Law of the Sea*) is one outstanding example.

Use of doctrine by judicial tribunals
"Where there is no treaty . . . resort must be had to the customs and usages of civilised nations, and as evidence of these to the works of jurists . . . well acquainted with the subject of which they treat. Such works are resorted to not for the speculations of their authors concerning what the law ought to be, but for trustworthy evidence of what the law really is." (*The Paquete Habana*, United States Supreme Court, 1900). This is still the position. However, more contemporary experience shows how little and not how much courts are inclined to accept the views of writers. "It is indicative of the present potentialities of [the writings of publicists as a source of law] that the International Court of Justice has so far found

no occasion to rely on it." (*Oppenheim's International Law*, Vol. 1, p. 33, by Sir Hersch (later Judge) Lauterpacht.) Most judges of the International Court of Justice are themselves highly qualified publicists!

Role of government legal advisers

In international relations new situations are constantly arising on which there is little or no known state practice but to which states must react. The sudden appearance of "pirate" radio stations is a recent example. In such cases, it is normal procedure for a state to request a legal opinion about the position in international law before acting. In the United Kingdom legal opinions are provided by the Law Officers of the Crown, or by members of the Legal Department of the Foreign Office. Senior legal advisers to government are often themselves amongst the most eminent highly qualified publicists. In a typical opinion a legal adviser may set out the views of other "highly qualified publicists" which he will then analyse in the light of the interests of the state he represents and of other states, and will conclude by suggesting a course of action, or, if his opinion has been requested with reference to a proposed course of action, by stating whether it would or would not be "in accordance with international law". In this way, government legal advisers play an important, if indirect and often unrecognised, role in the shaping of state practice itself.

UNILATERAL ACTS

Acts and decisions of international conferences

The "confrontation" provided by an international conference can have an undeniable influence on state practice. The extent of that influence will naturally depend on the success of the conference.

Treaties of the law-stating kind, and acts and decisions (including declarations) of successful international conferences, would appear to be of almost equal potential law-making value. Such acts and decisions differ from treaties in that they impose no immediate legal obligation on the states participating to act in accordance with the declaration or other act or decision in question. However, since the rules of procedure normally provide for a two-thirds majority for the adoption of "agreed" texts the participating states demonstrate a willingness to substitute the new text, if it can be agreed, for their existing state practice.

Even where a conference is unsuccessful, it may influence state practice. In theory, state practice need not suffer any change, since the formal rule is that positions adopted in negotiations (of any kind) which are unsuccessful are to be discounted, each state being free to revert to its previous practice. However, where an absolute majority, but not a two-thirds majority, are in favour of one solution, it becomes difficult for any state to maintain with much realism that another rule is "a general practice accepted as law." Thus, for example, the United Nations conferences in 1958 and 1960 on the Law of the Sea attempted to agree a limit to the width of the territorial seas: the second conference failed by one vote to agree on a two-thirds majority for a "six plus six-mile" limit. The United Kingdom apparently continued to regard the three-mile limit as representing a customary rule of international law.

Acts and decisions of international organisations
International organisations are originally created by treaty. Any subsequent act or decision can therefore formally be regarded as having its source in the treaty. However, normally such treaties also set out the special procedure by which the matters falling within the powers and functions of the organisation are to be regulated in future. It is therefore more realistic to regard certain of the acts and decisions of international organisations as being a joint statement of the legal position with regard to the matter in issue.

III. CODIFICATION OF INTERNATIONAL LAW

THE INTERNATIONAL LAW COMMISSION
The International Law Commission was established in 1949, to help the General Assembly of the United Nations make recommendations for the purpose of encouraging the progressive development of international law and its codification (Article 13(1)(a) of the Charter of the United Nations).

The "progressive development of international law" means "the preparation of draft conventions on subjects which have not yet been regulated by international law or in regard to which the law has not yet been sufficiently developed in the practice of states"; while the expression "codification of international law" means "the more precise formulation and systematisation of rules of international law in fields where there already has been extensive state practice, precedent and doctrine" (Article 15 of the Statute of the International Law Commission, set out in General Assembly Resolution 174 (II)).

Composition and function
The International Law Commission has twenty-five members, nominated by governments for their individual competence in international law (rather than as representatives of states) and elected by

the General Assembly of the United Nations. The function of the Commission is to prepare reports, generally in the form of draft articles with a commentary. These reports are submitted to the General Assembly which may *(a)* take no action; *(b)* take note of or adopt them by resolution; *(c)* recommend the draft to member states with a view to the conclusion of a convention; *(d)* convoke a conference for the purpose of concluding a convention (Article 23 of the Statute of the International Law Commission).

Status of the International Law Commission draft in international law

International Law Commission drafts are a mixture of evidence of existing international law *(de lege lata)* and suggestions for its development *(de lege ferenda)*. In practice, codification and progressive development are so interwoven as to be inseparable; and the Commission has abandoned the attempt to present its proposals in separate categories. The drafts are submitted to governments for comment both during the course of their discussion in the Commission and again before their submission to the General Assembly. Moreover, most members of the Commission enjoy the full confidence of their governments. For both these reasons it is unrealistic to regard the drafts as a specialised example of "doctrine". On the other hand, when a draft is examined by an international conference, it is usually changed, sometimes substantially; nor are individual states likely to adapt their state practice solely on the evidence of a Commission draft.

CHAPTER 3

Subjects of International Law

The subjects of a legal system are those upon whom the law bestows, or in whom it recognises, a capacity to act. In international law these include states, international organisations and certain other entities such as the Vatican. These are treated in sections I, II and III respectively of this Chapter. The question whether and to what extent individuals are to be considered subjects of international law is treated in Chapter Four.

The personality of a subject of international law is the measure of its capacity to act. Some subjects have, like individuals in national law, the full measure of legal personality. These are the fully sovereign and independent states. Others, like companies in national law, have only such personality as has been specially accorded to them. The legal personality of international organisations is of this sort.

The two following questions should therefore be carefully distinguished: does an entity have international legal personality; and if so, what is the extent of this personality? If the answer to the first question is no, then it is not a subject of international law. If the answer is yes, the second question must be asked: "how much" legal personality, or as it is more commonly put, what is the extent of its capacity?

I. STATES

This section deals with the rules which concern states as subjects of international law. They are set out under four headings: international status; recognition; types of states; and the formation, continuity and succession of states. Other rules, such as those relating to treaties and international responsibility, which apply not only to states but to all subjects of international law, are dealt with in separate Chapters.

INTERNATIONAL STATUS

Sovereignty and independence

States with the full capacity to act, or in other words with full international personality, are sovereign. They are able to take any action they think fit which is not prohibited by international law so long as it does not interfere with the rights of other states.

Within these limits, and subject to what is said in Chapter Four about human rights, a fully sovereign state has complete freedom of action to deal with its own nationals (personal sovereignty) and with its own territory (territorial sovereignty); to make use of the public domain (the high seas, the air beyond the territory of states, and outer space); to enter into legal relations with other states; to demand respect for its nationals abroad; and to become a member of all international organisations of universal vocation. In former times it included the right to make war; today all that remains is the right to use force in self-defence, and the right to remain neutral in armed conflicts between other subjects of international law.

If a state is sovereign it is independent, and vice versa. Independence is here treated as a legal, not a physical phenomenon. In the *Palmas Island Arbitration* (1928), Max Huber, as arbitrator, explained that "sovereignty in the relations between states signifies independence. Independence in regard to a portion of the globe is the right to exercise therein, to the exclusion of any other state, the functions of a state." A state which is sovereign may voluntarily, for example by treaty, accept a role of complete political dependence upon another state, entrust to it the entire conduct of its foreign policy and yet remain legally independent. Such was the position of Morocco in relation to France as a consequence of the Treaty of Fez of 30th March 1912. In the *Rights of Nationals of the U.S.A. in Morocco Case* (I.C.J., 1952), the court stated:

> "It is not disputed by the French Government that Morocco, even under the Protectorate, has retained its personality as a State in international law.... Under the [Treaty of Fez] Morocco remained a sovereign State but made an arrangement of a contractual character whereby France undertook to exercise certain sovereign powers in the name and on behalf of Morocco, and in principle, all the international relations of Morocco."

It is a consequence of the independence of each sovereign state that it is not subject to decisions taken by other states to which it does not consent. A state is not obliged to appear before an international court or arbitral tribunal unless it consents thereto.

Non-intervention and domestic jurisdiction

International law is concerned with the relations of states with each other. It is not concerned with nor does it permit interference by one state in the internal affairs of another. The same idea lies behind the insistence of the International Court of Justice that, before a state can bring proceedings against another state, the complainant state must show an interest — a legal interest — of its own in prosecuting the case. Only if it can prove such an interest is there any justification for interfering, or intervening, in the affairs of another state. Only in such a case is there any "relation" between the states.

Each state is sovereign and independent in the conduct of such of its affairs as are not affected by the need to respect the rights of other states. International law has forged a series of rules to ensure such respect, and these affect the treatment of foreign nationals, foreign state property, aircraft, ships, etc. Recently, international concern for human rights has in some respects introduced rules of international law even in relation to a state's treatment of its own nationals. But in other matters such as the right to confer nationality, control of imports and exports, immigration and emigration laws, the granting of visas and the issue of work vouchers, states act without reference to any interests but their own, and this is in full accordance with international law. Interests of other states may well be involved when a state comes to enforce its legislation, since international law itself prescribes the limits of the personal and territorial jurisdiction of states.

A matter within the domestic jurisdiction of a state may well cease to be so as a result of new developments in international law. The conclusion by the state of a treaty — under which rights are accorded to other states — will also remove the matters affected by the treaty from the reserved domain to the extent of the treaty obligation. In other words, the concept of domestic jurisdiction is purely relative: it is a convenient expression for the group of matters over which the state does not have to act in accordance with obligations under international law.

Equality of states

The equality of states is a general principle of international law. It is a necessary corollary of the concepts of sovereignty and independence of states. However, it is only the legal equality, or equality before the law, which is in question. States are of course not equal in fact. The general consequence is that each state is entitled to equal treatment under the law. One specific consequence of the equality of states is that each state is entitled to the same voting rights in international conferences and international organisations unless they agree to accept some other system.

RECOGNITION

In general
In this section we deal only with recognition of states and governments. Recognition of belligerents and insurgents is dealt with below.

Nature of the act of "recognition". "Recognition" is a political act with legal consequences. No state has a duty to recognise another state or its government; no state or government has the right to be recognised. Moreover, since there is no definition of "state" for general purposes of international law there is no legal measuring rod by which to determine whether a new state exists, and thus whether to recognise it. On the other hand the rules of international law cannot fully govern the relationship of the two states until each has recognised the other.

Meaning of the word "recognition". "Recognition" is used throughout this chapter in a limited and technical sense to include only the act by which one state recognises another state, its government, a belligerent entity or insurgent rebels.

It is to be distinguished from the same word when used in the context of a claim to territory. When one state claims territory, and another state accepts the claim, or acquiesces in it, the claim may be said to have been "recognised" by the other state. This "recognition" is not a political but a legal act, since (at least between those two states) the legal title to the territory is settled definitely by the act of recognition. "Recognition" of neutrality is also a legal act and must be recognised.

Purpose of recognition in international law. The act of recognition makes it possible for each state to identify the other members of the international community and their governments. In the absence of any body empowered to give a collective decision on this matter, each state decides for itself. Not all states recognise the same entities as making up the international community. Unless recognised by at least one state, the entity will have no claim to be considered as a subject of international law.

Recognition of states
Recognition of a state must be distinguished from recognition of the government of a state. A state, once recognised, does not itself require to be recognised by newly formed states. The question of recognition is important only for the latter. The contemporary world

no longer contains inhabited territory which is not already part of an existing state (except for South-West Africa which is a special case) so that today a "new" state can spring only from an existing state or states. The only internationally accepted measure of its separate identity from the former state is provided by recognition.

Recognition of a state as a political act. The emergence of a new state from an existing state is, generally speaking, the result of political struggle, and, frequently, of armed conflict. In deciding to recognise the new entity as an independent state a third state is taking sides — in other words, making a political choice.

Legal relations before recognition. A third state may require to have some relations with the new body politic even before recognition in order to protect its own interests in the disputed territory. Such relations are necessarily of a provisional character. Any agreement entered into is unenforceable since it is not possible to enter into a treaty with a non-recognised entity: a state which wishes its agreement to be binding in international law must accord recognition. Recognition can indeed be implied from the conclusion of a bilateral treaty. The fact that a state becomes a party to a multilateral treaty, some of the other parties to which it has not yet recognised, does not imply recognition. States normally enter a protest or disclaimer to this effect. Israel, which is not recognised by Arab states, is a party to several multilateral treaties, including the Charter of the United Nations, to which those states are also parties.

Legal effects of recognition of a state. When one state recognises another as an independent state the consequences extend only to the two states concerned. The full international legal personality of the new state is recognised. All future relationships between the two states will take place on a basis of legal equality. The new state is recognised to exercise sovereignty within its frontiers, to have the capacity to confer its nationality and to exercise diplomatic protection on behalf of its nationals.

The new state is considered responsible in international law for all its acts. Moreover, the acts of insurgents — who become the government of the new state — are imputed to the new state, which is made retroactively responsible for them. The reason is that the government of the former state was absolved from responsibility by *force majeure*; it could not have avoided the damage even had it wanted to. Rather than hold no one responsible, the rule is to attach responsibility to the government of the new state which is estopped from disclaimer because the damage was caused by its attempt to become the government of a new state.

Recognition of governments

Successive changes of government do not require any deliberate decision as to recognition, which will be implied if the change-over of governments is constitutional and therefore non-violent. Withdrawal of recognition in such circumstances might constitute interference in the domestic affairs of the state.

Where the new government is installed unconstitutionally (whether with or without the use of force), recognition of the former government cannot be assumed to extend to the new. A new government will be recognised only after reconsideration of the political position. For example, after the Bolshevik Revolution in Russia in 1917 the United States refused to recognise the Communist Government and continued to recognise the former Kerensky Government until 1936. Similarly, although the Communist Government of Mao Tse-tung was in effective control of mainland China from 1950, the United States Government continued to recognise the Government of Chiang Kai-shek as that of the whole of China until 1978.

Governments not in effective control of the whole territory. During an armed rebellion, or as the result of war, the recognised government may lose effective control over part of its territory. It may then happen that some states recognise one authority and some the other as the sole government of the state, as, for example, in the cases of Germany and Vietnam. It is probably not possible for one state to recognise two governments in the same state without thereby recognising two separate states unless the second body is recognised *de facto*, or as an insurgent or belligerent.

Governments in exile. During war-time, or in other exceptional circumstances, governments may be recognised while yet being unable by *force majeure* to operate within, let alone control, the territory of the state. Such a government is nevertheless considered by the recognising state able to represent and enter into undertakings on behalf of the whole state, since it is assumed that these will be honoured once the government resumes control of its territory. It is thus enabled to speak for and exercise public authority over its nationals outside the territory of the state, and in particular within the territory of the recognising state.

Recognition of government as a political act. Since no government has any right to be recognised, states may make their decision on the basis of whatever political criterion they wish. They may, for example, object to the political ideology of that government. On the other hand, governments may be recognised, the members of which do not even have the nationality of the population of the state; or which do not — because they cannot — operate within the territory of their own state; and governments may continue to be recognised after they have ceased to exist in fact.

The only relevant criterion is whether the government has sufficient control over its territory and population to give effect to its obligations under international law. But this is merely a matter of common sense: it is pointless conducting relations with a body lacking the ability to implement agreed decisions within his own territory.

Legal relations before recognition. No normal diplomatic relations are possible before recognition. Neither diplomatic nor consular relations are maintained with a non-recognised government. The good offices of some third state are required if it is desired to conduct diplomatic talks, as, for example, the talks between the United States and North Vietnam in Paris.

Legal effects of recognition of government. To recognise the government of a state is, as between the two states concerned, to recognise its right to represent the state in its international relations, whether bilateral or multilateral, as for example the right to represent the state in international organisations.

Recognition does not necessarily imply, however, that normal diplomatic relations will be resumed. In spite of the United States' recognition of the Chinese Communist Government of Huo Kwo Feng in 1978, diplomatic relations were not immediately resumed.

On the municipal law level, all property belonging to the state which is, at the moment of recognition or subsequently, within the jurisdiction of the recognising state will be at the disposal of the recognised government.

Moreover in certain circumstances the effects of recognition are retroactive. Thus the acts of insurgents who succeed in replacing the former government of an existing state, or who become the government of a new State, are retroactively attributed to, and recognised as the acts of, the government of that state. Thus in the case of *Luther* v. *Sagor* (Court of Appeal, England, 1936) certain timber was confiscated from the plaintiff by Bolshevik communist insurgents in Russia, and sold by them to defendant, who transported it into the United Kingdom. Since the United Kingdom had, subsequently to the act of confiscation, recognised the Bolshevik government as the Government of the U.S.S.R., the Court of Appeal held that the defendant had a valid title.

Forms of recognition

Since recognition is a political act, the various forms which it can take are also to be explained by reference to political rather than to legal considerations.

"De facto" and "de jure" recognition. Sometimes it may be convenient to recognise a state or a government, subject, however, to some reserve. In such cases recognition may be accorded *de facto*. This may be converted later into recognition *de jure* or withdrawn entirely, as the case may be.

During a civil war it may be in the interests of a state to accord the rebel authority some measure of recognition. Recognition *de facto* in this case would give the rebels the status of an independent administering authority, but not a "government". The legitimate government would then be recognised as the government of the whole state (*de jure*) and as the government of that part of the territory, if any, remaining under its control (*de facto*). Thereafter the government would be considered responsible only for acts performed in that part of the territory under its *de facto* control.

There is, however, no difference between recognition *de facto* and *de jure* in international law so far as the legal consequences are concerned. State practice indicates that it is not normal for recognition *de facto* to be followed by the establishment of diplomatic relations. However, the establishment of diplomatic relations is not a necessary consequence of recognition *de jure* either.

Collective recognition. States have occasionally recognised new states in a multilateral conference or treaty, as for example in a peace treaty where the territorial situation is defined afresh. Recognition enshrined in a legal instrument is no less of a political act.

Admission of a state to membership of the United Nations. Admission into the international community is signified today by the admission of a state into the membership of the United Nations rather than by an act of collective recognition. Admission signifies only that the state satisfies the requirements of membership of the United Nations: in casting their vote, states legally may have regard only to the conditions of membership, to the exclusion of all political considerations (see *Conditions of Admission to Membership of the United Nations* (I.C.J., 1947-48)).

A state voting in favour of admission is not implying thereby recognition as a state. Nor does admission to the United Nations give the state any claim to be recognised by other states. Most Arab states decline to recognise the state of Israel, though all are members of the United Nations.

Representation of a state in the United Nations. The question which government may represent a state admitted to the United Nations is distinct from the question of the recognition of the government; a vote in favour of admission would not imply recognition.

Entitlement to represent the state in the United Nations is in principle a mere procedural question, decided at the time of checking the credentials of delegates. Moreover, each organ of the United Nations decides this question for itself. It would thus have been possible, for example, for the credentials of the communist government of China to have been accepted as entitling it to represent the state of China in the General Assembly, but not in the Security Council.

Conditional recognition. Since recognition is a political act, it may be made subject to conditions. State practice contains many examples of recognition being made subject to assurances as to readiness to carry out international obligations and to conform to the existing framework of international law. The Litvinov Agreement of 1936, by which the Government of the U.S.S.R. assigned its own claims and the property rights of former Russian companies in the United States to the Federal Government, was a condition of the recognition of Stalin's Government by the United States.

Modes of recognition

The act of recognition of a state or government may be expressed or implied. Normally it is express. Thus in the Helsinki Treaty of 1976 the NATO powers recognised the German Democratic Republic, while the Warsaw Pact states recognised the Federal Republic of Germany.

One form of implied recognition is for a head of state or government to pay a state visit to a hitherto unrecognised state. Egypt recognised Israel by the visit of President Sadat to Prime Minister Begin in 1978.

However, it is not possible for the deed to replace the intention. Thus since the United States did not intend to recognise either the State of Rhodesia or the Government of Mr Smith, the fact that certain representatives of the latter, visiting the territory of the former, were permitted to have talks with government officials could not displace such intention. The talks therefore did not imply recognition.

Non-recognition

Withholding recognition from a state or government has occasionally been elevated into a "policy of non-recognition", designed as a sanction for breach of rules of international law. "Non-recognition" is a concerted policy by several states not to recognise an entity as a sanction for a breach of international law by the entity in question. The absorption of Manchuria by China, and of Estonia, Latvia and Lithuania by Russia in 1940, was met by such a policy.

TYPES OF STATES

Unitary states, federal states and confederations

A unitary state, causes no problem in international law. This is a state which, under international and constitutional law, is considered as an entity. France is a good example. The United Kingdom is an entity in the eyes of international law but not under constitutional law.

A federal state is also considered as one entity in international law. It may happen that the constitution, which regulates the position of the component states *vis-à-vis* the federation, permits the former to enter into international relations with other states on certain restricted matters. This may be permitted with the agreement of the federal government, for example, in the Federal Republic of Germany, or without this agreement, for example, in Switzerland.

The difficulty of a federal government arises when it is expected to enter into agreements with other states, the implementation of which requires action to be taken by the component states over which the federal government has no control. This difficulty is avoided by the use of the "federal state clause" which makes the international obligations of the federal state conditional upon the co-operation of the component states — an unsatisfactory but inevitable compromise in certain circumstances.

Confederations no longer exist, although the official title of the state of Switzerland is still the "Swiss Confederation". This term describes the condition in which two or more independent states decide to "pool" the exercise of certain competences, without, however, creating a central authority to replace that exercised by the "pooling" states. This situation is inherently unsatisfactory (in that the displaced authority is never effectively exercised) and historically has always been transitory. States either revert to full independence, or else become a federation. A confederation during its existence is not a state in international law.

Personal unions: real unions

A personal union occurs when two states have the same head of state. The contemporary world contains no examples of personal unions.

A real union takes place when two territories merge for the purposes of international law into one, while remaining separate for all internal purposes.

Permanently neutral states

Austria, Sweden and Switzerland are all neutral states, but the position in international law of each is different. The neutrality of Austria results from the "State Treaty", signed with the U.S.S.R. in 1955. Austria alone is unable to change this status. This status has subsequently been recognised by other states.

Sweden's neutrality is self-imposed, and is not recognised by other states. If Sweden decided to join NATO no other state could object on legal grounds.

Switzerland's neutrality is also self-imposed, although in this case not only is it one of the foundations of the Constitution of the Confederation, but it has been recognised by all the surrounding states as a permanent feature. Nevertheless, if the Swiss people agreed to change the Constitution, no state could object on legal grounds if Switzerland ceased to be neutral.

A permanently neutral state is a "neutralised" state: its neutrality is made "permanent" by the action of other states. A recent example is Laos, whose declaration of neutrality in July 1962 was guaranteed by a Thirteen Power Declaration.

FORMATION, CONTINUITY AND SUCCESSION OF STATES

Formation

"No rule of international law requires a State to have a definite or pre-determined structure." (*Status of Continental Sahara Case* (I.C.J., (1975)). In that case the International Court of Justice expressed the opinion that a state can be described (but not defined) as possessing four characteristics: having a settled population, inhabiting a territory, being organised under a government and being independent of any other state.

Population. The population must be settled, not nomadic. There are no requirements as to common language, culture, ethnic background or religion; or as to the size of the population.

Territory. Some territory must be inhabited by the population, although there is no requirement as to its size, area or extent. The outward limits or frontiers do not need to be established in detail. Israel, for example, was admitted to the United Nations before the outward limits of its territory were known. Separate portions of its territory may even be situated on different continents, as for example, the Netherlands and Surinam.

"Territory" in this context means land territory, and not air, water (including perpetually frozen ice), nor artificial constructions built on the sea-bed.

Organised under a government. We are here describing a state in the context of its international relations, and of the application of international law to those relations. But the state is represented in its relations with other states by its government, and would be unable to maintain any such relations without a government of some sort. It follows that every state must have a government, in the sense that a people not organised under a government cannot be considered to constitute a state.

A temporary anarchic situation during which a people formerly organised under a government lose all governmental control through the eruption of civil war will not deprive the state of that quality. So long as the anarchy is caused by the opposition of diverse groups seeking to gain control and become the government of the state, the international community will merely suspend international relations, and await the outcome (in the meantime making such temporary and provisional arrangements, especially of a humanitarian nature, as the circumstances may require). The state of the Congo was admitted to membership of the United Nations at a time when the government which had made the request for admission had been overthrown, the country was in the midst of a bloody civil war, and no one was able any longer to speak in the name of the government.

The government must satisfy three condition:

(a) it must represent the state, in the sense that it speaks in the name of the population;

(b) it must be able to govern this population, in the sense that it can impose its will;

(c) it must have some likelihood of permanence, in that, even if the actual government loses office it will be replaced by another. It is the institution of government, not the members of any particular government, which must have the appearance of being firmly established.

The government need not satisfy any other conditions; the matter is sufficiently often misunderstood for it to be worth stressing that there are no requirements of international law with respect to:

(a) the name or powers of head of state (monarch (whether constitutional or otherwise), emperor, president, etc.);

(b) the method or system of government (democratic, fascist, totalitarian, despotic, oligarchic);

(c) the political ideology (capitalist, socialist, communist);

(d) the internal organisation of the government (cabinet system, caucus, one-man rule);

(e) the place where the government is located (governments in exile may be located outside the territory);

(f) the nationality of the members of the government (the Italian Government of Mussolini was recognised as the Government of Abyssinia after the conquest of that country by Italy, and the Allied Powers as the Government of Germany after the Second World War).

Qualifications possibly introduced by recent developments of international law concern human rights and the right of all peoples to self-determination. The right to vote in free elections in order to choose a government is now widely accepted by states as a "human right" and it would appear to follow from this that the government must be democratically elected. Both the substance and the effect of the principle of self-determination are obscure, but it might prevent a government whose members were fundamentally alien to the population (for example, of a different nationality or ethnic background) being recognised as capable of "representing" the population of the state.

Independent of any other state. "A settled population, inhabiting a territory, organised under a government" — such a description would fit the state of Massachusetts, the Bylorussian Soviet Socialist Republic, the *Land* of Baden-Württemburg, the Canton of Geneva, or the State of Mysore. Moreover, it would apply to Puerto Rico or South-West Africa. The condition which excludes all these entities from being considered "states" for the purposes of the application of international law to international relations, is independence.

Unlike the first three conditions, independence is a legal and not a factual condition. The assessment of one state's legal independence will be made by each other state separately and will be measured by the extent to which the new state is recognised: the retention of foreign military bases on the territory, by agreement, does not affect the new state's legal independence. A state which has once acquired independence may, by treaty, revert to a dependent status. For example, Morocco, an independent state subsequently, by treaty accepted the status of protectorate, giving France control of its external affairs. This did not rob Morocco of its status as a state: it merely limited the exercise of its legal independence for the duration of the treaty. The suspension or termination of the treaty would have led to Morocco re-acquiring complete control over its own affairs. The case of Morocco was discussed in the case concerning the *Rights of Nationals of the United States in Morocco* (I.C.J., 1952). The external affairs of Liechtenstein are by agreement in the hands of Switzerland who thus exercises two votes in elections for Judges of the International Court of Justice. But if a state has previously by treaty agreed not to compromise its independence, preservation of this status becomes a duty. In the *Customs Regime between Germany and Austria Case* (P.C.I.J., 1931) a much-divided court considered that adherence to a customs union might in certain circumstances compromise the independence of a state.

Identity and continuity

Changes affecting the identity of the state. When after dynastic, constitutional or territorial changes, a state re-emerges on the international scene the question arises whether the new entity continues the identity of the former state, or whether it is a new state, the former having become extinguished.

Dynastic changes will never interfere with the identity of the state, as the history of France illustrates. Constitutional changes will do so only when and only to the extent that states voluntarily renounce their independence by merging into a federal state (as the United States merged the thirteen states of the Union, Italy merged the kingdoms of Lombardy, Piedmont, etc.). Under the original German and Swiss constitutions, the principalities and cantons nevertheless retained a measure of independence and to this extent continued the identity of the former states.

Territorial changes will interfere with the identity of the state only when they lead to total dismemberment of the original state. When the territories of the Austro—Hungarian and Ottoman Empires were redistributed, Austria and Turkey were considered to continue the identity of the former empires (*Ottoman Debt Arbitration* 1925)). When the Indian Empire was split into India, Pakistan and Burma, India continued the identity of the former Empire. Yugoslavia is (probably) a continuation of the legal personality of Serbia, so that a treaty of extradition of 1901 between the United States and Serbia was binding on Yugoslavia (*Kolovrat, et al.* v. *The State of Oregon* (U.S. Supreme Court, 1961)).

Changes wrought by conquest and absorbtion during war or by act of aggression are in principle to be considered as temporary situations; only the treaty of peace or subsequent international settlement can decide whether the identity of the state has been submerged or merely suspended for the duration of hostilities.

Consequences of the continuity of the state. The general rule is that if the state continues in existence, so do its rights and obligations. Changes of dynasty, head of state or government do not affect the rights and obligations previously incumbent upon the state. The refusal of the Soviet Government of the U.S.S.R. in 1918 to recognise Russian debts incurred by previous Russian governments was contrary to international law (and was a reason why certain governments refused to recognise the Soviet Government).

However, debts incurred by an insurrectionary force during or in anticipation of civil war or revolution and arising out of loans to raise funds for the carrying on of hostilities do not bind the opposing force which, by winning the struggle, becomes or remains the legitimate government. *Contra* where the force administers part of the territory and the debt was contracted as an incident of normal administration (*Hopkin's Case* (U.S.A. — Mexico Claims Commission, 1926)). State property seized by the rebel or insurrectionary forces may be claimed by the winning side (the government) as of right. Property acquired or funds raised by the rebels during the insurrection may be claimed by succession, but subject to any corresponding obligations in connection with such property. All debts of the winning force become state debts from the moment of their inception. These rules apply irrespective of recognition by the state pursuing the claim (*Tinoco Arbitration* (1923)).

The principle of permanent sovereignty over natural resources may affect a government's obligation to respect concessions, whether by treaty or contract, awarded by a previous government.

The right of self-determination may affect a government's obligation to respect treaties entered into by a previous government which was not representative.

These exceptions to the general rule are apparent but not real, since in each case they rest on the assumption that the debt or obligation in question never was binding on the state but was merely opposable to the entity which entered into it.

Where the identity of the state continues after a lapse of time. Austria was merged into Germany by the *Anschluss* in 1938; "Austria" re-emerged in the post-war settlement of 1945. Syria and Egypt merged into the United Arab Republic in 1958. Subsequently Syria seceded and took the name Syrian Arab Republic. The Governments of Austria and of the Syrian Arab Republic acted on the assumption that the "new" state had continued the identity of the "former" state. For example, the Austrian Government accepted liability for the pre-*Anschluss* Austrian debt. (The Syrian and Egyptian Governments had retained independence with respect to all financial matters throughout, so that the same problem did not arise.)

For these cases the rule appears to be that the government may opt to continue the identity of the state, but that this requires acceptance of all rights and obligations up to the moment of merger. Rights and obligations arising during the interruption are treated in the same manner as cases of state succession (*see* below) subject to the application of the principle of *force majeure* where the intervening merger was not voluntary.

Succession of states

The difference between state continuity and state succession. Apart from the above case which is exceptional, state continuity involves no interruption of legal continuity between the state as it was before, and the state as it is after, the change. State "succession" (as the word implies when used in national law) does involve an interruption of legal continuity.

This interruption arises out of the fact of replacement of one state by another in the responsibility for the international relations of territory, leaving aside any connotation of inheritance of rights or obligations on the occurrence of that event.

Partial succession and total succession. The body of rules known as the rules of "state succession" apply to two situations: partial succession, where there is a change of sovereignty over territory, one state replacing another; and total succession, where one state is totally extinguished. In the former case the rules of state succession regulate the extent to which rights and obligations — whether arising under treaties or otherwise — previously applying to the territory and population pass to the new sovereign. In the latter, the rules regulate to what extent the treaties, rights and obligations of the former state pass to the states incorporating its territory or population, and to what extent they lapse for lack of an entity in which to vest.

Succession with respect to treaties. In cases of partial succession the state losing territory remains in existence, and will remain party to all treaties by which it was bound before the loss of territory. This is a consequence of the rules of state continuity. To this rule there is one exception, in that the principle of treaty law *rebus sic stantibus* may apply to extinguish a treaty which has been so undermined by the change of circumstances wrought by the change of territory as to have lost all point. However, it is thought that this principle can apply only when the change of territory is involuntary and occurred by *force majeure*. Where the change of territory was voluntary it is difficult to see how a state can find its treaty relations with third states affected thereby. But treaties may lapse with the passage of time through the non-applicability of their provisions in the new territorial circumstances.

"Personal" rights and "territorial" rights. Certain questions of succession concern the state as an international person. These give rise to the succession of "personal" rights and obligations. Other questions concern rights and obligations which devolve with, and are inseparable from, territory. These may be called "territorial" rights or obligations or rights and obligations *in rem*.

The difference between extinction through the principle *rebus sic stantibus* and lapse through non-applicability becomes important when the preceding territorial situation is revived, or when in some other way the treaty once again becomes of practical importance through some succeeding change of circumstances. For an extinct treaty cannot revive; whereas a lapsed treaty may do so. After the First World War notices reviving the Anglo—Austrian Treaty of 1873 were given to Austria and Hungary; but a new treaty was entered into in 1924 with Czechoslovakia, a new state created out of the territory of Austria—Hungary.

Conversely, the state acquiring the territory will not become party to any new treaty by the mere fact of having acquired the territory. There is thus no "direct" succession to treaties. In the case of *Gil* v. *Polish Ministry of Commerce and Industry* (Supreme Administrative Court of Poland, 1923), the plaintiff alleged that a treaty of commerce between Austria—Hungary and the Russian Empire of 1906 "continued in force" between the Republic of Poland (in respect of those parts of its territory acquired from Austria—Hungary) and the Russian Empire. The court rejected this contention; a state could not become party to a treaty for the sole reason that part of its territory formerly belonged to a state which was a party to the treaty.

On the other hand, the other party to a bilateral treaty may, by notice, agree to consider a treaty previously applicable between it and the state losing territory as henceforward applicable between it and the state acquiring the territory, whether this be an already existing state, or a newly created state. The legal effect is then dependent upon the agreement of the states concerned, and not upon the succession. In the case of *Re Westerling* (High Court of Malaya, Singapore, 1950) the question was whether Indonesia had succeeded to the Anglo—Netherlands Extradition Treaty of 1898 in relation to Java, to which territory the treaty (and the Extradition Act 1870) had previously been applied. The Attorney-General of the United Kingdom informed the court, and the court accepted as binding, that this treaty now applied between the United Kingdom and Indonesia.

The principle of "movable treaty frontiers". The acquiring state may be required to extend, and the losing state will necessarily have to restrict, the territorial application of existing treaties. However, the question whether the acquiring state is obliged to extend the application of any particular treaty to the newly acquired territory is solely a matter of interpretation of the treaty, for it is not the treaty obligation which has changed, but its application to the territory of the state, The general rule of treaty law is that the rights and obligations arising out of treaties apply to the whole territory of the state unless otherwise stated or implied. Naturally, any treaties meant to apply to the state irrespective of its territorial boundaries, will be automatically extended. Thus a Franco—Belgian convention of 1899 on reciprocal enforcement of judgments was applied in the case of *Société Lebrun* v. *Dussy* (Brussels Court of Appeal, 1926) to a decision given by a court in Alsace after the annexation of Alsace-Lorraine by France under the 1919 Treaty of Versailles. On the other hand, any treaty concluded as a bargain can only be considered to extend to newly acquired territory if the bargain is not thereby upset.

Treaties creating rights or obligations "in rem". Treaties establishing frontiers are unaffected by state succession. Treaties concerning river-banks, waterways, railways, telegraph lines and other rights in territory may also survive the accident of change of personality of the parties to the treaty. Treaties whose object is to impress an area with a particular status may also be unaffected. Thus, by a treaty of 1856 between France and Great Britain on the one hand and Russia on the other, Russia undertook to demilitarise the Aaland Islands in the Gulf of Bothnia. These islands, which occupied a strategic position in relation to Stockholm, became in 1918 part of the territory of Finland. Sweden alleged that this special demilitarised status had to be respected by Finland as the successor state, and that any "interested party," whether or not a party to the treaty, could insist on it. A Committee of Jurists appointed in 1920 by the Council of the League of Nations, to which Finland and Sweden had referred the dispute, reported that the special international regime must be respected and could be invoked by Sweden, and rested its decision on the existence in this case of real obligations independent of the actual holder of sovereignty.

Another example occurs in the *Free Zones Case* (P.C.I.J., 1932). The Treaty of Turin, 1817, established the political frontier between Switzerland and Sardinia, and restricted the levying of customs duties in the zones of St. Gingolph and Gex, which separated Geneva from the frontier. A dispute arose over the interpretation of this treaty, which was, however, settled by a manifesto of the "Royal Sardinian Court of Accounts" in 1829. This abolished the customs house in the village of St. Gingolph and designated the area as a "free [customs] zone". This zone was included in the territory incorporated in France in 1860. In 1919, France suggested to Switzerland that the status of this zone should be regarded as having lapsed since it was no longer consistent with existing conditions. The Treaty of Versailles accordingly included an article which stated that France and Switzerland were to agree to its alteration.

A dispute arose out of Switzerland's refusal to regard the status of this zone as having been altered without its consent (not being a party to the Treaty of Versailles). The court upheld Switzerland's position and also stated that the manifesto of 1829 had settled the law between the parties to the treaty of 1816 and that France, as Sardinia's successor, must abide by the latter's interpretation of it.

New states and treaty succession. The legal problems confronting the government of a newly independent state concerning succession to treaties include not only the application of the rules set out above, but also the question whether there are any rights or obligations which devolve upon a newly created state, but which would not devolve upon an already existing state.

The answer to this problem, so far as treaties are concerned, is now to be found in the Vienna Convention on the Succession of States in Respect of Treaties, concluded on 23rd August 1978, being the most recent fruit of the work of the International Law Commission. Part III of this Convention is entitled "New Independent States" and sets out the general rule that a "newly independent state is not bound to maintain in force, or to become a party to, any treaty by reason only of the fact that at the date of succession of states the treaty was in force in respect of the territory to which the succession of states relates".

New states and bilateral treaties. If the new state decides not to prolong the treaty this becomes extinct. If the new state wishes to prolong the treaty it must ask the other party whether it accepts subrogation by succession, since the new state can no more oblige the other party against its will to be in treaty relationship with a state which did not exist at the moment the treaty was made, than the new state itself can be obliged against its will to be bound by such treaties.

The rule is stated thus in the Vienna Convention:

"A bilateral treaty which at the date of a succession of states was in force in respect of a territory to which the succession of states relates is considered as being in force between a newly independent state and the other state party when: *(a)* they expressly so agree; or *(b)* by reason of their conduct they are to be considered as having so agreed."

New states and multilateral treaties. In relation to multilateral treaties the matter is otherwise. Irrespective of whether the new state becomes a party to it the treaty will generally continue in force as between the other parties. However, the change of circumstances wrought by the attainment to independence of the new state might be such that the parties prefer to consider it as terminated. Otherwise the treaty continues in force and the parties continue to benefit from it. The equity requires that the new state should also be given that opportunity. This only applies however to treaties having some relation to the territory or population of the new state. The parent state often prepares a list of such treaties, but this merely represents its own opinion on the matter. It does not bind, but may be accepted by, the new state.

A state may, by accession or subrogation, become party to a treaty after it has entered into force. Any state may accede to a treaty which permits unconditional accession at any time, and may accede to those which permit accession subject to fulfilling a condition, on fulfilment of that condition. But, in pursuance of the principle of equity, a new state may claim the additional right to become party to a treaty where the treaty does not permit accession. This can only occur where the parent state numbered amongst the original parties and where the treaty specifically relates to the territory or population of the new state, or was made by the parent state on behalf of the territory in question. Where the application of the new treaty had merely been extended to the territory of the new state, its government has the right to ask to become a party thereto, and must accept the reply of the other parties (in the same way that a state which puts in a reservation accepts the decision of the other parties as to whether or not they regard the state making the reservation as a party to the treaty). Where the parent state does, but the new state does not, satisfy one of the objective conditions of accession, the new state may at least ask to have the conditions waived.

The principles are set out in the Vienna Convention in the following manner:

"A newly independent state may, by a notification of succession, establish its status as a party to any multilateral treaty which at the date of the succession of states was in force in respect of the territory to which the succession of states relates, [unless] it appears from the treaty or is otherwise established that the application of the treaty in respect of the newly independent state would be incompatible with the object and purpose of the treaty or would radically change the conditions of its operation; [or unless] under the terms of the treaty or by reason of the limited number of the negotiating states and the object and purpose of the treaty, the participation of any other state in the treaty must be considered as requiring the consent of all the parties, [in which case] the newly independent state may establish its status as a party to the treaty only with such consent."

Succession with respect to matters other than treaties:

(a) The legal system. Most state practice and the majority of decisions of national courts support the rule that civil and commercial (or private) law continues in force unless and until the new sovereign changes it. The same is true with respect to penal and administrative (or public) law, subject to two exceptions. Rules of the former state which are considered repugnant, contrary to natural justice, or in contradiction with *ordre public* will be considered as being impliedly changed without any express action being required. Rules of basic constitutional importance whether in relations between individuals, or between an individual and the state, will be incorporated by implication into the law of the predecessor state even while this law in other respects continues to apply.

(b) State debts. Dismemberment of a state always has taken place by agreement of the successor states. This agreement generally also concerns the division of responsibility for debts. If this problem is not settled by agreement, a court may be asked to effect some *pro rata* settlement. (*See* the *Ottoman Debt Arbitration* (1925)).

(c) Obligations. Successor states are responsible neither for breaches of obligation of the predecessor state (whether contractual or delictual) nor for the reparation due as a result thereof. Thus in *Robert E. Brown's Claim* (1923), the claim of Brown, a United States citizen, against the United Kingdom in respect of illtreatment received at the hands of the Boers, prior to the conquest of the Transvaal by the British, was rejected by the tribunal on the ground that private wrongs of the predecessor state cannot be imputed to the successor state.

II. INTERNATIONAL ORGANISATIONS

GENERAL
The term "international organisation" in its broad sense refers both to organisations created by states and to those established by private persons or bodies. By the end of 1979 there were approximately 4,000, of which, however, only 320 were "intergovernmental", the others being "non-governmental organisations". This section is not concerned with these, except in the limited sense mentioned in the next paragrah, since their independent legal existènce is not recognised in public international law.

The Economic and Social Council of the United Nations, most of the specialised agencies of the United Nations, and the Consultative

Assembly of the Council of Europe have established procedures for according certain non-governmental organisations "consultative status". As well as providing the organisations concerned with specialist advice in their fields of competence, this gives the chosen non-governmental organisations a privileged status so far as concerns their participation in the activities of the governmental organisations, including the right to receive information where this is not classified, and to make known their views concerning questions falling within their recognised sphere of competence.

The term "international organisation" will henceforward be used to designate only intergovernmental organisations.

Definition of an "international organisation"

An "international organisation" is an organisation established by a treaty to which three or more states are parties. An "organisation" is an entity legally distinct from any other and composed of one or more organs. An "organ" has been described as a "collectivity of powers grouped under one name".

Strictly speaking, it is inaccurate to incorporate the expression "intergovernmental" in this definition, for the parties to the treaty by which an organisation is created are necessarily states and not governments. The latter merely act on behalf of the former. However, by becoming a party to a treaty constituting an international organisation a state may accept obligations the performance of which falls exclusively upon its government and not upon the state as a whole. This is the case, for example, of the "Intergovernmental Maritime Consultative Organisation", one of the specialised agencies of the United Nations.

Diversity of international organisations

International organisations differ considerably both in size and in importance. The largest and most important is, of course, the United Nations. A table could be drawn up of the size of all international organisations measured by reference to state membership, but there is no necessary correlation between size and importance. In any case, the importance of an international organisation is difficult to assess.

The aims and purposes of international organisations, and therefore their activities, are equally various; indeed to such a point that it is probable that the only thing they have in common (besides their common origin in treaties) is their legal status. The same remark, however, might be made about corporations under national law.

LEGAL STATUS

In general

The constituent instrument. Every international organisation is created by a treaty between states. This treaty becomes the constituent instrument of the international organisation. It follows that the source of the law of international organisation lies in the law of treaties.

Birth and demise. Since international organisations are created by treaty they come into existence at the moment of the treaty's entry into force (unless it otherwise provides); they thereafter continue to exist until the treaty is terminated. It is, however, rare for states to terminate treaties constitutive of international organisations by an express act. Nor can termination in most cases be implied from the conduct of the member states. Mere lack of interest or non-participation on their part will not be enough if the international organisation has once been active, for in this case it will have acquired physical existence (staff-members, premises, equipment, etc.) which cannot be just abandoned. For this reason, of the 320 international organisations listed in the *Yearbook of International Organisations* no less than one-fifth are considered inactive. Legally, however, they all still exist.

Succession. For the reason given above, there is little practice in respect to succession of international organisations. The League of Nations was wound up at a specifically convoked session of the Assembly of the League in 1946, and arrangements made for its property to pass to the United Nations. More frequent is the transformation of an existing organisation, as for example the Organisation for European Economic Co-operation into the Organisation for Economic Co-operation and Development (including Canada, Japan and the United States).

Merger. An interesting case of the merger of international organisations is to be seen in the circumstances of the creation of the European Space Agency (ESA), by a convention signed at Paris in 1975. This convention provides that as of its entry into force "the Agency shall take over all rights and obligations of the European Space Research Organisation (ESRO) and of the European Organisation for the Development and Construction of Space-Vehicle Launchers (ELDO)" (Article XIX) and that on the same date "the Convention for the establishment of ESRO and the Convention for the establishment of ELDO shall terminate" (Article XXI).

This "merger" by demise and rebirth was performed pursuant to a resolution of the European Space Conference which had decided that a new organisation with somewhat enlarged aims and purposes would be formed out of ESRO and ELDO. This operation was facilitated by the fact that, after the withdrawal of Australia as a member of ELDO, all the members of ELDO were also members of ESRO. To complete the transfer, which from a legal point of view is of considerable elegance, provision was made that the convention creating the new organisation should enter into force only after ratification by all the states members of the merged and dissolved organisations.

So far as the transfer of assets and liabilities were concerned, those relating to ESRO (principally research) were to be retained extended, but all the major projects of ELDO were to be terminated and the assets and liabilities liquidated. In the five year period between the conclusion of the European Space Agency Convention and its entry into force, this policy was carried into effect, but it was specifically provided by a resolution of the European Space Conference that any ELDO liability not so liquidated but taken over by the ESA would be met by such only of the member states of the Agency as had been members of ELDO.

The new convention provides (Article XIII) that any state not a party to the ELDO or ESRO Convention which becomes, by accession, a party to the European Space Agency Convention "shall make, in addition to its contributions, a special payment related to the current value of the assets of the Agency". It is thought that this example of charging, as it were, an entrance fee, is an innovation in international organisation law.

Transfer of competences. Different again is the case of the transfer of competences from one organisation to another. For example, in 1959, certain social and public health activities of the Western European Union were transferred to the Council of Europe, the Western European Union continuing to exercise its military and other political functions. This was possible because all its members are members of the Council of Europe, within which these activities are now carried on under a "partial agreement".

"Second generation" international organisations. Just as companies may, under municipal law, establish new companies, so international organisations can, under international law, set up new international organisations. This may happen wherever it appears that some activity coming within the general terms of reference of one organisation could be more effectively carried out by a separate organisation specially created to that effect. In the case of UNITAR (United

Nations Institute of Training and Research), and UNIDO (United Nations International Development Organisation), both established by resolution of the General Assembly, the aim was no doubt to ensure their functional independence. In setting up by resolution the Resettlement Fund to resettle refugees, the Committee of Ministers acting on behalf of the Council of Europe, was principally concerned to ensure the Fund's separate financing, and capacity to sue and be sued in its own name.

Legal personality in international law

Every international organisation has a legal personality in international law. The extent of that personality differs from case to case.

In establishing an international organisation, states are always guided by the same object, which is to substitute for their own individual and unconcerted actions in a certain field one entity capable of acting on behalf of all of them. Without legal personality such an entity is incapable of performing acts having legal significance, so that the bestowment of legal personality within *some* legal system is indispensable to the achievement of that object. By definition, international organisations perform governmental or other state functions (parliamentary or judicial). Since no part of the inhabited globe is outside the territory of a state, international organisations have to be established within state territory. Unless accorded immunity, their acts would be subject to the law of that state. Since it is inconceivable that states will permit the exercise of public functions carried out on their behalf to be subject to the law of another state, the activities of international organisations are exempt from the application of the local law. (*See* below: Privileges and immunities.) It follows that the grant of legal personality on the level of municipal law is not in itself enough to permit international organisations to perform their functions. Moreover, many of the functions (political, military, etc.) of international organisations fall outside the scope of municipal law and can only be performed on an international level. The endowment of an international organisation with a legal personality in public international law is, therefore, a *sine qua non* of achieving the object for which the organisation was set up.

International organisations and sovereignty. International organisations are not sovereign. Whereas, within the international legal system, a state may do anything not contrary to the general law or its particular obligations under treaties, an international organisation may, on the contrary, act only within the limits of its constituent treaty. For one of the principal functions of that treaty is to mark off the functions and powers of the organisation from those retained by the member states. Moreover, it may only act in accordance with agreed procedures. The analogy may usefully be drawn with the position of the individual and of the corporation, respectively, under municipal law. Only the individual has "full legal capacity", the corporation being required to act within the limits of its charter. This analogy must not be taken too far, for in setting up a corporation account has to be taken of the municipal law which contains certain rules mostly of form, breach of which may result in the corporation being invalid. In international law, states are sovereign in this as in other matters, there being no requirements as to form in the creation of international organisations, except that the constituent instrument must be a treaty.

The extent of the legal personality of an international organisation: legal capacity. Although each international organisation has a legal personality in international law to enable it to act in the performance of its functions, one may not invert that relation and assume that the mere possession of legal personality empowers the organisation to act by reference to that legal system. For as shown above, the legal capacity of an international organisation depends upon its powers, and the powers of an organisation are set out in or may be implied from its constituent instrument.

Subjective or objective personality. It is one thing for a group of states, by treaty, to create an international organisation, endowed with separate legal personality: it is quite another for other states to be obliged to recognise it.

In the case of the *Reparations for Injuries suffered in the Service of the United Nations* (I.C.J., 1949) the court was asked to give an Advisory Opinion on the question whether Israel, at that time not a member of the United Nations, was required to recognise the legal personality of the United Nations for the purposes of a claim to reparation made by the United Nations against Israel and arising out of the killing of Count Bernadotte and other persons while on special United Nations duty in Palestine. The court answered this question in the affirmative.

While this decision may be supported in the special case of the United Nations in view of the central place assigned to that organisation by the international community, it would be unwise for any other international organisation to work on the basis that it too had objective personality, in view of the rule regarding the effect of treaties on third parties. The United Nations must be considered in this, as in other important respects, as an organisation *sui generis*.

Legal personality in municipal law

Article 104 of the Charter of the United Nations declares that "The Organisation shall enjoy in the territory of its members such legal capacity as may be necessary for the exercise of its functions and the fulfilment of its purposes." Most international organisations are accorded a similar "functional" legal capacity, enabling them to acquire premises, purchase office equipment, enter into contracts, institute legal proceedings, etc.

Privileges and immunities. International organisations are subject to local law, unless exempted. Since there is no rule of customary international law that an international organisation is immune from the local law, such an exemption must be expressed in the constituent treaty. Provisions to this effect are rare. On the other hand, international organisations are, almost invariably, expressly exempted from the application and the enforcement of municipal law, and it is with this aspect of the matter that the whole question of privileges and immunities of international organisations is concerned.

General agreements on privileges and immunities. An article in the constituent instrument generally accords privileges and immunities under some general "functional" formula, and provides that these are to be set out later in detail in a separate instrument. Article 105 of the Charter of the United Nations is typical in this respect:

> "1. The organisation shall enjoy in the territory of each of its Members such privileges and immunities as are necessary for the fulfilment of its purposes.
>
> 2. . . .
>
> 3. The General Assembly may make recommendations with a view to determining the details of the applications of paragraph 1 . . . or may propose conventions to the members of the United Nations for this purpose."

Article 2 of the General Convention on the Privileges and Immunities of the United Nations adopted in 1946, states that: "The United Nations, its property and assets, wherever located and by whomsoever held, shall enjoy immunity from every form of legal process, except in so far as in any particular case it has expressly waived its immunities."

Agreements on privileges of other organisations contain almost identical provisions. The premises and archives of the organisation are normally inviolable, and it is accorded a range of fiscal and currency privileges the extent to which varies between organisation and organisation. The communications of all organisations are immune from censorship and some of the most important also have the right to use codes and bags and to have priority, equal to that accorded to foreign governments, and for their telecommunications. The United Nations has, in addition, the right to operate its own radio station, aircraft and vessels. Both the United Nations and the Council of Europe have the right to fly their own flags.

Headquarters agreements. The legal status, privileges and immunities accorded under the constituent instrument and the general convention or agreement on privileges and immunities apply within the territory of all member states, and not just within that of the host state. There is, however, a range of questions which affect only the organisation and the host state. These are regulated in a Headquarters Agreement. Such an agreement would for example specify the conditions under which the organisation's premises may be entered by the authorities of the host state, make provision for appropriate protection of the organisation's premises, and most important, delegate power to authorities within the state and within the organisation to regulate subsidiary administrative matters as and when they arise.

The security of the state and the independence of the organisation. Some agreements (*see* the Protocol on the Privileges and Immunities of the European Launcher Development Organisation (ELDO)) provide that "each member state retains the right to take all precautionary measures necessary in the interests of its security". Where this matter is not expressly regulated the question can only be resolved case by case, since it brings into conflict two principles of equal importance, namely, the security of the state, and the independence of the organisation.

Waiver. Privileges and immunities are accorded exclusively in the interests of the proper functioning of the organisation, and this is always expressly stated in General Agreements. It follows that the authority within the organisation having the power to invoke the immunity is also under the duty to waive it wherever this can be done without prejudice to the proper functioning of the organisation.

"Organs" of an international organisation

An organ which is endowed with original powers is, by conception, so constructed as to be able to act. It has a stated composition, and its procedure is governed by rules. Moreover, each organ is independent of any other, unless otherwise stated in the constituent instrument.

An international organisation, like a state, can act only through one of its organs. However, the legal entity remains the international organisation, since its organs do not normally have any legal personality, each organ merely acting on behalf of the organisation in respect of matters falling within its competence, unless the constituent instrument states otherwise. The Security Council of the United Nations appears to be an exception in view of the express terms of Article 24(1) of the Charter, which reads:

> "In order to ensure prompt and effective action by the United Nations, its members confer on the Security Council primary responsibility for the maintenance of international peace and security, and agree that in carrying out its duties under this responsibility the Security Council acts on their behalf."

While acting in this capacity the Security Council is thus clearly endorsed with a separate legal personality, since it exercises responsibilities directly on behalf of the member states of the United Nations, and not indirectly through the intermediary of the United Nations. It is believed, however, that the Security Council is the only case of an organ of an organisation having separate personality.

Some of the smaller international organisations have only one organ; the largest, the United Nations, has five principal organs, and a large (and ever increasing) number of subsidiary ones. The United Nations is the only organisation to operate such a distinction, and even there it has proved unworkable since there are organs which are neither principal nor subsidiary.

Statutory and non-statutory organs. As a general rule, the constituent instrument expressly names each of the organs of the international organisation. However, in rare cases the charter may provide for the participation of a body without naming it as an organ, as for example the "Secretariat" in the Council of Europe. Whether such a body is nevertheless an organ of the organisation will depend upon whether it can act, and whether it was designed as part of the structure of the organisation.

The representative organ. A reserve power necessary to deal with situations which occur in the life of the organisation, but which, unforeseen by the founders, are not dealt with in the constituent instrument, falls to the organ which is composed of a representative of each member state. The Treaty of Rome actually contains a rule to this effect: "Where action by the Community appears necessary to achieve one of the objectives of the Community, . . . and where this treaty has not provided the necessary powers of action, the Council shall adopt the appropriate provisions by a unanimous decision, after consulting the Assembly" (Article 235).

Sub-organs. For the fulfilment of its tasks an organ may have resort to such aids as it deems necessary or useful. These may include the creation of a sub-organ to fulfil one particular and limited task. It would appear that an organ has an inherent power to create sub-organs to perform specific tasks where this appears to be *necessary* (as opposed to being merely *useful*), subject to the evident rule that the sub-organ can never exceed the functions or powers of the parent body.

The addition of new organs. To discover the organs which constitute an international organisation, reference must be made to its constituent instrument. New organs may be created either by an amendment thereto, or through application of an "implied power" (as in the case of the Administrative Tribunal of the United Nations). Organs created by neither of these methods but through conclusion of a new treaty will not become organs of the organisation unless the treaty amends the constituent instrument. This is so even where the new treaty was concluded within the framework of the organisation with the avowed object of furthering its aims. Such is the case of the European Court of Human Rights, and the European Commission of Human Rights, commonly referred to as being "of the Council of Europe". In fact these organs were established under the Convention for the Protection of Human Rights and Fundamental Freedoms, a treaty drawn up within the Council of Europe and open only to its member states. There are many links between the Human Rights organs and the Council of Europe, just as there are between a holding company and its subsidiaries. Legally, however, they are separate entities, although in *Zoernsch* v. *Waldock and McNulty* (English Court of Appeal, 1964) the court unanimously came to a contrary conclusion in English law.

POWERS OF AN INTERNATIONAL ORGANISATION
The powers of an organisation are merely the sum of the powers of its organs, including the reserve power inherent in the representative organ. One of the principal purposes of the treaty which becomes the constituent instrument of the organisation is to separate the powers accorded to the newly created organisation from those retained by member states. Even after it has become a member of an international organisation, a state must retain the right to allege that the organisation is acting *ultra vires*, and this allegation is made by one subject of international law (the state) against another (the international organisation).

For one organ to assume to itself a power allocated to another is just as much *ultra vires* as for the organ to assume a power beyond those allocated to the organisation. Should the General Assembly of the United Nations act on the basis of a power which, under the Charter, is allocated exclusively to the Security Council, the act would be *ultra vires*, and member states would be under no obligation to comply with or to contribute to the expenses of such an operation. The validity of the establishment by the General Assembly of the United Nations Emergency Force in the Middle East was challenged by two members of the Security Council, France and the U.S.S.R., on such a ground. They accordingly refused to contribute towards the financing of it. The General Assembly referred this question to the International Court of Justice for an Advisory Opinion. The court advised, in the case of *Certain Expenses of the United Nations* (I.C.J., 1962), that the General Assembly did have the power under the Charter to establish such a force, from which it followed that these states, as members of the United Nations, had the duty to contribute towards its expenses.

Interpretation of the powers of an international organisation

Consideration of the implied powers of an organisation is inseparable from the question of interpretation of its constituent instrument, a question at present governed by customary law. The Vienna Convention on the Law of Treaties, which came into force on 27th January 1980, applies to any treaty concluded after that date, which is the "constituent instrument of an International Organisation . . . [without prejudice] to any relevant rules of the Organisation" (*see* Article 5). It will thus be the ordinary rules of treaty interpretation which will apply to such treaties. The main rule will then be that "a treaty shall be interpreted in good faith in accordance with the ordinary meaning to be given to the terms of the treaty in their context and in the light of its objects and purpose." But it is further provided that there shall be taken into account together with the context "(*b*) any subsequent practice in the application of the treaty which establishes the agreement of the parties regarding its interpretation" (Article 31(3)).

This rule runs perilously close to saying that whatever an organisation does is lawful because the acts constituting the "practice" establish "the agreement of the parties regarding its interpretation". However, this cannot be sufficient especially where some of those parties have voted against the act and have been outvoted, if the reason for their opposition was that the organisation was acting *ultra vires*. The phrase (in Article 5) "subject to any relevant rules of the organisation" includes those which lay down by which majority decisions shall be taken. Only where the organisation acts on the basis of a vote *nem. con.* can the act on which the practice is founded be considered to "establish the agreement of the parties regarding its interpretation": this, at any rate, is the position if any member state's objection is based, even partially, on the *ultra vires* argument.

The principle of "effectiveness"

With the passing of time, the text of the constituent instrument becomes less and less helpful for the interpretation of the legality of the acts of an international organisation. Situations arise which were, frankly, not envisaged by the founders, or if they were, were not regulated in the text from lack of agreement as to how to do so. Accordingly, it is the "objects and purpose" of a treaty constituting the international organisation which become of primary importance. This is the legal justification for the argument of "implied powers".

Implied powers

Any powers the possession of which are necessary for the effective use of powers expressly granted, may be implied. This may best be illustrated by an example: the Charter of the United Nations makes provision for a secretariat, "which shall comprise a Secretary General and such staff as the organisation may require" (Article 97). "The paramount consideration in the employment of the staff . . . shall be the necessity of securing the highest standards of efficiency, competence and integrity" (Article 101(3)). The General Assembly established an "Administrative Tribunal" to hear appeals from decisions of the Secretary General affecting staff members. The Secretary General dismissed certain officials. The Administrative Tribunal upheld their appeal, and awarded a large sum as damages. The General Assembly was divided over whether it was obliged to vote these sums, or whether it could overrule the decision of the Tribunal. In the *Effect of Awards of the United Nations Administrative Tribunal* case (I.C.J., 1954), the International Court of Justice, invited to give an Advisory Opinion as to the question whether "the General Assembly had the right on any grounds to refuse to give effect to awards of compensation" of this type, was confronted with the argument that because the General Assembly had established this Tribunal, the awards of the Tribunal could not be considered binding on the General Assembly. The court, in refuting this argument, pointed out that the Tribunal possessed a power, the judicial power, which the General Assembly did not itself possess, from which it followed that the one could not be subordinate to the other. This finding, however, raised the further question whether an organ had the power to create a body with powers it did not itself possess. The court found that, in this case at least:

". . . the power to establish a tribunal, to do justice as between the organisation and the staff members, was essential to ensure the efficient working of the Secretariat, and to give effect to the paramount consideration of securing the highest standards of efficiency . . . Capacity to do this arises by necessary intendment out of the Charter."

In creating the Tribunal, the General Assembly was thus doing something *necessary* for the continued operation of the United Nations through its Secretariat.

The same case illustrated the principle that, unless otherwise stated in the constituent instrument, each organ may act on behalf of the organisation within the field of its competence. This does not apply to a sub-organ, which can only act, if so empowered, on behalf of the organ of which it is a subsidiary. The Administrative Tribunal (which was not a sub-organ) was acting in the name of the United Nations in awarding these sums, and the General Assembly as an organ of the same organisation had no alternative but to vote in favour of them.

PARTICIPATION OF STATES IN THE ACTIVITIES OF INTERNATIONAL ORGANISATIONS

Participation

As distinct from membership. The only invariable rule so far as concerns the participation of states in the activities of international organisations is that it is the participating states which pay, or otherwise provide, the budget of the organisation.

Generally speaking, the form of participation is membership of the organisation, but there is no rule and no necessity that state participation should take this form. In creating by treaty an international organisation, states are establishing a body to perform a service for themselves, and it follows that they are prepared to pay for it. But it does not follow that they are obliged to participate as members of the organisation. So long as they are satisfied with the service, and have established a satisfactory system of control over the expenditure of the organisation, there is no need for their participation to extend further. It is therefore appropriate, before dealing with the membership of an international organisation, to deal briefly with the question of financial participation.

Financial participation. As a general rule, the budget of an international organisation is paid exclusively by the participating states. If other states are subsequently permitted to participate in some or all of its activities a proportionate contribution to the budget is generally required.

There is no fixed rule as to the manner in which the budget is divided up between member states. In some cases the basis of contribution is size of population; in others, size of population and gross national product are both taken into account. In some of the early organisations, for example the Universal Postal Union, a state could choose which of the different standards of membership it desired, members of Class I paying a higher proportional rate than those of Class II, and so on.

It is rare for the amount of the financial contribution to have any incidence upon voting rights. Only in financial organisations such as the International Monetary Fund does this occur. In such cases, the operational budget has to be distinguished from the administrative budget; but it is only in relation to the former that financial participation has a direct effect upon voting rights.

Membership

The members of international organisations are generally states but they may also be governments, individual departments of governments, or the national administrations of some public utility, such as the railways. An example of the latter is the European Company for the Financing of Railway Rolling Stock, the members of which are the national railway administrations of sixteen European states. Some international organisations do not have a fixed membership. For example, the Government of Belgium is authorised to invite all states and certain international organisations to each separate session of the Diplomatic Conference of International Maritime Law. There is no rule preventing non-sovereign states from becoming members of an international organisation: indeed, some of the oldest, the Universal Postal Union and the International Telecommunications Union, had separate representation for non-self-governing territories. It is even possible for the members of an international organisation to be specially chosen individuals, such as the nominees (chosen by governments) who collectively constitute the Asian—African Legal Consultative Committee. In fact, so long as the entity really is an international organisation, that is to say, has been established by an agreement to which three or more states are party, there is no restriction on who may become members of it. In general, however, the members of an international organisation are states or some authority within the state.

Organisations of unlimited membership. Certain organisations, all of which are within the United Nations family, aspire to universal membership, but none have achieved it. The United Nations apart, the organisation with the largest state membership is the Universal Postal Union with 147 members.

Organisations of limited membership. A special group of organisations are of a regional character (the Council of Europe, the Organisation of American States, the Organisation of African States, and the League of Arab States). Another group of organisations of limited membership are the Commodity Councils (coffee, tea, sugar, tin, etc.) generally confined to states importing and exporting the commodity.

Original membership. A treaty constitutive of an international organisation generally enters into force after ratification by a certain number of signatory states. These states are the original members of the organisation, unless the treaty otherwise provides. An example of a constituent treaty that does provide otherwise is the Charter of the United Nations which states that "The States signatory to the present Charter which ratify it *after* it has come into force will [also] become original Members of the United Nations on the date of the deposit of their respective ratifications" (Article 110(4)).

Subsequent membership. Unlike original membership, subsequent applicants must satisfy any conditions there may be as to membership.

Conditions of membership. All international organisations contain some condition as to membership even if it is only that the applicant be a "state", "government", etc. Consequently, some procedure is normally laid down to permit a decision to be taken as to whether the applicant fulfils this condition. This is generally a decision taken by vote in the representative organ of the international organisation. A distinction is often drawn between objective and subjective conditions. A condition that membership is restricted to "petroleum exporting" states, as in the case of the Organisation of Petroleum Exporting Countries, is objective, since whether a state exports petrol is a fact which may be verified. A condition that it be "peace-loving" is subjective, and cannot be verified.

However, since the decision-making procedure is the same whether the conditions are subjective or objective, this distinction is generally devoid of importance. Reasons do not have to be given for casting a vote within an organ of an international organisation. Thus, in the case of a subjective condition, it becomes impossible to control the exercise of the voting power, even where an appeal is provided to a judicial body. Again, while a state may not make its vote dependent upon any conditions other than those contained in the constituent instrument (*Conditions of Admission of a State to Membership of the United Nations* (I.C.J., 1948)) there is no way in which this rule can be applied unless the state voluntarily

gives reasons for the way in which it casts its vote. Where the condi-
is objective (for example, the Council of Europe is open to all European states) the same decision-making procedure (that is, a vote in
the representative organ, the Committee of Ministers) would be
decisive, even if, for example, the applicant were Israel. In other
words, the objectivity of a condition of membership cannot be
relied upon so long as the decision as to whether it has been fulfilled rests in the hands of a political body in which decisions are
taken by vote.

Representation of states within international organisations

In organisations of which the members are states, governments or
some department of government, that is to say the vast majority,
members are represented on the various organs of the organisation
by officials, Members of Parliament, judges, technical experts, trade
union officials, etc. For example, each member state is represented
in the Conference of the International Labour Organisation by four
persons, two officials, one employers' representative, and one trade
union representative. In the Consultative Assembly of the Council
of Europe, member states are represented by a delegation of members of Parliament varying in number from three to eighteen,
depending on the size of population.

"Courts", "tribunals", "commissions", and "committees". Generally
speaking, the persons elected or nominated to "courts", "tribunals"
and "commissions" are chosen for the special qualities they possess.
Although their election or nomination will generally depend upon
their nationality and although they may have been proposed by
their governments, it is not correct to regard them as "representatives". In performing the task for which they have been chosen,
they express nothing but their own views. By contrast (and again
speaking generally, for there are exceptions) the members of a
"committee" are generally the representatives of the participating
states and their views are given "on instructions".

Representation of states vis-à-vis international organisations. The
volume of activity of some of the more important international
organisations is such that states have found it convenient to be permanently represented at the seat of the organisation. There are thus
"permanent representations" (equivalent to ambassadors) at New
York, Geneva, Brussels and Strasbourg. The role is to represent
their state's interests *vis-à-vis* the organisation as a whole. In practice,
the same diplomat is often accredited as the representative of his
state in the most important permanent organ. In this latter capacity
he is a representative in the sense used in the preceding paragraph,

but to that organ or that committee alone, and not to the whole organisation.

Privileges and immunities of representatives of states to international organisations. All representatives on committees and all individual members of courts, tribunals and commissions functioning within international organisations are accorded "functional immunity". This covers words spoken and written during the performance of their tasks, freedom from arrest and detention during the course of the mission (unless caught *in flagrante delicto*), and freedom from customs search of official papers and immigration and visa control. The law on this question is, however, less clear-cut than it should be, and certain General Agreements are defective in this respect.

The legal regime governing permanent representations (or missions) and permanent representatives is, unless otherwise provided, that applicable to diplomatic missions and diplomats.

LEGAL EFFECTS OF ACTS OF INTERNATIONAL ORGANISATIONS

The acts of an international organisation

In a sense, everything that an international organisation does is an act. In the context of this section, however, the word has a narrower meaning, and refers only to those acts of the organisation which are in a form expressly provided for in the constituent instrument. In this respect, the word resembles the concept of the *acte* in French law, viz. an act or document invested by law with a special significance. That it is in substance *ultra vires* does not prevent it being an "act of the organisation".

The context of an act. The organs of international organisations are authorised to perform acts not in the abstract but — invariably — within a certain context. Most frequently this is within the context of the organisation itself, as for example Article 4(2) of the Charter of the United Nations: "The admission of any . . . .state to membership of the United Nations will be effected by a decision of the General Assembly upon the recommendation of the Security Council." Such acts — the "recommendation" and the "decision" — have legal effect solely within the organisation. Another common context is that of the relationship of the organisation with its member states. *See* for example Article 10 of the Charter: "The General Assembly may discuss any . . . matters within the scope of the present Charter . . . and make recommendations to member states." The context of the act will indicate whether it is the law of the organisation which will determine its legal effect or whether

regard must also be had to some wider legal context (public international law or, as the case may be, the national law of a member
or a non-member state).

The source of an act. The idea that an act can have a source is
strange unless it is realised that the "acts" in question are of a
special kind. It is not the host of administrative acts and decisions
that are in question but only those acts by and through which the
organisation is empowered to accomplish its aims. Examples taken
at random from the Charter of the United Nations are "decisions";
"recommendations"; "investigations"; that the Security Council
may "call upon" member states to do various things: that the
Secretary General may "bring to the attention of" the Security
Council the existence of certain situations; that the Trustee Council
may "hear petitioners", "examine reports"; and so forth.

As has been stated, an organisation may act only through one of
its organs. Nearly all organs (except the secretariat) decide matters
by a vote. The source of all such acts is therefore to be found in the
procedure, culminating in a vote, by which proposals are turned
into decisions. (A vote need not actually be taken; it is enough if
it could have been taken at the request of any one present.) It
follows that proposals which do not receive the number of votes
required for adoption do not lead to any "act" at all.

In the Advisory Opinion on the *Competence of the General
Assembly for the Admission of a State to the United Nations* (I.C.J.,
1950), the International Court of Justice was asked whether the
"admission of a state to membership of the United Nations pursuant
to Article 4(2) of the Charter could be effected by a decision of the
General Assembly when the Security Council has made no recommendation for admission by reason of the candidate having failed to
obtain the requisite majority . . . upon a resolution so to recommend." In returning the answer "No" to this question, the court
addressed itself to the argument that there were "positive recommendations" and "negative recommendations", the latter being
resolutions to recommend which had failed to obtain the requisite
majority. The court rebutted this argument by reference to the
general principles of treaty interpretation as applied to the Charter.
The short answer is, however, that where a proposal is put to the
vote and fails to receive the requisite support there is no act. This
does not depend on the interpretation of the particular instrument
or upon the rules of procedure of the organ in question but may be
considered an application of a general principle concerning the
functioning of international organisations.

The name of an act. Every international organisation has its own
name for its acts: "resolutions", "recommendations", "decisions",

etc. Some are in common use (particularly recommendations and decisions). It might be thought that the legal effect of all acts having the same name would be the same, whatever the organisation which performed them. This is not the case: on the contrary, the legal effect of the act of an international organisation, however called, can only be discovered from an analysis of the law governing the international organisation in question, as the following example will show.

Within the United Nations any course of action resulting from a vote is a "decision" — *see* the terms of Articles 18 (the General Assembly), 27 (the Security Council), 89 (the Trusteeship Council). If reference is now made to Articles 4(2) and 10 (*see* above: *The context of an act*) which refer to "recommendations", it must follow that these are also "decisions". Indeed, Article 18(2) seems to confirm this interpretation: "*Decisions* of the General Assembly on important questions shall be made by a two-thirds majority of the members present and voting. These questions shall include: *recommendations* with respect to the maintenance of international peace and security." It now becomes clear that the "decision of the General Assembly" in Article 4(2) must be something different from the "decision[s] of the General Assembly" in Article 18(2).

This analysis of the use of the same term as applied to the same organ of a single organisation will show what little significance can be attached to the name or term used to described the act in the search for its legal effect. It will also serve to show of what little use is "the ordinary meaning of the term" for the interpretation of treaties which are the constituent instruments of international organisations.

Legal effect of an act

In international law. The constituent instrument of the organisation may itself spell out the legal effect of the different classes of "acts". An example is the Treaty of Rome which instituted the European Economic Community. Five types of "act" are provided for: regulation, directive, decision, recommendation and opinion. It is specified that:

> "Regulations shall have general application. They shall be binding in every respect and directly applicable in each member state. ... Directives shall be binding, in respect of the result to be achieved, upon every member state, but the form and manner of enforcing them shall be a matter for the national authorities. ... Decisions shall be binding in every respect upon those to whom they are directed . . . . Recommendations and Opinions shall have no binding force" (Article 189).

Generally, however, the constituent instrument is vague about this important point (sometimes because the drafters of it were unable to agree). The Charter of the United Nations authorises the General Assembly to make "recommendations" to member states without giving any precise indication as to their effect upon the recipients. The International Court of Justice had occasion to state in the Advisory Opinion on the *Competence of the General Assembly for the admission of a State to the United Nations* (I.C.J., 1950) that "a recommendations must, by the very nature of things, precede a decision", but as indicated above no conclusions may be drawn from general observations of this nature.

The legal effect of acts directed towards member states can be divided into those that are merely hortative or indicative, those that are declaratory, and those that are binding. Much confusion was caused by the attempt to treat resolutions of the General Assembly as coming within either the first or the third category. In fact, however, certain resolutions such as "Declaration of Legal Principles Governing the Activities of States in the Exploration and Use of Outer Space" fall within the second category. They are authoritative in the sense that they constitute a declaration by member states as to the present state of international law on the matter in issue. Because nearly all the states in the world are members of the United Nations, their collective expression of the law on a topic immediately becomes more authoritative than any previous statement of the position. This does not however mean that the resolution is binding: their authority lies not in the fact that the rules are contained in a resolution, but in the fact that they are evidence of the formation of new rules of customary law.

In municipal law. Even where an act of an international organisation is binding upon a member state, the question arises whether it has direct application in its national law. It will only have such an effect if the constituent treaty expressly so provides (*see* for example the "regulation", Article 189 of the Treaty of Rome). Otherwise the "act" will take direct effect only on the international plane. Its effect on municipal law will be indirect and will depend upon the provisions of the constitutional law of the state in question. Such provisions concern the procedure by which treaty provisions and the acts of international organisations based upon such treaty provisions take effect in municipal law and vary widely between states.

Some states have a rule by which a treaty provision, as such, has no effect whatever in municipal law. This is the case in the United Kingdom. An Act of Parliament, or in the case of matters failing within the Royal Prerogative, an Order in Council, is necessary before a treaty provision can infringe upon English law. In other states, of which the United States is one, a distinction is made between treaties capable of direct application (self-executing treaties) and those that are not, only the latter requiring to be implemented by legislation in the official gazette, if necessary. In the Netherlands, publication is also sufficient since it has the character of an order to the courts to give effect to the treaty. In France, too, publication is sufficient to make the treaty applicable in French law. Before courts of the "administrative order" questions involving treaty interpretation are regularly referred to the executive, unless the interpretation is clear. Before courts of the "judicial order" only questions involving a point of treaty interpretation concerning a question of *ordre public* are referred to the executive. In Austria and Germany both parliamentary ratification and publication in the *Federal Law Gazette* are necessary. In Austria the treaty is then directly effective in Austrian law, to such a point indeed that it is the language used in the treaty, and not the national language, which constitutes the authoritative text! In Germany, no further action needs to be taken if the treaty is amended — the amended text is immediately applied as German law by the courts. Constitutional provisions which accord treaties the same force as federal or constitutional law are sometimes said to reflect a theory according to which there is a rule of international law that treaty provisions are hierarchically superior to the provisions of municipal law. There is no escaping the fact, however, that the effect in, for example, Austrian law of a treaty provision to which Austria has consented to be bound depends upon Austrian, and not upon international, law. Moreover, in view of the fact that the majority of states have rules which produce a different effect, it is difficult to assert that there is any customary rule of international law on the matter, far less that the "hierarchical" theory is a proper reflection of it.

INTERNATIONAL OFFICIALS

The secretariat
The concept of an "international official". Not all international organisations have an international secretariat, but those which do not have no continuing existence either. An institutionalised conference like the Diplomatic Conference of International Maritime Law, which meets once every two years, can make do with the assistance of some officials specially seconded for the occasion by the host state. However, where the organisation is required to function continuously, it needs a permanent staff. To provide this, member states might of course "second" members of their national civil service. This is, to a large extent, the case in NATO.

The conception of an international secretariat composed of international officials requires more than this. Such officials must be, in the first place, independent of governments. Their independence is most important, and most difficult, with regard to the state of their own nationality. For the allegiance owed to the state of his nationality an official must substitute a form of allegiance to the international organisations for which he is recruited. This substituted allegiance must not, however, be exaggerated: it applies only to the extent of the aims of the organisation, and to the scope of the official's duties within it. Outside this sphere the official is perfectly entitled, and is indeed expected, to preserve his national character, allegiance and culture. In no organisation, for example, is the official deprived of his vote in national elections by any rule of the organisation.

The role of an international secretariat. The role of the staff of an international organisation is to further its interests; the "interests" of the organisation are the interests of the collectivity of its members or the "general interest". This latter assertion follows logically from the hypothesis that the object of creating an international organisation is to substitute for the individual and unconcerted actions of a group of states, one entity capable of acting on behalf of them all. An offical who took as his point of departure the interests of a particular state would be incapable of working in the interest of them all — in the interests, that is to say, of the organisation. Such considerations explain why provisions to the following effect appear in the constituent instruments of most international organisations, in particular those entrusted with political functions.

(*a*) Officials are requested to make a solemn declaration that their duty will be to the organisation, and that they will not seek or receive instructions in connection with the performance of their duties from any government.

(*b*) Member states are required to accept an obligation not to seek to influence officials in the discharge of their responsibilities and to respect their exclusively international character.

Functions of an international secretariat. Every secretariat has one function, which is to provide secretarial and general administrative services to the other organs of the organisation. In the United Nations, for example, "[The Secretary General] shall be the chief administrative officer of the Organisation" (Article 97). "He shall act in that capacity in all meetings of the General Assembly" (Article 98). Beyond this, no general rule can be laid down. More illuminating is the possible classification of functions.

Original and derivative functions. An "original" function is one directly bestowed upon the secretariat by the constituent instrument: for example, "The Secretary General may bring to the attention of the Security Council any matter which in his opinion may threaten the maintenance of international peace and security" (Article 99). Functions performed by the secretariat on the orders, or at the request, of other organs of the organisation, are derivative. For example, "The Secretary General shall . . . perform such other functions as are entrusted to him by [the other principal organs of the United Nations] " (Article 98). Whether or not the Charter had contained such a provision, the Secretariat would have been obliged to perform these other functions. Whatever the nature of the functions so performed, whether political, military (as in the case of the United Nations Emergency Force in the Middle East) or administrative, their derivative status means both that the function is performed under the orders and the responsibility of another organ, and that it may be withdrawn by that organ at any time. Original functions (which are far more rare) are performed on the responsibility of the Secretary General, and cannot be withdrawn or amended without an amendment of the constituent instrument.

The organisation of the secretariat. A secretariat is normally organised hierarchically under a chief executive officer generally called the "Secretary General". More rare is the case of the European Community where the "Commission", one of the Community "institutions", is a collegiate body under a president but taking its decisions by a majority vote (Article 163 of the Treaty of Rome). Under this body is organised the remainder of the secretariat, the "officials" and "the other servants of the Community" (Article 212).

The legal status of a member of the secretariat vis-à-vis the organisation. Officials are recruited either by a contract, or, in the case of some organisations, directly appointed under a statute of service. Little importance attaches to the precise method adopted. Even if recruited by contract, the contract will refer to conditions of service governed by "staff rules". The rules or the statute of service are laid down by the "representative" organ of the organisation, and provision is always made for them to be changed by the same method. Thus in a sense the contract is not a contract, since it permits one party to it, the organisation, to change its obligations unilaterally.

However, it has become common practice to provide for the judicial settlement of disputes between members of the staff and the organisation arising out of their employment. A variety of "administrative tribunals" exist which have laid down a body of case-law from which certain principles may be deduced. Most important, so far as protection of staff is concerned, is the principle of the protection of the acquired rights of the staff. In application of that principle, although the conditions of service may be unilaterally changed, as indicated above, the staff must not be put in a worse position than they were before, once all such changes have been taken into account. In other words, changes which are to the prejudice of the staff are valid so long as there are other changes which improve their position, and the overall position is as good as, or better than, the previous one.

Privileges and immunities of international officials. In the exercise of his functions an international official is not subject to the sovereignty, and therefore to the public law, of the host state. Were it otherwise, he could not be an *international* official. In his daily life outside the organisation the official is subject to the local law and jurisdiction, so that any privileges he may have outside his official functions are by grace and favour of the host state rather than by legal right.

Applying these two propositions to the fiscal field, his salary and emoluments from the organisation are not subject to taxation, but revenue from other sources is; he is not subject to tax on the use of the car in which he drives to and from work, but he is obliged to pay rates or other taxes on private house occupation or ownership; he is not subject to national legislation imposing compulsory pension provisions, but he must participate in social security schemes which extend cover to his family, unless the organisation has itself made adequate provisions.

An official is not subject to immigration or visa restrictions in member states and any military service obligation is postponed during the course of his employment.

III. OTHER SUBJECTS OF INTERNATIONAL LAW

INSURGENTS

A civil war or armed uprising in one state may well have international repercussions. In the eyes of the existing government of that state any internal disturbance is a purely domestic matter. Where, however, other states find that the effect of the uprising is such as to endanger the lives or livelihood of their nations, or to disrupt commerce, these states are justified in reconsidering their attitude.

One possible attitude would be to regard the rebels as simple lawbreakers which would imply treating seizure of private property as the acts of robbers or pirates. This states habitually refuse to do for rebels are distinguishable from simple law-breakers by the political motive of their acts.

To overcome this difficulty, states may decide to recognise the rebels as "insurgents". This applies as much where the rebels' object is to establish a new state as where they aim at the overthrow and replacement of the government of an existing state.

Such recognition has the sole effect of absolving the recognising state from treating the rebels as law-breakers: the legitimate government is still owed all the rights (and still owes all the duties) that the government of a state habitually exercises over its territory and population. For example, treaties continue to apply to the entire territory of the state and the government is held responsible for damage caused by either side as a result of the uprising in the same way, and under the same conditions, as before the recognition of insurgency.

Any attempt by a foreign state to aid the insurgents would constitute intervention in the affairs of the state where the uprising has occurred. This applies to the transmission of broadcasts in their favour as much as to the supply of arms, or to the provision of training bases for recruits to the ranks of the insurgent force. On the other hand, other states may aid the legitimate government if they choose to do so, subject only to the limitations imposed by international law and the terms of the Charter of the United Nations.

BELLIGERENTS

If a state of insurgency shows signs of enduring, and if certain portions of the territory appear to have fallen under the control of an organised insurgent force, other states may feel obliged to adopt a more stringent attitude. This might (but in recent practice rarely does) take the form of recognition of a state of "belligerency" or of a declaration of neutrality. The one implies the other.

The belligerent power is recognised as the responsible authority in respect of the territory and population over which it exercises actual control. The legitimate government and the belligerent power are treated in most respects on a basis of complete equality. The laws of neutrality henceforward apply as if the conflict was an international rather than a civil one. The recognising state may engage in political discussions with the belligerent power through the sending and reception of official state agents, although since belligerents have no right to legation, these do not have the status of diplomats.

Recognition of belligerency is perhaps becoming obsolete. States have in any event the alternative of recognising the rebel party as the *de facto* government, and the legitimate government as the *de jure* government; of recognising the rebels as the government, and withdrawing recognition from the previous government; or, in the case of an attempt as secession, simply recognising a new state. Political considerations generally dictate which of these courses states will adopt. Each is a political decision having legal consequences, the effects of which are strictly limited to the relations between the recognising state and the recognised entity.

THE HOLY SEE

The position of the Pope is and always has been anomalous in international law.

The international legal personality of the Holy See is based on the fact that the Pope, as spiritual head of the Catholic Church, has for many centuries maintained international relations with states for the protection and promotion of the interests of the Catholic Church and the spiritual values on which it is founded. Thus states have concluded treaties with the Holy See, called Concordats, and have sent and received accredited diplomatic representatives. This aspect of the international legal personality of the Holy See has probably continued uninterrupted for several centuries.

The Pope's temporal position has, however, undergone severe changes. Until 1870 he was a monarch of the Papal States. His temporal position between then and the conclusion of the Lateran Treaty in 1929 was uncertain. That treaty, to which the parties are Italy and the Holy See, created the Vatican state, an area of less than one hundred acres, with a very small resident population, most of whom are there solely by reason of their office.

The significance of the Holy See in the field of international law "lies in the fact that international personality is here recognised to be vested in an entity pursuing objects essentially different from those inherent in States" (Lauterpacht, *Oppenheim*, eighth edition, Vol. 1, p. 254).

MANDATED AND TRUST TERRITORIES

Mandates and Trust Territories are almost a thing of the past. They did nevertheless constitute a noble experiment in international relations. Moreover, one Trust Territory still exists and the legal status of one mandated territory, recently terminated by the General Assembly, cannot be appreciated without a knowledge of the mandates system, so that these institutions cannot yet be considered a mere matter of history. Before the legal status of these territories can be understood, the mandate and trusteeship system must be briefly sketched.

The mandate system

In the words of Article 22 of the Covenant of the League of Nations:

"1. To those colonies and territories which as a consequence of
the [1914-1918] war have ceased to be under the sovereignty of
the states which formerly governed them [Germany and Turkey]
and which are inhabited by peoples not yet able to stand by
themselves under the strenuous conditions of the modern world,
there should be applied the principle that the well-being and
development of such peoples form a sacred trust of civilisation
and that securities for the performance of this trust should be
embodied in this covenant.

2. The best method of giving practical effect to this principle
is that the tutelage of such peoples should be entrusted to advanced
nations who by reason of their resources, their experience or
their geographical position can best undertake this responsibility,
and who are willing to accept it, and that this tutelage should be
exercised by them as mandatories on behalf of the League."

Article 22 then set out the three types of mandate, A, B, and C.
The A and B mandates have all become independent and so are no
longer relevant. The Covenant described C mandates in the following way:

"6. There are territories, such as South-West Africa and certain
of the Pacific Islands which, owing to the sparseness of their
population, or their small size, or their remoteness from the
centres of civilisation, or their geographical contiguity to the
territory of the mandatory, . . . can be best administered under
the laws of the mandatory as integral portions of its territory,
subject to the safeguard above mentioned in the interests of the
indigenous population."

The safeguards referred to are given in the previous paragraph in
the context of the B mandates, and read as follows:

"The mandatory must be responsible for the administration of
the territory under conditions which will guarantee freedom of
conscience and religion, subject only to the maintenance of public
order and morals, the prohibition of abuses such as the slave
trade, the arms traffic and the liquor traffic, and the prevention
of the establishment of fortifications or military and naval bases
and of military training of the natives for other than police purposes and the defence of the territory."

The mandate for South-West Africa was given to the Union of
South Africa. The Pacific Islands were split into four — Samoa

(mandatory, New Zealand); Nauru (mandatory, the British Empire, i.e. Great Britain, Australia and New Zealand jointly); other Pacific Islands south of the Equator (mandatory, Australia); Pacific Islands north of the Equator (mandatory, Japan).

The trusteeship system

At the time of the dissolution of the League of Nations in 1946 none of these territories had achieved independence. This was one of the reasons why the Charter instituted, as Chapter XII, an international trusteeship system. This was to apply to:

(a) territories now held under mandate;
(b) territories which may be detached from enemy states as a result of the Second World War; and
(c) territories voluntarily placed thereunder by states responsible for their administration.

Of the former C mandates, Samoa and Nauru were turned into Trust Territories and have since achieved independence. The Pacific Islands south of the Equator were known as the Trust Territory of Papua New Guinea and were administered by Australia. This has now terminated, Papua New Guinea having achieved independence. The Pacific Islands north of the Equator were detached from Japan and became a Trust Territory administered by the United States as a strategic area.

However, South Africa refused to convert South-West Africa into a Trust Territory, and expressed its intention of making it part of its own territory.

In its Advisory Opinion on the *Status of South-West Africa* (I.C.J., 1950) the court advised the General Assembly that South Africa was under no obligation to conclude a trusteeship agreement, but had no authority to modify the status of the mandated territory without the consent of the United Nations.

Trusteeship agreements. Territories became Trust Territories by the conclusion of a trusteeship agreement "between the States directly concerned". The terms of the trusteeship had to be approved by the Security Council in respect of strategic areas, and by the General Assembly in all other cases. The Pacific Islands, an area comprising the Maricana, Caroline and Marshall Islands, was the only strategic area trusteeship agreement. The General Assembly approved ten trusteeship agreements.

Objectives of the trusteeship system. The objectives of the international trusteeship system are set out in Article 76 of the Charter. Except for the mention of the furtherance of international peace and security (an implied reference to the "strategic area"), these are, broadly speaking, the same as for the mandates, viz. "to promote the political, economic, social and educational advancement of the inhabitants and their progressive development towards self-government or independence . . . as may be founded by the terms of the Trusteeship Agreement." In fact, no trusteeship agreement refers to self-government as the final aim.

The trusteeship council. The administration of the trusteeship system was entrusted to the trusteeship council (*see* Chapter XIII of the United Nations Charter). It was to consist of members which administer Trust Territories, the other permanent members of the Security Council, and as many other members as may be necessary to ensure equality between administering and non-administering authorities (Article 86). With only one state, the United States, still administering Trust Territories, this article can no longer be complied with. The trusteeship council now consists of this state plus the other four permanent members of the Security Council: China, France, U.S.S.R. and the United Kingdom. Administering authorities are obliged to submit to the council annual reports, to accept periodic visiting missions and to forward petitions, so that they may be examined by the council in consultation with the administering authority.

The legal status of mandated and trust territories

No territories have been voluntarily placed under mandate or converted into Trust Territories; they were all territories which had been "detached" from states as the result of the two World Wars. In other words, these states had lost their sovereignty over the territories in question by force of arms. The mandate and trusteeship systems hinged on the fact that the power or powers to whom the people and territories were entrusted did not acquire sovereignty over them. The residual aspects of sovereignty were bequeathed to the League of Nations and — in this respect as its successor — to the United Nations. Only when the international community, in the shape of the League of Nations and the United Nations, considered that the peoples of these territories were ripe for independence, could the sovereignty reappear in the form of a new independent state, or as part of an already existing state.

This is so in the case of, *inter alia,* South-West Africa. In spite of the fact that the Covenant authorised the mandatory to administer territory "under its laws as an integral portion of its territory" this does not mean that the mandatory has the powers of sovereignty — see the *Status of South-West Africa* case.

In the same case, the International Court of Justice was confronted with the problem that the League of Nations had disappeared without provision being made for the continuance of the supervisory functions exercised by its Permanent Mandates Commission. There appeared, therefore, to be no body in existence to ensure that "securities for the performance of [the] trust" (in the words of Article 22(1) of the Covenant) were being complied with. In these circumstances the court boldly declared that these supervisory functions had devolved upon the United Nations (as *ultimus heres*).

In two further Advisory Opinions, the court developed this conclusion in respect of the voting procedure to be adopted within the United Nations and the treatment of petitions. In their capacity as former members of the League, Liberia and Ethiopia then started contentious proceedings against South Africa *(South-West Africa Cases (Preliminary Objections)* (I.C.J., 1962), *(Merits)* (1966)), alleging that the introduction of apartheid into the territory constituted a breach of the mandate. Article 7 of the mandate specified that "if any dispute whatever should arise between the Mandatory and another member of the League of Nations relating to the . . . application of the provisions of the Mandate, such dispute . . . shall be submitted to the Permanent Court of International Justice." On the merits of the claim, the court decided that these states had no legal rights or legally protected interests arising out of the mandate: that South Africa owed its obligations with regard to the treatment of the inhabitants to the League as such, and not to the individual members — obligations now owed therefore to the United Nations.

The advisory opinion handed down by the International Court of Justice on 21st June 1971 in the case concerning the *Legal consequences for States of the continued presence of South Africa in Namibia (South-West Africa) notwithstanding Security Council Resolution 276 (1970)* appears to have clarified the situation in two respects: it has confirmed the legality of General Assembly Resolution 2145 (XXI) which purported to have "terminated the Mandate for South-West Africa"; and it upheld Security Council Resolution 276 (1970) which declared the continued presence of South Africa in Namibia — the name by which the former territory of South-West Africa is now known — to be illegal, and called upon all members states of the United Nations to act accordingly.

Although these opinions were adopted by large majorities, 13:2 and 11:4 respectively, it is difficult to see how the court overcame the objection that the General Assembly did not have the power unilaterally to terminate the mandate. The two key pronouncements appear to be the following:

"To deny to a political organ of the United Nations which is a successor of the League in this respect the right to act on the argument that it lacks competence to render what is described as a judicial decision, would . . . amount to a complete denial of the remedies available against fundamental breaches of an international undertaking" (paragraph 102 of the judgment).

". . . the General Assembly declared that, the mandate having been terminated, 'South Africa has no other right to administer the Territory.' This is not a finding on facts but the formulation of a legal situation. For it would not be correct to assume that, because the General Assembly is in principle vested with recommendatory powers, it is debarred from adopting, in specific cases within the framework of its competence, resolutions which make determinations or have operative design" (paragraph 105 of the judgment).

The objection to both these passages is that they assume what they set out to prove, i.e. whether remedies are available, and whether it is within the framework of its competence for the General Assembly to make the pronouncements in question. The reasoning in the judgment is unsatisfactory.

CONDOMINIUM

Nothing prevents two states agreeing to exercise sovereignty jointly over territory. When this happens a condominium is created. Each state may exercise its rights to sovereignty over the territory, the inhabitants of which may become entitled to the nationality of one or other or both states. Alternatively, each state may, by agreement, accord nationality to a part of the population. Each will, in any event, exercise separate jurisdiction over such of its subjects as are already resident before, or reside in the territory after, the condominium is established. But neither state is obliged to confer nationality as a mere consequence of the exercise of sovereignty over the territory. Where they do not so do, they are nevertheless each internationally responsible towards other states for the well-being and misdeeds of the resident population.

France and the United Kingdom used to exercise joint sovereignty over the New Hebrides Islands, until this territory achieved independence. Andorra, on the Franco—Spanish border, is a condominium administered by these two states.

SPECIAL TERRITORIAL SITUATIONS

Territory held on lease

It is not unknown for one state to obtain a leasehold over territory belonging to another. Thus part of the British colony of Hong Kong is on lease from China. The lease expires in 1997. During the period of the lease the lessee may exercise such rights as the lease agreement provides and this amounts, in the case of Hong Kong, to the exercise of full sovereignty.

Another species of the "lease" occurs when one state grants another the right to construct and use military bases on its territory. On the basis of an agreement made with the United Kingdom during the Second World War, the United States was given the right to build and operate bases in certain parts of the territory which subsequently become the Federation of the West Indies, in exchange for 48 destroyers. On the attainment of independence by the Federation the United States readily recognised that its rights had lapsed, thus demonstrating that the analogy with the municipal law concept of lease is not exact in international law.

The polar regions

In the Arctic, Canada and the U.S.S.R., and in the Antarctic, Argentina, Australia, Chile, France, New Zealand, Norway and the United Kingdom, have laid claim to certain areas. Other states have not accepted these claims. It is doubtful whether the requirements as to the acquisition of sovereignty over *terra nullius* apply, for most of these regions are composed of perpetually frozen ice, and as such are inherently incapable of supporting natural settlement.

The status of the Antarctic has been affected by the Antarctic Treaty of 1st December 1959 which stipulates a special regime for the region for a duration of thirty years, without, however, any of the claimant states having thereby renounced their claims over the territory. Inversely, their activities within this area in the meantime may not be considered as advancing their claims. Since all seven claimants as well as Belgium, Japan, South Africa, the United States and the U.S.S.R. have ratified this treaty, it may be considered as having impressed the region with a special regime in international law.

NATIVE TRIBES AND CHARTERED COMPANIES

Although today native tribes do not exist independently the measure of their former international personality as subjects of international law may not always be a matter of merely historical interest. For example, recently the chiefs of certain tribes in what had by then become part of Nigeria claimed from the Government of the United Kingdom the special status and privileges granted to them in a nineteenth-century treaty by the East India Company. The Legal Department of the Foreign Office advised the Government that, although the East India Company was acting under the authority and on behalf of the Crown, the native tribes had not been recognised as possessing any international personality. Accordingly, the agreement, although binding, was not one governed by international law (with the result that on the attainment by Nigeria to independence the United Kingdom's obligations thereunder had lapsed).

CHAPTER FOUR

The Position of the Individual (Including Corporations) in International Law

I. NATIONALITY

Nationality in relation to an individual is his quality of being a member or "subject" of a certain state. "It is a legal bond which constitutes the judicial expression of the fact that the individual . . . is more closely connected with the population of the state conferring nationality than with that of any other state" (*Nottebohm Case* (I.C.J., 1955)).

It is for each state to determine under its own law who are its nationals. Consequently, any question as to whether a person possesses the nationality of a particular state shall be determined in accordance with the law of that state (Rule 1). This law shall be recognised by other states in so far as it is consistent with international conventions, international custom, and the principles of law generally recognised with regard to nationality (Rule 2).

Rules 1 and 2 are taken from Articles 1 and 2 of the Convention on the Conflict of Nationality Laws of 1930, although in a slightly revised word order.

For any municipal law purpose, Rule 1 is sufficient, but for purposes of international law it is merely the starting point. While international law cannot confer nationality on one who does not enjoy that status under the law of some state, this nationality will have no effect under international law unless the requirements of Rule 2 are satisfied.

EFFECT OF NATIONALITY UNDER INTERNATIONAL LAW

Customary international law

An individual having an internationally valid nationality will be in a better position than one who has not in two principal respects:

his state may not deny him entry to its territory, and he will qualify for protection by his state while he is abroad.

Admission to the territory of the state

Strictly speaking, the rule is not that the individual may enter as of right, but rather that should any state other than that of his nationality wish to expel him, the state of his nationality may not refuse to admit him. The right thus belongs to states, not to individuals. Indeed, the individual may be obliged to return if expelled from a foreign state whether he wants to or not unless another state agrees to admit him.

Diplomatic protection of nationals

This topic is dealt with in a separate section (*see* section II below: Diplomatic Protection). Suffice it to say here that although a national qualifies for protection by his state while he is abroad, whether he will receive it will depend entirely upon the decision of his government. He has no protection as of right. He may also be "protected" while resident within his own state, for many states refuse to extradite nationals in circumstances which would otherwise have justified such extradition.

States have, on rare occasions, asserted the right to protect abroad persons who were not nationals, either because the person concerned had begun but not completed a naturalisation procedure, or because he had undergone service in the protecting state's armed forces. Such cases may be regarded as anomalous.

Conventional international law

In the contemporary world, the chief advantages of the possession of a nationality are conferred by treaties rather than by customary international law. The object of the conclusion of most treaties is to confer benefits upon the nationals of the contracting states. This applies to treaties of "friendship, commerce and navigation", consular treaties, treaties on establishment, treaties concerned with telecommunications, postal services, international travel by road, rail or aircraft, the administration of justice, etc. For every treaty dealing with military alliances or such matters of high politics, there are a hundred falling into these mundane categories.

Most-favoured nation clause

One frequently employed technique by which benefits are accorded under treaties to nationals is the "most-favoured nation" clause. A bilateral treaty containing such a clause confers upon the nationals of each contracting party treatment within the territory of the other as favourable as that given to the nationals of the "most-favoured" foreign state. An agreement to accord "national" treatment confers an even more favourable status, but this is more rare.

These two clauses apply not only to the position at the time this treaty comes into force but to any subsequent changes. State A may therefore find that a treaty with state X to improve the position of the nationals of X in A's territory will have the effect of improving the position also of the nationals of states M, N and O, because there are most-favoured nations clauses in force between A and those states.

Proof of nationality for the purpose of a treaty
If, under a treaty, benefit is conferred upon the "nationals" of a contracting party, the matter ceases to be a question purely of municipal law; for the question then is not whether the individual has a certain nationality for the purposes of that state's national law, but whether he has it for the purposes of the treaty. Under international law, any question of municipal law is treated as a fact. Just like any other fact, nationality requires to be properly proved. Under the Treaty of Peace with Italy of 1947, Italy agreed, in certain circumstances, to pay over compensation to "United Nations Nationals" (i.e. nationals of the Allied Powers). In the *Flegenheimer Case* (United States — Italian Mixed Claims Commission, 1958), the Mixed Claims Commission decided that the claimant, Flegenheimer, had failed to establish that he had United States nationality for the purposes of the treaty at the relevant time. This finding was without prejudice to the question of his status under American law. The case is a strong one, since the United States Government had submitted to the Commission Flegenheimer's "certificate of citizenship". In the somewhat confused circumstances of that case the Commission did not consider this sufficient proof.

"Nationality of claims"
When one state presents a claim before an international tribunal against another state based upon an injury suffered by an individual or a corporation, the admissibility of the claim depends upon the claimant state proving that the person or body concerned possesses its nationality. (*See also* Chapter Eleven.)

ACQUISITION AND LOSS OF NATIONALITY
A state may well not have any nationality law, and international law does not require that it enact one. The Yemen Arab Republic apparently had no nationality law for some years after its creation. Moreover, the question of a person's nationality only becomes of international significance in practice if he desires to go abroad. Possession of a passport is then normally sufficient evidence of the holder's nationality.

Passport and nationality

A passport is merely the name given to a document issued by the state attesting the nationality of the bearer. The issue of a passport need not depend upon the existence of any national law, but merely requires a decision of the government in relation to the applicant. States may prevent their nationals leaving the territory unless they are in possession of a passport. The actual document is, however, the property of the issuing state, and it is probable that its confiscation from the person to whom it has been issued by an authority of the host state with a view, for example, to preventing that person leaving its territory, is an inimicable act towards the issuing state involving its responsibility. In any event, nothing prevents the issuing state immediately issuing a new passport. (*See* further section III below: Visa.)

Effect of recognition of a state

Recognition of a "new" state and of its government amounts to recognition of the right of that government to speak for and represent in its international relations the population resident within the territory over which it claims sovereignty at the moment of recognition. The expression "population" in this context includes persons present in the territory other than those of a different nationality and those who are there in some capacity other than as residents. The same rule applies in relation to the population of any territory subsequently acquired, whether by cession or conquest. Where that population previously had a nationality (that of the ceding or partly conquered state), the inhabitants may be granted, at the discretion of the new sovereign, the option of retaining the former nationality, or acquiring a new nationality. Retention might in such a case, in conformity with international law, involve leaving the territory, for a state cannot be expected to keep on its territory large numbers of persons of a foreign nationality if it considers that to do so would constitute a threat to its internal or external security.

This is the original mode by which a state "acquires" its nationals. It may then decide by a "law" that henceforward persons shall acquire its nationality either through the *jus soli*, the *jus sanguinis*, or some combination of the two. In relation to the state, these become merely derivative modes of acquisition of nationality.

Acquisition of nationality by individuals

It is "generally recognised", *vide* Rule 2 above, that nationality can be acquired by birth, marriage or subsequent choice.

A person may acquire a nationality through birth either because of the place of his birth (*jus soli*) or because of the nationality of his father (or, if born illegitimate, of his mother) at the time of his birth (*jus sanguinis*). Where the nationality of the mother is different from that of the father, some states (for example France) allow the child to choose the mother's nationality on coming of age. The nationality of a child changes during minority with that of the parent.

A married woman may always acquire her husband's nationality. Some states require, while others merely permit, her to do so. Moreover, while some states allow her to retain their nationality after acquiring that of her husband, other states deprive her of her original nationality. Indeed, there is no reason why a husband should not obtain the nationality of his wife if municipal law so permits.

Nationality acquired by subsequent choice is called "naturalisation". Each state permits non-nationals to acquire its nationality if they want to, and if they fulfil certain conditions, of which a fairly long period of residence is normally one. However, the first and essential condition is the exercise of a free choice. No state can be allowed to "nationalise" the nationals of another state by, for example, imposing nationality on all who buy property, or establish or direct companies in its territory. Some former state practice, involving South and Central American Republics, provides examples of laws which provided that all persons who acquired real property within the territory would thereby acquire the nationality of the state in question. These laws gave rise to vigorous protest on the part of the other states, and were short-lived.

Loss of nationality by individuals

The nationality laws of all states provide certain circumstances in which a person may lose his nationality. He may be deprived of it against his will; he may be entitled to renounce it; or he may lose it as the automatic consequence of the acquisition of another nationality, through marriage or naturalisation.

Deprivation. The Universal Declaration of Human Rights states that "no one shall be arbitrarily deprived of his nationality" (Article 15(2)). Article 8 of the Convention on the Reduction of Statelessness, of 1961, sets out four grounds of deprivation which are not considered arbitrary:

(*a*) taking an oath of allegiance to another state;

(*b*) other evidence of repudiation, or desire to repudiate, allegiance to the state of nationality;

(*c*) rendering services to, or receipt of emoluments from, another state (in relation to espionage, in particular);

(*d*) conduct seriously prejudicial to the vital interests of the state of nationality.

Another ground, in both United States and Russian law, is failure to return to the territory to fulfil any obligation (for example, military service) of nationality.

All the above grounds apply irrespective of whether the person concerned has acquired a new nationality, or of his wishes in the matter. Loss of nationality by deprivation is thus a form of sanction.

Renunciation. The Universal Declaration of Human Rights states that "everyone has the right to a nationality" (Article 15(1)). If this nationality is to be a benefit rather than a burden to the individual, it should follow that he has the right to renounce one nationality on acquiring a new one (the so-called "right of expatriation"). This is unfortunately not the case. Apart from persons born with double nationality, few states permit their nationals the option of renouncing their nationality on acquiring a new one.

Automatic loss of nationality. On the other hand, all states provide some circumstances in which nationality is automatically withdrawn. These circumstances include the acquisition of a new nationality by naturalisation or marriage, and the failure to perform some act such as registration with a consul in the case of persons with an option to take up nationality at a certain age. This is a separate category in that there is no notion of sanction involved, and the automatic effect of the withdrawal distinguishes it from renunciation which concerns only withdrawal at the option of the person concerned.

Dual nationality of individuals

The variety of generally accepted methods of acquiring nationality leads to the phenomenon of dual nationality. If the nationality law of state X is based upon the *jus soli,* and of state Y on the *jus sanguinis*, a person born in state X of parents having the nationality of state Y would acquire the nationality of both states at birth. In such cases some states provide that their nationality may be renounced in favour of the other on the attainment of legal majority. Dual nationality may also be acquired by a woman through marriage, and more rarely by a person who is naturalised. The phenomenon of dual nationality can only occur as a result of the joint application of the nationality laws of two states, not just as a result of the application of that giving the second nationality. For the law of the state of the original nationality will also contain rules as to its withdrawal. Acquisition of a new nationality by a voluntary act is, for example, a common ground of automatic loss of the original nationality.

The Convention on the Reduction of Cases of Multiple Nationality and Military Obligations in Cases of Multiple Nationality 1963, accords to persons having the nationality of two or more parties the faculty of renouncing the nationality of one or more of them. Such persons are required to fulfil their military obligations in relation to one state only. Nationals of one party who acquire the nationality of another by their own free will, for example by naturalisation, are to lose their former nationality.

The effect of dual nationality of individuals in international law depends upon the place where the question has to be judged. "When in the country of their second nationality persons of dual nationality cannot avail themselves of the protection of the representatives of the state of the first nationality against the authorities of the foreign country, and are not exempt, by reason of possessing their first nationality, from any obligation (such as military service) to which they may be liable under the foreign law." This statement, which appears on the inside back page of a British passport, is a formulation of international law valid not only in relation to British nationals, but generally. Where a dual national seeks diplomatic protection whilst in some third state, that state is not answerable to both the states of his nationality, but only to one of them. It is in this situation that the "effective link" test was first enunciated. With which of the two states concerned does the person have the most "real connection"? The third state is entitled to judge this question for itself, and to recognise the nationality of that state only.

Nationality of corporations

How nationality is decided. The nationality of a corporation is decided by reference to the law of the state whose "nationality" is alleged. Under the law of the United Kingdom and of the United States, a corporation has the nationality of the state in which it is incorporated (the criterion of incorporation). States on the European continent use various criteria: the *siège social* in France, the *siège réel* in Germany, or the principal place of business in Italy. International law thus makes a *renvoi* to the appropriate municipal law to determine the nationality of a corporation.

There are special rules for deciding upon the nationality of "enemy" and "neutral" corporations in the context of the law of war. Here, the criterion of control is used almost exclusively. In a company limited by shares this requires an estimation of the nationality, or in some circumstances, the domicile of the directors and/or controlling shareholders.

The above rules do not necessarily apply in relation to a treaty where everything will depend upon the context. Where rights are given in favour of "citizens", "subjects" or "nationals" (in French, *ressortissants*), the treaty may be interpreted as applying only to individuals and not to corporations. Even if this is not the case, the treaty itself may specify which criterion is to be applied to determine the nationality of corporations. The mention of "corporations" in treaties of peace must thus be interpreted with particular caution.

Dual nationality of corporations. The multiplicity of acceptable criteria for according nationality to corporations may lead to a corporation having a dual nationality. A company incorporated in the United Kingdom but having its principal place of business in Italy would have, by British law, British nationality, and, by Italian law, Italian nationality. The rules set out above relating to this dual nationality of individuals apply to corporations. (*See also* section II below: Diplomatic Protection of Corporations.)

II. DIPLOMATIC PROTECTION

Protection can be viewed from several points of view: that of the state exercising protection; that of the state against which protection is being exercised; or that of the individual being protected.

"Diplomatic protection" is the protection by a state of its *nationals* abroad; section III below is concerned with international law rules governing the treatment by a state of *aliens* resident within its territory, and consequently with their protection from that state; while the international protection of human rights (*see* section VII below) is concerned with the protection of individuals *qua individuals* by the international community from states in general and the state of residence in particular.

DIPLOMATIC PROTECTION OF INDIVIDUAL NATIONALS

A state may exercise protection in favour of its nationals. This right is a right of states only, for although nationality entitles the bearer to seek protection, whether he will *receive* it depends entirely upon the discretion of the government. A national thus has no right to diplomatic protection. Moreover, if, as the result of a claim made on his behalf, a sum of money is paid by way of reparation to the state, the person concerned has no right, at least under international law, to a share of it.

Effective nationality

Nationality only entitles a state "to exercise protection *vis-à-vis* another state, if it constitutes a translation into juridicial terms of the individual's connection with the state which has made him its national" (*Nottebohm* (I.C.J., 1955)). This connection must be real; it must express the fact that the national is "more closely connected with the population of the state conferring nationality than with that of any other".

Mr Nottebohm, a German national, had been granted Liechtenstein nationality by naturalisation in 1939, thereby probably causing the loss of his German nationality. Both before and after this date he was a permanent resident in Guatemala, from which he was eventually expelled as an "enemy" national and refused readmission. Before his expulsion from Guatemala, his sole connection with Liechtenstein (a state which was neutral during the Second World War), was a visit to his brother, who resided at Vaduz. During this visit, he completed the formalities necessary for the acquisition of nationality (swearing an oath of allegiance, payment of certain sums of money and taxes). The International Court of Justice decided that Mr Nottebohm had acquired Liechtenstein nationality in circumstances which failed to demonstrate any effective link with that state. The court concluded that Guatemala was not obliged to recognise Liechtenstein's right to exercise diplomatic protection in his favour.

Although the International Court of Justice decided that Leichtenstein could not allege its right of diplomatic protection against Guatemala, the state of his former permanent residence, the court carefully refrained from stating what would have been the position in relation to any other state.

Since nationality acquired at birth, through application either of the *jus soli* or of the *jus sanguinis*, constitutes in itself a sufficient real link, the "rule in Nottebohm" can only apply, it is thought, to nationality acquired otherwise than at birth; and is perhaps even further limited to nationality acquired through naturalisation.

DIPLOMATIC PROTECTION OF CORPORATIONS

It is now well established that a state can exercise diplomatic protection in favour of a corporation which has its nationality.

Nationality based on the registered office (*siège social*), the centre of control (*siège réel*) or the principal place of business (*centre d'exploitation*) provides a sufficiently real link to satisfy the test of an effective nationality. In most cases, so does the criterion of incorporation, but there is, perhaps, one exception. A claimant state whose law employs the sole criterion of incorporation may not be able to exercise protection on behalf of its national when it is controlled by nationals of the state against which protection is being exercised. The sole authority for this proposition, however, is the somewhat equivocal case of the "I'm Alone" (Special Commission 1935).

A third state, however, cannot in any event rely upon this exception. In the *Agency of Canadian Car and Foundry Company Case*

(American—German Mixed Claims Commission, 1939), the United States claimed the right to exercise protection on behalf of the Agency, a corporation incorporated in the United States and thus having American nationality according to United States law. Germany alleged that this nationality was not effective, since the controlling shareholder was a Canadian corporation. This defence was rejected.

Protection of shareholders

The protection of foreign investments is today the most common form of diplomatic protection. However, in the Convention on the Settlement of Investment Disputes between States and the Nationals of other States 1965, drafted under the authority of the Executive Directors of the International Bank for Reconstruction and Development (I.B.R.D., or "World Bank"), a means has been found of substituting for diplomatic protection a more direct means of protection for the investor. For the states which are parties to that convention undertake to submit to conciliation or arbitration any legal dispute arising directly out of an investment with a foreign investor, whether individual or company, with whom they have agreed that disputes should be settled in this way. An International Centre for the Settlement of Investment Disputes is created with its seat at the World Bank, and provision made for the constitution of conciliation commissions and arbitration tribunals, as the case may be. Resort to this procedure excludes the use of diplomatic protection. This consensual approach made it unnecessary to define "investment".

The term investment does, however, include a shareholding in a foreign corporation. Protection may of course be exercised in favour of a corporation having the nationality of the protecting state. In certain cases a state may protect the "real interests" of its nationals in a foreign corporation. Where the corporation has the nationality of the defendant state, the right of other states to protect their shareholders is clear. Thus in the *Shufeldt Case* (United States — Guatemala Mixed Claims Commission, 1930) Guatemala granted Shufeldt, an American citizen, a concession subject to the condition that he created a Guatemalan company, and assigned the concession to it. This he did. The concession was then exploited for two years, after which Guatemala annulled the concession, thus bringing the activity of the company to a standstill. Guatemala argued that *(a)* the company continued to exist; *(b)* it was the sole concessionaire at the time the concession was cancelled; and *(c)* it had Guatemalan nationality. Admitting all three propositions, the Arbitrator nevertheless awarded damages to the United States, observing that it was not the rights of the company which were in dispute but the personal interests of Shufeldt in the company:

international law "was not bound by the national law (of Guatemala) nor by anything other than natural justice", and "puts aside the legal person in favour of the real interests in question".

Where the corporation has the nationality of some state other than the defendant state, third states have no right of protection of their shareholders unless *(a)* the corporation has meanwhile been wound up in the state of its nationality; or *(b)* the injury has been caused directly to the shareholders and not to the corporation; or *(c)* it is the shareholders' rights in the corporation rather than the rights of the corporation itself which have been allegedly violated. Thus in the *Barcelona Traction, Light and Power Company Ltd. Case* (Belgium—Spain) Second Phase (I.C.J., 1970), the Belgian Government claimed the right of diplomatic protection of its nationals as shareholders in the Barcelona Traction Company. This company, which carried on certain operations in Spain, was incorporated in Canada where it had since been put into receivership but not wound up. The court held that Belgium had no *locus standi* in other words no right to protect its shareholder nationals in this case.

III. ALIENS OR NON-NATIONALS

THE CATEGORY "NON-NATIONAL"

The division commonly drawn between nationals and aliens leaves out of account an intermediate category, the "non-national". The true distinction is between nationals and non-nationals, the latter category including aliens. A citizen of the Republic of Ireland in the United Kingdom, and of Costa Rica in the United States, is neither a "national" of the latter states, nor an "alien". He is therefore simply a "non-national". As such, he has, while within the territory, all the rights and capacities, but also all the obligations, of a national (except in relation to certain political rights).

ALIENS

Stateless persons and refugees apart (as to whom *see* section V below), aliens are the "nationals of foreign states". A foreign state is, potentially at least, unfriendly. The presence of the nationals of foreign states within its territory may constitute for the state in question a menace to its security. In wartime, for example, it is not unknown for a state to imprison, or subject to detention, all resident enemy aliens for the duration of hostilities. Even in peacetime a state may expel resident aliens.

Nevertheless, so long as a state's security is not threatened, every state has an interest in ensuring reasonably tolerable conditions for visiting aliens, and demanding similar conditions for its own nationals abroad. Thus has state practice developed an international minimum standard of treatment for aliens (*see* Chapter Eleven below) and rules requiring that if aliens are expelled, their expulsion takes place in reasonably humane conditions.

The rules of international law concerning aliens show an uneasy balance between these two conflicting positions, the one permitting the state to treat aliens with discretion, the other insisting on a minimum standard of treatment.

Entry of aliens

A state may refuse aliens permission to enter its territory at all, from which it follows that it may subject their entry and residence to any conditions it may think fit. (*See* below section IV: Immigration.) Conversely, it may admit any alien it wishes at any time, and in doing so will be accountable to no one. (*See* below section IV: Asylum.) An alien will not normally be admitted without a valid passport issued by the state of his nationality.

Visa. A visa, normally stamped into the blank middle pages of a passport, is the foreign state's authorisation to enter its territory. The issue of visas is a consular function. They may be obtained from the local consular post before setting out on the journey. Visas are generally issued for a stated period. Before a visa is granted, the local consul may, for security or other reasons, be required to report on the applicant's background. Without a visa, a national of a state from which visas are required will be turned back at the frontier. However, by treaty, most states have dispensed with the visa requirement for nationals of other friendly states.

Expulsion of aliens

There are various circumstances in which a state may require aliens to leave its territory (*see* section IV below: Expulsion).

Treatment of aliens

While a state may treat its nationals at pleasure, the same does not apply to its treatment of aliens. International law asserts an international minimum standard of treatment of aliens, and any state which does not live up to it will be liable to make reparation in a claim based on state responsibility (*see* Chapter Eleven). That nationals are treated no better is no defence in such a case.

On the other hand, a state may accept aliens into its territory subject to such conditions of residence as it may see fit. There can accordingly be no question of aliens claiming equal rights with nationals. Some states, for example, do not permit aliens to vote, acquire real property, own ships or aircraft, exercise certain professions or activities, or benefit from legal aid or social security. Moreover, special measures may be imposed upon the residence or movement of aliens. Aliens may thus be required to register at a police station and to make periodic visits to it, or a visa may be issued to an alien to work as a technical expert in a factory subject to a prohibition against his travelling more than a certain distance from the factory where he is employed, without special authorisation. Breach of such a condition would lead to expulsion.

Apart from such legislative discrimination as applies between nationals and aliens generally and from such special conditions as may be imposed upon particular individuals, the general law will be taken to apply as much to aliens as to nationals. An alien has, in particular, the "equal protection of the law" (access to the courts, protection of his security and property, remedies for his rights), but he must pay taxes, and even, if this is a condition of continued residence, perform military obligations. A state which insists on this latter requirement is likely to provoke retaliation against its own nationals abroad, for enlistment in the armed forces of a foreign state is, according to many nationality laws, a ground for depriving the person concerned of his original nationality.

IV. IMMIGRATION, EMIGRATION, EXTRADITION, EXPULSION, ASYLUM

IMMIGRATION

The existence in most states of restrictive laws on immigration provides the proof of the rule that each state has discretion in relation to the admission of aliens. While tourists and students are normally admitted freely, those who wish to immigrate into the state and make it their permanent home are subject to more stringent conditions. Those who are considered physically, morally or even socially unfit may be excluded altogether. In addition, quotas for different nationalities may be established so as to limit the overall number.

Although treaties of commerce and establishment seek to improve the position of the nationals of one contracting party in the territory of the other contracting party, they do not generally affect the application of the immigration laws.

If the state permits the "bread-winner" of a family to immigrate the "right of a family to live together" requires that the dependent members of that family shall also be admitted. Only where a state has accepted specific treaty obligations for the international protection of human rights is there any remedy for the failure to respect this right.

EMIGRATION

Subject to any rules as to the international protection of human rights, international law is indifferent to the manner in which a state treats its nationals within its territory. This applies for example to the question whether it permits them to leave that territory. It is the hallmark of a totalitarian state that its nationals are not permitted to do so, without special leave. All democratic states, on the other hand, permit unqualified emigration. These political differences, however, are of no concern to international law.

On the other hand, no state is permitted to prevent the emigration of resident aliens. Moreover departing aliens must be permitted to take their possessions with them, subject to such restrictions (currency controls, payment of taxes, etc.) as apply to nationals and aliens alike.

EXTRADITION

No state may exercise physical control over an individual within the territory of another state. On the other hand a state may admit an alien to reside within its territory at discretion. It is thus possible for a law-breaker to escape justice by the simple expedient of crossing the frontier. Having committed no crime in the state of refuge, the police of that state have no valid cause to arrest him and hand him over. It is this situation that extradition treaties are designed to meet.

An extradition treaty provides that persons accused of having committed a crime in state A, who are in refuge in state B, will be handed over by the police of state B to state A on demand, and vice versa. Some states, as the result normally of a constitutional rule, will not extradite any national to a foreign state, but in this case undertake to try him themselves for the alleged crime in order that he may not escape justice altogether.

Extraditable crimes

The basis of the treaty is an agreed statement of what will be considered a "crime" for the purposes of the treaty. In general only "objective" crimes are included (acts which would be considered criminal offences wherever committed). "Subjective" crimes are excluded. Treason, espionage and other "political offences" are good examples of subjective crimes (i.e. acts which appear "criminal" only in the eyes of the government of the state making the application). However, a bomb explosion by an anarchist is not considered a political offence since destruction as a political creed is viewed with distaste by all governments. Whether a political assassination will be considered a political offence or murder may well depend merely on the political relations between the states concerned.

The request for extradition
A mere request for extradition is not sufficient; some evidence must generally be provided that the wanted person was guilty of the extraditable act. A warrant of arrest from the requesting state is always required as a formality. In democratic states, the person may not be extradited without authorisation by a judge after a hearing in public and in the presence of the accused. The actual surrender is carried out by the executive.

Definition of extradition
Extradition may thus be defined as "the formal surrender of a person by one state to another state for prosecution or punishment". This normally takes place only as the result of a treaty.

The principle of specialty
It may be stated as a rule of customary international law that, without the consent of the requested state, the surrendered person may not be tried or punished for an offence other than that for which he was surrendered.

EXPULSION
A state may expel aliens at discretion. The only rule imposed by international law is that the expulsion be not arbitrary. This power is a consequence of the fact that a state may take whatever steps are required to ensure its own security and well-being within its territory. In wartime a state may expel or intern all enemy aliens, whether visitors or residents, and even in peace time the mass expulsion of aliens of certain specific nationalities is not treated, in state practice, as illegal in itself. But it can be no part of that requirement that persons be expelled with force, cruelty or generally in inhumane conditions. Accordingly a state is responsible in international law for the manner of the expulsion, although never for the expulsion itself.

The power of expulsion is not interpreted as being limited by treaties of establishment in spite of the fact that the object of such treaties is to guarantee nationals of one contracting state a right of continued residence within the territory of another contracting state on fulfilment of certain conditions.

The nature of expulsion

Expulsion, also known as deportation, is an executive act which consists in the implementation of an order that a named person leave the territory of a state. It differs from extradition in that:

(a) there is no request from another state that the person be handed over;

(b) the expelled person's presence within the territory of the state of his residence is considered undesirable by the authorities of that state; and

(c) the expulsion order is put into effect immediately and is implemented as soon as the person has left the territory, his final destination being of no concern to the expelling state. Since, however, the alien must enter the territory of another state once he leaves the state from which he was expelled, and since the only state which has any duty to receive him is the state of his nationality, cases have been known of a deportation order being withdrawn from a stateless person, no state being found which would accept him (*Staniszewski* v. *Watkins* (United States District Court, 1948)).

Reconduction

In some states the police have powers to arrest certain types of aliens, vagabonds or persons whose identity papers or residence or work permits are not in order, and to forcibly conduct them to the frontier: this is known as reconduction, and does not require the issue of any order.

Refoulement

Refoulement, or the turning back at the frontier, or point of entry, is an administrative measure consequent upon refusal of entry or residence to an alien. The person concerned is sent back to the state of his last residence if it will admit him; otherwise he is returned to the state of his nationality which, as we have seen, is under a duty to receive him.

Grounds for expulsion

While it is not possible to give a list of causes of expulsion which are considered acceptable in international law, that is to say which are not arbitrary, one general category is involvement in political activities. For an alien to take an active role in the political affairs of the "host" state is now universally recognised as a valid ground for expulsion. For example in 1896 Ben Tillet, a British subject, was expelled from Belgium for organising a dockers' union. The United Kingdom argued that his expulsion was unnecessary, but the Arbitrator, after a full investigation of the reasons given and the facts, upheld Belgium's right. A more recent example is the expulsion from France of a university student, Danny "le rouge", a German national, during the "May rising" in 1968.

Mass expulsion of aliens

Recent state practice has provided several examples of mass expulsion of aliens. As the result of an over-liberal policy of immigration a state may find that an unduly large proportion of the total population are aliens (for example Switzerland and Ghana). This may lead to rapid expulsion of large numbers of people. The technique employed is either to introduce a new condition of residence (such as a work or residence permit), or to cancel systematically such permits as have already been issued. Such measures may also be taken at the onset of unemployment during an economic recession (for example the Federal Republic of Germany). In such cases the states whose nationals are affected intervene vigorously to ensure that the manner of the expulsion is as humane as possible and if necessary threaten retortion either in kind (i.e. to expel all resident nationals of the expelling state) or in some other manner.

Arbitrary expulsion

The power of a state to expel aliens may not be abused. The state of the nationality of an expelled alien, in the exercise of its diplomatic protection or for other purposes of its own, may ask the expelling state to give a reason for the expulsion. Refusal to give any reason would make it impossible to criticise (and thus set any limit to) the power of expulsion, and is considered equivalent to an abuse of the power. If the reason given is one of state security an international tribunal would normally require no further explanation but in other cases a complete explanation may be required. Once given, it may be possible to attack it successfully.

In the *Boffolo Case* (1903), Boffolo, an Italian, was expelled from Venezuela. The matter went to arbitration on the question of whether the right to expel was absolute. In support of this thesis Venezuela argued that it had no duty even to admit the reason for the expulsion. The Umpire said that the state had a "general power to expel foreigners at least for cause, but that it must, when occasion demands, state the reason of such expulsion . . . and an inefficient reason or none being advanced, take the consequences." In that case it appeared that his expulsion was for publishing an article reflecting unfavourably on the local authorities. To sanction such an act was in itself contrary to the Venezuelan constitution. For this reason damages were awarded against Venezuela.

ASYLUM

Territorial asylum

"The competence of the state to allow political offenders or political refugees to enter and remain in its territory under its protection, and thereby to grant asylum to them, has never been doubted in international law" (*Carnegie Manual of Public International Law,* ed. Max Sorensen, p. 491). An individual has no right to asylum. He merely has, according to Article 14 of the Universal Declaration of Human Rights, the right to "seek" asylum from persecution and if asylum is granted to "enjoy" it. The constitutions of certain states promise political asylum to the persecuted. It is, however, for the states granting asylum to judge the circumstances of each particular case. If a claim is made out the usual immigration laws and requirements will normally be waived. Nor may the state from which the person seeking asylum has fled regard his reception as a hostile act: the state, in granting asylum, is exercising a right of territorial sovereignty.

Diplomatic asylum

Territorial asylum must be distinguished from diplomatic asylum, which occurs when an embassy grants asylum to a person seeking protection from the authorities of the state in which the embassy is situated. The inviolability of embassy premises prevents his forcible arrest by the territorial authorities: but once he leaves the embassy he loses his protection. The embassy has no right to insist that a person to whom it has given asylum be given a safe-conduct to leave the territory (*Haya de la Torre Case* (I.C.J., 1951).

In that case, Mr Haya de la Torre, a former Minister of Peru, sought and was granted asylum within the Colombian Embassy in Peru, when as the result of a change of government, he had reason to fear for his life (as he alleged). The Colombian Government requested the Peruvian Government to grant Mr de la Torre a safe conduct to enable him to be brought to the frontier and so into Colombian territory where the Colombian authorities were prepared to grant him territorial asylum. The Peruvian Government refused. Before the International Court of Justice, Colombia invoked the existence both of a rule of general international law, and, or in the alternative, of a rule of regional international law applicable only in South and Central America, in favour of this right to a self-conduct. The court, after a careful survey of state practice, and especially that of South and Central American republics, considered that Colombia had failed to make out the existence of such a rule and rejected the claim.

Indeed it is probably correct to assert that for an embassy to extend such protection (for other than purely humanitarian purposes) constitutes an abuse of its privilege of inviolability of premises.

V. STATELESSNESS, REFUGEES, SLAVERY

STATELESS PERSONS

A stateless person is one who does not have, according to its law, the nationality of any state. This situation may arise through conflicts of nationality laws, changes of sovereignty over territory, or denationalisation by the state of nationality. A person thus deprived of the protection of any state was beyond the protection afforded under traditional international law. International efforts to improve this situation took two directions, the one aimed at reducing the incidence of statelessness, the other at introducing a measure of special protection.

Efforts to reduce statelessness

The Convention on the Conflict of Nationality Laws of 1930, in conjunction with the Convention on the Reduction of Statelessness of 1961, provides that contracting states shall accord nationality to a person who would otherwise be stateless:

(a) if he were born in their territory (*jus soli*); or
(b) if one of his parents had, at the time of his birth outside the territory, the nationality of that state (*jus sanguinis*).

REFUGEES

Refugees are persons who have fled from their state of origin out of a well-founded fear of being persecuted for reasons of race, religion, nationality or political opinion. Refugees may thus include both nationals and stateless persons. A refugee, being in flight from his state or origin, no longer enjoys the protection of the government of that state.

Travel documents for refugees

Once a refugee has been admitted and allowed to reside in the territory of a state, what is the position when he wishes to go abroad? Since a refugee has no passport, the problem has been solved by the issue of a special travel document for refugees. This includes a "return clause" allowing him to return to the territory of the issuing state within a certain period of time. On the strength of such a document a refugee may visit other states. A visa would in principle be required. As between the parties to the European Agreement on the Abolition of Visas for Refugees 1960, the visa requirement has been waived.

Protection by states

The possession of a travel document does not carry any right to protection by the issuing state. Recent state practice contains some indications that the idea of according a right of protection to the state which allows a refugee to reside in its territory is now being considered. An example is found in Article 2(2) of the Protocol to the European Convention on Consular Functions concerning the Protection of Refugees of 1967 which gives to the consular officer of a state where a refugee has his habitual residence the right "to protect such a refugee and to defend his rights and interests."

Protection by joint international action

The vast increase of the number of refugees brought about by the two World Wars, and the ideological revolutions in China and South-East Asia generally (in 1952 it was officially estimated that there were sixteen million refugees) led states to decide upon the need for joint multilateral action to aid and protect them. At first within the League of Nations, and subsequently in the United Nations, a special body was created (now called "The Office of the High Commissioner for Refugees"). The legal basis for the protection thus accorded is provided by a series of conventions, and by Resolution 428 (V) of the General Assembly of the United Nations (14th December 1950) by which the "Office" was set up, and subsequent resolutions.

The competence of the High Commission extends over any person considered as a refugee under previous conventions (now consolidated in the Convention Relating to the Status of Refugees adopted in 1951 and the protocol to that convention adopted on 31st January 1967), as well as any person who, "as a result of events occurring *in Europe* [unless the contracting states decide to apply the provisions of the convention to refugees from outside Europe] and owing to a well-founded fear of being persecuted for reasons of race, religion, nationality or political opinion" has been made a refugee. Its object is to promote the conclusion and ratification of conventions for the protection of refugees, to provide for the execution of measures designed to improve the situation of refugees, by special agreements with governments, and to assist all efforts, whether governmental or private, to facilitate their assimilation in new national communities, or their voluntary repatriation.

Status of stateless persons and refugees

In the state which has received them into habitual residence, the status of stateless persons and refugees is governed by the provisions of the Convention relating to the Status of Stateless Persons of 1954, the Convention relating to the Status of Refugees of 1951 and the Protocol of 1967 respectively.

With regard to freedom of religion and religious education of children, they are accorded the same treatment as is granted to nationals. The same applies in respect of elementary education of children, labour legislation and social security, public relief and assistance, and fiscal charges. In relation to most other matters, their status is assimilated to that of aliens generally; however, in relation to the access to, and the participation in, wage-earning employment by refugees, most-favoured nation treatment is accorded.

In relation to expulsion, both refugees and stateless persons are accorded a more favourable status than that applicable to aliens generally, for they may not be expelled except to preserve public order or national security, and then only after due process of law. Moreover, a refugee is not to be expelled or returned in any circumstances to the frontiers of any territory where his life or freedom would be threatened on account of his race, religion, nationality, political opinion or membership of a particular social group.

SLAVERY

The complete abolition of slavery was the object of the Slavery Convention of 1926, which, as amended in 1953, assigns to the United Nations certain duties and functions to safeguard its effective implementation. To this was added a supplementary convention adopted at Geneva in 1956, designed to bring about the complete abolition of institutions and practices analogous to slavery, such as bondage, serfdom, bride-price and exploitation of child-labour, and to outlaw the transport of slaves by ships and aircraft of the contracting states. A slave setting foot in such a vessel is free *ipso facto*.

Prohibitions of slavery and the slave trade in all its forms are contained in the Universal Declaration of Human Rights and the International Covenant on Civil and Political Rights.

VI. MINORITIES

Unlike the protection accorded to aliens and to stateless persons and refugees, minority protection is concerned with the international protection of certain groups of nationals from discrimatory treatment by their own state authorities. The "minority" in question might be based on language, religion, ethnic or national origin.

This type of protection was first given concrete form in Articles 86 and 93 of the Treaty of Versailles, 1919. The principle was incorporated into the Treaty of Peace concluded with Austria, Bulgaria, Hungary and Turkey after the First World War; the treaties concluded with Czechoslovakia, Greece, Poland and Romania; and the treaties concluded by Poland with Danzig, and in particular with Germany (the treaty of 15th May 1922 concerning Upper Silesia). Each of these treaties guaranteed:

    (a) life, liberty and free exercise of religion to all *inhabitants* of the territory;

    (b) equal treatment before the law and the same civil and political rights to all *nationals*;

    (c) the same treatment and security in law and in fact to all linguistic, religious or ethnic *minority groups of nationals*;

    (d) the right of such *minority groups* to establish schools and religious institutions, and to use their own language for publications, at public meetings and before the courts.

The right of minorities to their own culture, religion and language is mentioned in the International Covenant on Civil and Political Rights adopted by the General Assembly of the United Nations in 1966. However, generally speaking, this notion has now been replaced by the concept of "elimination of racial discrimination" and more generally the "protection of human rights for all people without distinction as to race, sex, language or religion."

VII. HUMAN RIGHTS

RIGHTS AND DUTIES

For every right there is a corresponding duty, and in the context of human rights the duties fall upon states (but *see* below: "Human duties"). This section is accordingly concerned with the recognition of human rights by states and their protection against states.

"Human rights"

The recognition by states that all human beings regardless of nationality possess rights deserving international recognition and protection marked a revolution in international law, for hitherto the treatment by a state of its own nationals had been considered a matter of "domestic jurisdiction", beyond the reach of international law.

The use of the word "right" in the context of human rights may cause some difficulty to lawyers trained in the Anglo–American jurisprudential tradition. It should be remembered however that while there can evidently be "no remedy without a right", it is not necessarily true that there can be "no right without a remedy". A lawyer trained in the civil law system is familiar with another

analysis, namely, that a remedy is itself a species of right, a procedural right permitting the right (which may be called the substantive
right) to be recognised and enforced by the court. Since it is clear
that the acceptance and recognition by the states of human rights
preceded their protection by remedies, the latter analysis is preferred.
Accordingly, the recognition of human rights is hereafter treated
separately from their international protection.

"Human duties"

It follows from the proposition that duties are the corollary of
rights, and from the fact that human rights are owed to the individual
by the state, that "human duties" are owed by the individual to
the state. But the state has always had other means at its disposal
to ensure that duties are fulfilled. The whole movement for the
protection of human rights arose as an attempt to redress the balance
between the power of the state to impose duties on individuals and
the powerlessness of the individual to ensure a correlative respect
for his rights.

The American Declaration of the Rights and Duties of Man,
adopted in 1948, contained ten articles setting out the duties of
Man, including the duty to support, educate and protect his minor
children; to acquire at least an elementary education; to vote; to
obey the law; to pay taxes; and to work. It is also said to be "the
duty of the individual so to conduct himself in relation to others
that each and every one may fully form and develop his personality."

The Universal Declaration of Human Rights (*see* below: Stages of
development) contains merely a revised draft of the last-mentioned
article, which, however, specifies to whom this duty is owed: "Every
one has duties to the community in which alone the full and free
development of his personality is possible." Subsequent statements
and conventions on human rights merely contain the stipulation
that all states, bodies and persons have the duty to abstain from any
act aimed at the destruction of any of the recognised human rights.

THE RECOGNITION OF HUMAN RIGHTS

From their very nature, human rights which are often characterised
as "basic" or "fundamental" can hardly be considered as having
been "created" at any given moment: on the contrary, they must
have existed, in however nascent a form, for as long as man has
lived in communities. Successive stages of their "recognition" can,
however, be traced. This process started on the national level with
the French Declaration of the Rights of Man, but the present work
is concerned only with their international recognition. The various
important steps are set out on p. 100.

Developing recognition

It should be noted that the rights in question were developed at each stage of their recognition. Moreover, the later universal statements included some rights or freedoms which did not appear in earlier statements. One may assume that this process of "developing recognition" of human rights will continue, and that existing texts are not necessarily definitive. The same conclusion follows from the fact that certain economic and social rights are framed in elastic terms, for example, the right to "a continuous improvement of living conditions".

Dynamic nature of human rights

Statements of human rights must be considered by reference to time and space: in other words, far from being absolute as one might be tempted to conclude at first sight, they are relative to existing conditions in the various parts of the world. This is particularly true of economic and social rights. Sometimes this is explicit from the terms in which a particular right is stated, for example "the right to an adequate standard of living". More striking though only implicit, is the existence of regional statements of human rights. Certain regional groupings have found it possible to run ahead of the international community in the recognition (and particularly the protection) of human rights (*see* below).

Stages of development

(a) One of the first examples of international recognition of human rights and protection occurred in the "minorities treaties" concluded after the First World War which guaranteed life, liberty and freedom of religion to all inhabitants of the territories concerned.

(b) A further step was marked by the creation of the International Labour Organisation as an autonomous part of the League of Nations by the Treaty of Versailles, 1919. As restated in the Declaration of Philadelphia, 1946, the International Labour Organisation was based on the ideas that *(i)* labour is not a commodity, *(ii)* freedom of expression and association are essential to sustain progress, and *(iii)* poverty anywhere constitutes a danger to prosperity everywhere.

(c) The first universal and comprehensive recognition of "human rights and fundamental freedoms" occurred in the Charter of the United Nations, 1945, whose preamble speaks of the determination of the "peoples" of the United Nations to reaffirm faith in human rights. One of the aims of the United Nations is to achieve "international co-operation . . . in promoting and encouraging respect for human rights" (Article 1).

(d) The first attempt to spell out the individual rights occurred

in the Universal Declaration of Human Rights adopted on 10th December 1948 by the General Assembly of the United Nations (Resolution 217(III)). The declaration was to be considered as "a common standard of achievement for all people and all nations".

(e) On 16th December 1966, the General Assembly adopted the International Covenant on Civil and Political Rights, and the International Covenant on Economic, Social and Cultural Rights (Resolution 2200(XXI)). These two treaties entered into force early in 1976.

REGIONAL STATEMENTS OF HUMAN RIGHTS

Two regions of the world, Europe and America, have felt the need to institute regional statements of human rights, and regional agencies for their international enforcement.

Europe

On 4th November 1950, the Committee of Ministers of the Council of Europe adopted the text of the Convention for the Protection of Human Rights and Fundamental Freedoms, which covers the whole range of civil and political rights. While their formation was modelled on that of the Universal Declaration, the measures set out in the convention to ensure their protection were quite new (*see* below).

The European Social Charter, adopted at Turin on 18th October 1961, sets out most of the rights which are to be found in the International Covenant on Economic, Social and Cultural Rights and provides for their protection, although the expression "human rights" does not appear in the text of the charter.

America

On 22nd November 1969, most of the states members of the Organisation of American States (apart from the United States) signed the Inter-American Convention on Human Rights. This convention will enter into force after ratification by eleven states. It provides "civil and political" rights as well as "economic, social and cultural" rights, the latter, however, being treated in a single article headed "Progressive Development" to be achieved "within the limit of available resources". The measures for protection are closely based on the European model (*see* below).

CATALOGUE OF HUMAN RIGHTS AND FUNDAMENTAL FREEDOMS

The following list of rights appears both in the Universal Declaration and the appropriate international covenant (also in the European and American conventions).

Civil and political rights

These are: the right to life, liberty and security of the person; freedom from slavery and servitude; freedom from torture and inhumane treatment; freedom from arbitrary arrest and imprisonment; the right to vote and to participate in government; the right to equality before the law and to equal protection of the law; the right to a fair trial, including the presumption of innocence, and non-retroactivity of penal laws; freedom of conscience and religion, opinion and expression; the right to peaceful assembly and association; freedom of movement and residence; the right to respect for private life, home and correspondence; the right to marry and to found a family.

Economic, social and cultural rights

These are: the right to work; the right to an adequate standard of living; the right to safe and healthy conditions; the right to just and favourable conditions of work; the right to rest and leisure; the right to education and to participate in the cultural life of the community.

Additional rights appearing in the Universal Declaration

These are: the right to recognition as a person before the law; the right to nationality; the right to leave any country including one's own; the right to return to one's country; the right to equal access to the public service; the right to periodic elections; the right to own property; the right to equal pay for equal work; and the right to special protection for motherhood and childhood.

Rights mentioned in the Covenants but not in the Universal Declaration

These are as follows:

Civil and political rights: freedom from forced or compulsory labour; freedom from imprisonment on the ground of inability to perform a contractual obligation; freedom of an alien from arbitrary expulsion; the right to compensation for unjust conviction.

Economic, social and cultural rights: the right to strike; the right to the highest attainable standard of health; the right to the protection of interests resulting from scientific, literary or artistic productions.

Beneficiaries

One feature common to all texts on human rights is that the range of persons who benefit from their provisions is very extensive. Each state party to the instrument undertakes to apply its provisions to "everyone within the jurisdiction". Only in the case of the European Social Charter is this not the case, for there the beneficiaries are restricted to the nationals of member states. However, that instrument was not conceived in a human rights context.

INTERNATIONAL PROTECTION OF HUMAN RIGHTS

International protection is achieved when the state is made responsible to some international body or authority for the implementation of its obligations in the field of human rights.

It is in relation to such measures of protection that the distinction between civil and political rights, and economic, social and cultural rights become vital, for the measures appropriate to the protection of each are quite distinct.

Civil and political rights

Universal texts. Since the Universal Declaration contains no measures of protection, the only text to consider is the International Covenant on Civil and Political Rights. States which are parties to the covenants undertake to submit reports on the measures they have adopted to give effect to the rights mentioned in the covenant (Article 40). A human rights committee is established (Article 23), composed of eighteen members acting in their personal capacity, nominated by states which are party to the covenant, elected in a special session convened by the Secretary General of the United Nations. The function of the committee is to study the reports, and submit them together with its own comments thereon to the Economic and Social Council of the United Nations and to the states which are party to the covenant.

Regional texts: the European Convention on Human Rights. Under the European Convention remedies for violation by a contracting state are given in favour of other contracting states and also in favour of individuals. *State applications* may be lodged against a contracting state as a result of its ratification of the convention. *Individual applications* require a separate and additional declaration of acceptance.

European Commission of Human Rights. A European commission was established, now composed of fifteen members acting in their personal capacity, elected by the Committee of Ministers of the Council of Europe from a list of names drawn up by the parliamentary members of the Consultative Assembly of that organisation. Both states' and individuals' applications (petitions) are addressed to the commission, whose tasks are:

(*a*) to decide whether they satisfy the conditions of admissibility; if so, *(b)* to investigate with a view to effecting a friendly settlement; and

(c) to submit a report to the Committee of Ministers of the Council of Europe in which the commission declares whether, in its view, there has been a violation of the convention.

Within the three months following the transmission of the report, the commission, any state whose national is alleged to be a victim, any state which referred the case to the commission, or any state against which the complaint has been lodged, may bring the matter before the court *(see* below). If on the expiry of this period the case has not been brought before the court, the Committee of Ministers must decide by a two-thirds majority whether there has been a violation of the convention, and, where appropriate, the period of time granted to the state to bring its law into harmony with the provisions of the convention or to take other corrective measures.

The commission is the most efficacious body concerned with the international protection of human rights in the world today.

The European Court of Human Rights. The European Court of Human Rights is composed of one judge from each member state of the Council of Europe (irrespective of whether that state has ratified the convention). The method of election closely resembles that adopted for the commission. In the case of state applications, the parties before the court are the state against which a violation of human rights is alleged, and the body (state or commission) which submitted the case to the court. The competence of the court extends only to such states as have accepted its compulsory juris-diction, either by a separate declaration, or in relation to a particular case. Where individual applications are concerned, the case is present-ed by the commission. It is, however, inexact to describe the role of the commission before the court as that of a "plaintiff": the role is more that of *amicus curiae* or "Advocate General". The court may also decide to hear the individual, but in his capacity as a witness rather than as a party. The implementation of the judgment of the court is the task of the Committee of Ministers.

Beneficiaries of remedies.

(a) State applications. The mere fact of being a contracting party to the convention provides a sufficient *locus standi* to bring a claim against another state. No connection need be established whether of nationality, residence or kinship, with the persons against whom the violation is alleged. The application by the Scandinavian countries and the Netherlands against Greece (1969) was for the protection of the Greek people against their own government (*Greek Case*)!

(b) Individual applications. States undertake to ensure the rights of "everyone within their jurisdiction". Once a state has accepted, by declaration, the "right of individual petition", everyone within the jurisdiction may benefit from the remedy. "Everyone" means all individuals (irrespective of nationality), groups, corporate and unincorporated bodies, and non-governmental associations.

Inter-American Convention on Human Rights. Largely modelled on the European Convention, the American Convention on Human Rights differs only in that mere ratification of the convention carries with it the obligation to accept individual applications, whereas state applications are only admissible against contracting states which accept this procedure by a separate declaration. The convention has not yet entered into force.

Inter-American Commission of Human Rights. This commission is an organ of the Organisation of American States (O.A.S.). Its statute was adopted by the O.A.S. council in 1960, and its powers enlarged to include dealing with petitions from individuals in November 1965. The commission "represents the member states" of the O.A.S. The seven members are elected in a personal capacity by the General Assembly. As well as the examination of petitions, its functions include the power to make recommendations to governments to adopt measures for the increased production of human rights; to prepare studies; and to conduct investigations as to the manner in which the internal laws of contracting states ensure the protection of human rights. If the commission is unable to effect a friendly settlement, it is to draw up a report on the petition and send it to the "states concerned", together with any recommendations, etc. If the dispute is not then submitted to the court, the commission itself, if its jurisdiction is admitted (presumably by a special agreement or a declaration), may give an opinion and state its conclusions, including recommendations, to the states concerned to take measures necessary to remedy the situation within a specified period. The commission's decisions are taken by an absolute majority vote. If the state has not complied within the stated period, the commission may decide to publish this report.

Inter-American Court of Human Rights. Save that it is composed of only seven members, the provisions governing the functioning and powers of this court are parallel with those of the European court. Only states which are parties to the convention and the commission can bring cases before the court. Should it consider that a right guaranteed by the convention has been violated, the court can order that the person prejudiced be guaranteed the benefit of the right or freedom violated, and in addition, where appropriate, the making of full reparation.

Beneficiaries of remedies. Besides contracting states, any person or group of persons and any non-governmental entity recognised within "at least one state" of the O.A.S. can submit petitions.

Economic, social and cultural rights

Universal texts: the International Covenant on Economic, Social and Cultural Rights. Contracting states must submit reports on the measures which they have adopted and the progress they have made in achieving the observance of the rights set out in the covenant. These reports are examined by the Economic and Social Council for the United Nations (ECOSOC). This body may submit the report to the Commission on Human Rights, a subsidiary organ, for study and general recommendations. ECOSOC is required to submit a general report from time to time to the General Assembly.

Regional texts: the European Social Charter. A committee of experts, composed of seven members acting in their personal capacity, nominated by contracting states and appointed by the Committee of Ministers of the Council of Europe is established to ensure the application of the provisions of the charter. Each contracting state is required to submit an annual report. These reports are then examined by the independent committee, which submits its observations to a governmental body, the sub-committee of the Governmental Social Committee of the Council of Europe. The Consultative Assembly of the Council of Europe, and particularly its Social Affairs Committee, then studies the reports and stimulates the member governments to take appropriate remedial action.

Inter-American Convention on Human Rights. This deals with the whole question of economic and social rights in one article as follows: "The parties undertake, both on the national level and by international co-operation — notably economic and technical — to take, within the framework of available resources, and by the adoption of legislative provisions or by any other appropriate method, the measures designed to ensure the progressive enjoyment of the rights which flow from the economic and social, the educational, scientific and cultural standards laid down in the charter of the Organisation of American States."

INDIVIDUAL, COLLECTIVE AND GROUP RIGHTS

It is useful to distinguish individual rights from collective rights, and individual and collective rights from group rights.

Individual rights are inherent in Man's being and personality, as for example, the right to life, to liberty, to a decent living standard, to freedom of expression.

Collective rights are those which an individual acquires as a result of his living in a collectivity, or society, such as the right to marry, to freedom of association, to join a trade union, to vote.

Group rights are those which exist not in relation to the individual but only in relation to the group, such as the rights of minority groups and the right of peoples to self-determination.

Whereas individual rights are basic, no matter what may be the level of development of the state, collective rights may well take a lower priority in less developed states if it is thought that the rapid achievement of individual rights requires strong government.

Before there can be any question of group rights, a group must be shown to exist. While objective criteria exist to demonstrate the existence of minority groups, the same does not always apply in relation to a "people". This fact, plus the absence of any body capable of deciding the question with authority, renders the existence of these rights somewhat subject to hazard.

Right of self-determination

The most important of the group rights is the right of a "people" to become a state. The assertion of this right to self-determination may be traced through three stages:

(a) Chapter XI of the Charter of the United Naitons, entitled the Declaration Regarding Non-Self-Governing Territories, in particular Article 73 which reads (in part): "Members . . . which have . . . responsibilities for the administration of territories whose people have not yet attained a full measure of self-government, recognise the principle that the interests of the inhabitants . . . are paramount, and accept . . . the obligation to promote . . . [their] well-being, and to this end *(i)* to ensure . . . their political economic, social and educational advancement; *(ii)* to develop self-government."

(b) Resolution 1514 (XV) adopted by the General Assembly on 14th December 1960 on the Granting of Independence to Colonial Countries and Peoples, which declares that "the subjection of people to alien . . . domination . . . constitutes a denial of fundamental human rights."

(c) The International Covenants on Economic, Social and Cultural Rights and on Civil and Political Rights each declare in Article 1 that "all peoples have the right to self-determination. By virtue of that right they freely determine their political status."

Plebiscites

One of the means whereby a "people" may determine its own political future is the institution of the plebiscite. In the case of the plebiscite to determine the future status of the Trust Territory of the Northern and Southern Cameroons in 1960, the General Assembly of the United Nations decided to give the "people" of that territory only two choices, that of becoming independent as part of the state of Nigeria, or becoming a part of the state of the (former French) Cameroons, refusing to add the third choice of becoming an independent state. It might be thought that through this decision the General Assembly itself denied the inhabitants of those territories the right of self-determination.

CHAPTER FIVE

Organs of the State

This Chapter is concerned with the organs of states in their relations with other states. The relations of states with international organisations has already been considered in Chapter Three, section II.

I. GENERAL

PERMANENT ORGANS OF THE STATE

Although in the Continental Sahara Case, 1976, the International Court of Justice expressed the opinion in the majority judgment that "no rule of international law requires a State to have any definite or pre-determined structure", most states, in the course of time, institute a structure which includes the following five permanent organs:

    (a) a head of state;
    (b) a government;
    (c) a diplomatic service;
    (d) a consular service; and
    (e) the armed forces of the state.

Thus although not necessary — in the sense that international law does not require their existence — these organs are, in terms of the state's international relations, highly useful; indeed, without them no state can fully take advantage of the body of rules and permitted faculties comprised within the international legal system. A state lacking a consular service can hardly protect the interests of its nationals abroad. A state without armed forces, as Japan, must depend for its survival upon the protection of another state or states. The Swiss Government is a seven-man Federal Council, with a rotating Presidency, the President for the time being having the status of head of state. Under the constitution the President is forbidden to go abroad during his term of office, so that, were he to do so, the question whether he would be treated with the dignity of a visiting head of state must remain hypothetical.

Representation of the state

A state may be represented either by an organ or by an agency. An "organ" is a part of the state while an "agency" is separate from it, the relationship being one of principal and agent.

How a state organises itself for its internal affairs is a matter of little direct concern to international law. The constitution of each state will lay down the division of powers and functions between such of its organs as it may deem useful and necessary. Since the constitutions of states differ, the organs used for the conduct of their internal affairs will also differ from state to state.

By contrast, all states possess the same organs for the conduct of their external relations, a phenomenon which is both an illustration and a consequence of the legal equality of states.

State agents or agencies

In addition, states may send or maintain abroad temporary or permanent establishments of various kinds, as for example, trade delegations, information centres, tourist offices, state airline offices, hostels for visiting members of the merchant marine, offices for the payment of state pensions. None of these can be considered an organ of the state for its external relations, although each of them represents the state abroad for matters falling within its competence as an agent or agency of the state. Moreover it may be represented by as many different agents or agencies as it wishes. We are only concerned with state agencies in the context of the immunity of the state from the courts of other states (*see* sections VII and VIII below).

TEMPORARY ORGANS OF THE STATE

A state may find it convenient to conduct *ad hoc* diplomacy, that is, to regulate certain matters through the use of a diplomatic mission not part of the regular diplomatic service but specially created for the purpose of the mission, and dispersed on its termination. This institution is now known as the "special mission".

THE GRANTING OF IMMUNITIES IN INTERNATIONAL LAW

It is a consequence of the sovereignty which each state exercises over its territory that no other state may, without permission, exercise its authority therein in any form whatsoever. However, for the daily conduct of its external relations, each state grants permission to other states to establish such permanent missions (diplomatic and consular missions) as may be necessary for the sending state and convenient for the receiving state. Such permission is granted on a basis of reciprocity. With respect to diplomats and consuls, the nature and extent of the authority which the sending state may exercise within the territory of the receiving states is well defined in the enumeration of the functions of diplomats and consuls. In other cases the extent of this authority must be agreed with the receiving state in advance of the visit (for example, with respect to heads of states, members of the government, and the armed forces).

However, the public authorities of two different states cannot operate under the law of one of them, so that a necessary corollary of the grant of permission to perform any public function of the sending state in the territory of the receiving state is the allocation to the former of as extensive an immunity from the law of the latter as may be necessary to permit the function to be performed.

A state may refuse to permit a foreign state to establish an embassy or consulate on its territory, but if it permits it to do so, it is bound by a rule of international law to grant the requisite amount of immunity from the operation of its law.

The general rule may therefore be postulated that a state is bound to accord to the representatives of other states admitted into its territory and permitted to perform there some function involving the exercise of public authority, such measure of immunity from its own law as may be required to permit this function to be performed. The precise extent of this immunity will depend in the first place upon the nature and scope of the function of each type of representative. However, other considerations besides the "functional" have been taken into consideration in considering the extent of immunity in certain cases (for example, the dignity due to a visiting head of state or government).

Thus, the granting of immunity to the organs of states, and to the state itself in the person of its agents and agencies, is merely the consequence of permitting such organs, agents and agencies to perform their state functions abroad.

II. THE HEAD OF STATE

Traditionally, intercourse between states was considered to flow between one sovereign and another. Treaties were agreements between monarchs, which, consequently, bound the state; and diplomatic envoys were accredited personally to the head of the receiving state from his "brother" in the sending state. Traces of this "personalised" state may be found in modern international law, in the rule that obliges the sending state to accredit ambassadors, envoys and ministers to the head of the receiving state, and in the rule which treats the head of state as competent to speak for and bind the state in its international relations, for example, by his signature of a treaty. These rules apply irrespective of his constitutional position, of whether he is "monarch" or "president", and of whether the office of head of state is vested in one man or a council. Certain rules of protocol (precedence in state processions, etc.) still distinguish between monarchs and presidents.

THE PROTECTION OF THE HEAD OF STATE

In general

Several states have made it a criminal offence to offend the dignity of a friendly foreign head of state. This is of particular importance in relation to the law of defamation. This may be considered a rule of comity. Where the head of state is also the effective head of government, as with the Presidents of the United States of America and of France, any restrictions on the freedom to criticise political decisions, through criticism of the person having taken them, seem unjustified.

Abroad

The matter, however, is quite different where, at the request or with the consent of the receiving state, a foreign head of state visits its territory. In this case, the duty on the receiving state to protect the life and dignity of the visitor must be considered absolute. Whether and if so under what conditions the personal bodyguard and secret service escort of the head of state may accompany him is a matter for bilateral agreement.

THE IMMUNITIES OF A HEAD OF STATE

A visiting head of state would appear to be absolutely immune from the operation of the criminal law of the territorial state. So far as immunity from the civil (or private) law is concerned, state practice and the case-law of national courts is uncertain. Some states act on the assumption that the head of state can enjoy no greater immunity than the state itself, while others consider that he can be afforded no less immunity than that granted to the highest ranking diplomatic agent, the ambassador.

The correct approach may very well depend upon the status of the visit: it is inconceivable that while on a "state visit" a head of state should be inconvenienced by court proceedings of any sort.

Where the visit of the head of state is officially announced but is not a "state visit", immunity must cover all official acts; moreover, the fact of receiving the permission of the authorities of the territorial state to enter the territory may be assimilated to the accrediting of an ambassador, thus entitling him to extensive immunity in relation also to his non-official acts.

On incognito visits, which are unknown to the authorities of the receiving state, there is, not surprisingly, hardly any state practice. The sole existing case would appear to be *Mighell* v. *Sultan of Johore* (English Court of Appeal, 1894). In this case the plaintiff sued the defendant for breach of promise to marry without having any idea of the latter's real name or position. The Sultan claimed, and was accorded, "sovereign" immunity in his capacity as a "head of state". Nothing prevents a state from according a greater measure of immunity than is required by international law, nor from according such immunity to heads of "states" having no independent existence in international law, and this case must be read in the light of these remarks. As a matter of principle, a head of state, being unannounced, cannot claim a similar immunity to that extended to his ambassador, although he may be thought entitled to the immunity accorded to his state. In view of the recent trend (*see* section VIII below) to restrict state immunity to acts of public authority only and not to private law acts, this is less favourable than diplomatic immunity.

As in all cases, immunity may be waived, and such a waiver must be expressed. However, unlike any other case, the waiver of the immunity of the head of state can be made only by himself.

Persons entitled to the immunity accorded to a head of state
Immunity (and protection) are afforded to the office and not to the person. Thus a monarch who has abdicated or a retired president ceases to be entitled. A state may, nevertheless, extend some measure of protection as a matter of comity. The members of the head of state's family are entitled to the like immunity afforded to the head of state. State practice is silent with respect to presidents, although the case of monarchs is better illustrated. The members of the "retinue" are considered entitled to some immunity in relation to the performance of their official duties. However, the meaning of the term "retinue" is unclear, although the members of the secret service of the visiting state and the personal bodyguard of the head of state probably fall within this category. State practice has not yet elucidated these points.

III. THE GOVERNMENT

The government represents the state in all external relations. The role of head of state in international law was developed at a period when he was assumed to be in effective charge of the government. In some instances this is still the case, but where he fulfils a merely constitutional role reliance is placed not on the head of state's ability to represent his state (except on a symbolic level), but rather on that of the "head of government", an office which was not recognised in international law until recent times.

THE HEAD OF GOVERNMENT AND THE MINISTER FOR FOREIGN AFFAIRS

The head of government has no claim to be considered a separate organ of the state: he is merely the mouthpiece of his government, fulfilling the same role as his minister for foreign affairs. The latter officer is accorded a special place in international law because "the orderly conduct of international affairs requires that communications between governments should pass to and from the minister for foreign affairs" (*Carnegie Manual of Public International Law,* ed. Max Sorenson, p. 391). The state must speak with one voice, that of the government; but it is the minister for foreign affairs (unless the head of government intervenes personally) who acts as its spokesman and who collects, through the diplomatic channel, all messages addressed by other governments to his own. In the absence of agreement or permission to the contrary, "all official business with the receiving state entrusted to the [diplomatic] mission by the sending state shall be conducted with or through the ministry for foreign affairs of the receiving state" (Article 40(2) of the Vienna Convention on Diplomatic Relations, 1961). Conversely, no other minister or official is recognised as being able to speak for, or represent, his state abroad unless specially authorised. At diplomatic conferences there is a rule that representatives of the state, other than the head of government or minister for foreign affairs, must produce their credentials (in the form of a certificate specifying the powers given to the representative and signed by the minister for foreign affairs).

Capacity of the minister for foreign affairs to commit the state

The minister for foreign affairs, as spokesman for the government, may commit his state even by his spoken word. Thus in the *Eastern Greenland Case* (P.C.I.J., 1933), the court considered it "beyond all dispute that a reply orally given . . . by the minister for foreign affairs, in response to a request by the diplomatic representative of a foreign power, in regard to a question falling within his province, is binding upon the state to which the minister belongs." The same applies *a fortiori* to the head of government.

Immunities accorded abroad to the head of government and the minister for foreign affairs

In principle such persons would seem to be entitled to as extensive an immunity as is accorded to the head of state, and for the same reasons: they too represent a state in its external relations (although as spokesman for its government and not directly) and each of them is senior in rank to an ambassador. In *Chong Boon Kim* v. *Kim Yong Shik* (Circuit Court, State of Hawaii, 1963) the Korean Foreign Minister was served with a writ while in transit through Hawaii on an official visit. The United States State Department filed a suggestion of immunity that "under customary rules of international law, the head of a foreign government, its foreign minister and those designated by him as members of his official party, are immune from the jurisdiction of the . . . courts."

OTHER MINISTERS OF THE GOVERNMENT

With the increasing complexity of international relations, it is becoming more and more common for ministers other than the minister for foreign affairs to become actively involved in the external policy aspects of the matter within their competence. Conferences of ministers (of transport, justice, education, regional planning, etc.) are becoming a regular feature of European governmental co-operation. Even in these cases, however, it will be found that the name of the minister is communicated through the diplomatic channel to the minister for foreign affairs of the host state, by the foreign ministry of the sending state.

IV. THE DIPLOMATIC SERVICE

THE VIENNA CONVENTION ON DIPLOMATIC RELATIONS

The establishment of diplomatic relations is a bilateral operation requiring mutual consent. It normally results in the setting up of permanent diplomatic missions in the capitals of both the states concerned.

The rules set out below are now codified, and are contained in the Vienna Convention on Diplomatic Relations of 1961 which entered into force on 24th April 1964. It has been ratified by 134 states. Its preamble states that matters not dealt with in the Convention continue to be regulated by customary international law. However, all important matters were regulated in the Convention, which was adopted at a United Nations sponsored conference on the basis of a draft prepared by the International Law Commission.

THE DIPLOMATIC CHANNEL

The chief purpose of establishing diplomatic relations and permanent missions is to serve as a means by and through which states are able to communicate with each other. Such communications, which may for example take the form of conversations between the minister for foreign affairs of the state receiving the mission (the receiving state), and the ambassador of the state sending the mission (the sending state), pass from one government to another through the "diplomatic channel". Since each state normally has not only its own diplomatic mission in the capital of the foreign state, but also a diplomatic mission of the foreign state in its own capital, there are two diplomatic channels. To communicate a message to a foreign state the minister for foreign affairs can either send instructions to his ambassador in the foreign state, in which case the ambassador would request an interview with the minister for foreign affairs of that state, or summon the ambassador of the foreign state and give him the message himself for the ambassador to send back to his ministry. Where no answer is required the latter method is the simplest; but where an answer is required the former method offers the best chance of obtaining the answer quickly, since the ambassador can only reply in terms of the instructions given him by his minister.

Secrecy of communications through the diplomatic channel

If diplomacy is to serve any useful purpose it is evident that instructions and other messages passed through the diplomatic channel must remain secret, and in particular not come to the attention of the receiving state. The secrecy and security of official communications is secured by the following rules.

Communication by wireless. A diplomatic mission may, with the consent of the sending state, install a wireless transmitter. In practice, consent will only be given on the basis of reciprocity. Messages may be sent to and from the government in code.

Communications by means of the diplomatic bag. The diplomatic bag, containing packages (bearing visible external marks) of diplomatic documents, or articles intended for official use, may be entrusted to a diplomatic courier, who is to be provided with a certificate attesting his status and the number of packages constituting the diplomatic bag. He is to be "protected" by the receiving state, enjoy personal inviolability, and is not liable to any form of arrest or detention. Alternatively, the bag may be entrusted to the captain of a commercial aircraft, in which case the mission may send one of its members to take possession of it "directly and freely" from the captain. The diplomatic bag may not, in any event, be opened or detained. Messages may be sent in code or cipher.

Communication by ordinary means. The mission may also send messages in code or cipher by telegraph, telegram or telephone. A "government telegram" has priority: priority may also be obtained on request for a telephone communication.

Inviolability of "official correspondence". All correspondence relating to the mission and its function is inviolable, whether or not contained in the diplomatic bag.

The principle of "free communication"
In general, the receiving state undertakes to "permit and protect" communication on the part of the mission for all official purposes with its government, and with other missions and consulates wherever situated.

FUNCTIONS OF THE MISSION
The receiving state is obliged to accord full facilities for the performance of the functions of the mission. These are:

(a) representing the sending state in the receiving state;
(b) negotiating with the government of the receiving state;
(c) protecting the interests of the sending state and of its nationals;
(d) reporting conditions and developments in the receiving state "by all lawful means";
(e) promoting friendly relations and developing economic, cultural and scientific relations.

A diplomatic mission may also perform consular functions.

The receiving state must ensure freedom of movement and travel to all members of the mission, subject to its law regarding zones into which entry is prohibited or regulated for reasons of national security.

THE MEMBERS OF THE MISSION
The members of the mission are the head of the mission and the members of the staff of the mission. The latter include the members of the diplomatic staff, of the administrative and technical staff, and of the (domestic) service staff.

Diplomatic agents
Heads of mission and members of the diplomatic staff are called diplomatic agents. A head of mission may have the title of Ambassador, Envoy or Minister (in which cases he is accredited to the minister for foreign affairs). Other diplomatic agents include counsellors, secretaries of embassy and attachés.

Nationality of diplomatic agents

Members of the diplomatic staff should in principle have the nationality of the sending state. However, two or more states may appoint the same person as head of mission to another state unless objection is offered. The consent of the sending state, which may be withdrawn at any time, is required for the appointment of persons having the nationality of the sending state, and also for that of nationals of third states not also having the nationality of the sending state.

Prior approval of appointment by the receiving state

The sending state "must make certain" that the *agrément* of the receiving state has been given for the person it proposes to appoint as head of mission. The receiving state is not obliged to give reasons for its refusal. In the case of naval, military and air attachés, the receiving state may require their names to be submitted beforehand for approval.

Persona non grata

The receiving state may at any time and without having to explain its decision notify the sending state that any diplomatic agent is *persona non grata,* or that any other member of the mission is not acceptable. The sending state must then recall its diplomatic agent or recall or terminate the employment of other members of the staff of the mission; failing this the receiving state may, after a reasonable time, refuse to recognise the person concerned as a member of the mission.

Size of the mission

In the absence of a specific agreement as to its size, the receiving state may require that the size of a mission be kept within limits considered by it to be reasonable and normal, having regard to circumstances in the receiving state and the need of the particular mission. The receiving state may also refuse to accept officials of a particular category.

Protection of the person of a diplomatic agent

Since his person is inviolable a diplomatic agent is not subject to arrest or detention. Moreover, the receiving state is to take "all appropriate steps" to prevent any attack on his person, freedom or dignity. He is immune from criminal jurisdiction and, with the three following exceptions, from civil and administrative jurisdiction:

(a) real action relating to private immovable property;

(b) an action relating to succession, in which the agent is involved as executor, administrator, heir, or legatee;

(c) an action relating to professional or commercial activity; unless in any of these cases he was acting on behalf of the state.

A diplomatic agent is not obliged to give evidence. He is moreover exempt in the receiving state from all personal and military services, from social security and from all dues and taxes except indirect taxes incorporated in the price of goods or services; dues and taxes on private immovable property; certain succession and inheritance duties; taxes on private income having its source in the receiving state and capital taxes on investments there; charges for specific services rendered; and registration, etc., fees and stamp duties.

Waiver of diplomatic immunity

It is generally considered that a diplomat is immune not from the law itself, but only from the application and implementation (or execution) of the law through and by the courts and other authorities of the receiving state. This immunity can be expressly waived by the sending state (but not by the diplomatic agent himself). A waiver cannot be implied from the conduct of the agent, although if he institutes proceedings he thereby submits to the jurisdiction of the court in respect of any counter-claim "directly connected" with the principal claim. Waiver of immunity of jurisdiction does not imply waiver of execution, for which a separate and express waiver must be obtained from the sending state.

Status and immunity of other members of the mission staff

A lesser scale of privileges and immunities is provided for the administrative and technical staff, and for the service staff. Those which are "locally recruited" (nationals or permanent residents) enjoy full immunity only in respect of official acts. It is not clear who is to decide when an act is official.

Duty to "respect the law" of the receiving state

All persons enjoying diplomatic privileges and immunities have a duty to respect the laws and regulations of the receiving state, and not to interfere in its internal affairs.

End of diplomatic functions

A diplomatic agent's functions are normally terminated on notification of this fact by the sending state to the receiving state; if, however, he has been declared *persona non grata* and has not been withdrawn, the receiving state may notify the sending state that he refuses to recognise the agent as a member of the mission.

Duty to facilitate departure

The receiving state must, finally, facilitate the departure of persons enjoying diplomatic privileges and immunities and members of their families, irrespective of nationality, at the earliest possible moment. If need be the necessary means of transport must be placed at their disposal. This duty applies even in the case of armed conflict.

PREMISES OF THE MISSION

The premises of the mission include the embassy building, offices and land (irrespective of ownership) used for the purposes of the mission, and the residence of the head of mission. Without the express consent of the receiving state, the sending state may not establish offices forming part of the mission in localities other than those in which the mission itself is established. The flag and emblem of the sending state may be used on the premises, including the private residence and means of transport of the head of mission.

Inviolability of the premises of the mission, and of the private residences of members of the diplomatic staff

"Inviolability" means that the receiving state may not use any means of coercion to enforce its will or its law. The agents of the receiving state are forbidden to enter the premises of the mission or the private residences of diplomatic agents except with express permission. All mission property, including means of transport, is immune from search, requisition, attachment or execution, while the archives and documents are inviolable at any time and wherever they may be.

Protection of the premises of the mission

The receiving state is under a special duty to protect the premises of the mission against any intrusion or damage and to prevent any disturbance of the peace or impairment of its dignity. This duty may require the state to take special measures over and above those it takes to discharge its general duty of ensuring order.

In the *Case concerning United States Diplomatic and Consular Staff in Tehran* (U.S.A. v. Iran), (I.C.J., 1980) the court had occasion to state and apply a large number of the rules of diplomatic law, in particular the duty of protecting foreign embassies. The case arose out of the armed attack on the United States Embassy by "militants" on 4th November 1979, which led to the overrunning of the premises and the seizure of the inmates as hostages, as well as the appropriation of its property and archives. As the court noted: "The attack and the subsequent overrunning of the whole Embassy premises was an operation which continued over a period of some three hours without any body of police, any military unit or any Iranian official intervening to try and stop or impede it from being carried through to its completion."

Although the court found that, at this stage, the action of the militants was not imputable to the state, nevertheless ". . . this does not mean that Iran is free of any responsibility in regard to those attacks; for its own conduct was in conflict with its international obligations. By a number of provisions of the Vienna Convention of 1961, Iran was placed under the most categorical obligations, as a receiving state, to take appropriate steps to ensure the protection of the United States Embassy and Consulates, their staffs, their archives, their means of communication and the freedom of movement of the members of their staffs."

RECIPROCITY AND NON-DISCRIMINATION

The above rules of law are of general application: (receiving) states must not, in applying them, discriminate as between (sending) states whether on the basis of their political friendship or on any other. Diplomatic relations are actually most valuable between two mutually hostile states. However, these rules constitute a minimum, and there is nothing to stop two states, whether on the basis of custom or agreement, from according each other more favourable treatment than is set out above. Conversely, if one state applies the above rules restrictively, the other state may, without being considered discriminatory, accord as a sanction exactly reciprocal treatment to the diplomatic mission of that state in its territory.

V. CONSULS AND CONSULATES

THE CONSUL AND THE SOURCES OF CONSULAR LAW

The institution of the "consul" is older than that of the permanently established diplomatic envoy. Consular law has been developed through a network of bilateral treaties, whereas diplomatic law was largely based upon unwritten agreements between states. The law is now set out in the Vienna Convention on Consular Relations of 1963, which entered into force on 19th March 1967 and to which to date 98 states are parties. The preamble asserts that customary international law continues to govern matters not expressly regulated therein. The provisions of the convention do not, however, affect other international agreements in force as between states which are parties to them and there are in practice a large number of bilateral agreements in force between states; moreover, a number of new bilateral agreements have been concluded subsequently. Unless otherwise stated, however, the rules set out below are taken from the Vienna Convention.

It should be noted that, since there are different classes of "consul" and "consulate", the Vienna Convention uses the term "consular officer" and "consular post" and "head of consular post".

THE ESTABLISHMENT AND SEVERANCE OF CONSULAR RELATIONS

The establishment of consular relations depends upon mutual consent: their severance is a unilateral act and one which is extremely rare in practice. Whereas consent to the establishment of diplomatic relations will be taken to imply consent to the establishment of consular relations (where these do not already exist), severance of diplomatic relations does *not* imply severance of consular relations. But consular relations may not only outlast diplomatic relations, they may also precede them, as may be implied from the rule that where a state has no diplomatic relations with another, it may, with the latter's consent, authorise a consular officer to perform diplomatic acts.

THE CONSULAR SERVICE

The close interrelationship between the functions of consuls and of diplomats, the growing practice of allowing diplomatic missions to perform consular functions, and the practice referred to above of permitting consular officers to perform diplomatic acts, have led to a trend in favour of amalgamating the consular and the diplomatic services of a state into a single foreign service. In any event, the consular service, like the diplomatic, is normally under the sole authority of the minister for foreign affairs. In the eyes of the receiving state, the consular service nevertheless remains a separate organ of the sending state for the performance of certain government functions abroad. Some states, however, have always made a practice of filling consular posts, or some of them, with the persons who are outside government service.

THE CONSULAR POST

There are four types of consular post: consulate-general, consulate, vice-consulate and consular agency. The consent of the receiving state is required for the establishment in its territory of a consular post; the choice of its seat; its classification and the district to be allocated to it; the opening of any office in a locality other than that in which it is itself established; and the opening by a consulate-general or consulate of a vice-consulate or consular agency.

THE CONSULAR DISTRICT

Unlike the diplomatic mission, the consular post is of a local character. States may thus appoint several consular posts in the territory of a receiving state, assigning to each a consular district within which it alone can exercise its functions. For this reason a consular officer may address himself only to the competent authorities of the receiving state within his district. Only where an international agreement or the laws of the receiving state so permit may a consular officer contact the central authorities directly. Consuls are not accredited to the government of the receiving state: they do not, even within their district, represent the sending state for the whole range of its external affairs. In general each consular post and district is independent of every other, although they are all under the authority of the head of the diplomatic mission.

CONSULAR FUNCTIONS

Consular functions are exercised by consular posts and diplomatic missions. There is no exhaustive list of consular functions, for a consular post may perform any functions entrusted to it by the sending state to which the receiving state makes no objection. There are, however, a number of functions generally recognised as pertaining to the consular office.

Functions to which the receiving state may make no objection

Once a state has agreed to the establishment of consular relations it cannot object to the consular post performing any of the following functions.

(a) Protecting the interests of the sending state and furthering the development of its commercial and economic interests (as also of its social, cultural and scientific interests).

(b) Seeking information by all lawful means on economic and other conditions and development in the receiving state and reporting thereon to the government of the sending state.

(c) Issuing passports and travel documents to nationals of the sending state and visas to persons wishing to travel to that state.

(d) Helping nationals of the sending state and protecting their interests (nationals include individuals and bodies corporate).

(e) Inspecting vessels and aircraft having the nationality of the sending state and supervising and assisting such vessels and aircraft and their crews.

Functions whose performance is subject to the laws of the receiving state

In relation to the following list of functions the receiving state may object only if, and to the extent that, performance would be contrary to its law and regulations.

(a) Acting as notary and civil registrar and in capacities of a similar kind, in relation, for example, to registers of birth, death and marriage of nationals, to consular marriages, voting and call-up papers, attesting documents, taking oaths.

(b) Transmitting judicial and extra-judicial documents, executing letters rogatory or commissions to take evidence for the courts of the sending state.

(c) Representing nationals in court proceedings when they are unable to defend their rights at the proper time.

(d) Safeguarding the interests of minors and other persons lacking full capacity, particularly in cases of guardianship or trusteeship; and the interests of nationals in cases of succession *mortis causa.*

(e) Conducting investigations into any accidents which occurred during the voyage of a vessel, and settling disputes of any kind between master, officers and seamen.

The European Convention on Consular Functions concluded at Paris on 11th December 1967 deals with the matter of consular functions in more detail.

Communication with nationals, including those who are imprisoned
Consular officers are free to communicate with nationals of the sending state anywhere in their district. If, within the consular district, a national of the sending state is arrested or committed to prison, the competent authorities of the receiving state must, *if the national so requests*, inform the consular post without delay and forward any communication made by him to the consular post. The authorities are under a duty to inform the person concerned of this right without delay. Many bilateral consular agreements and one multilateral agreement, namely the European Convention on Consular Functions, 1967, provide that notification of detention must be made to the consul automatically and irrespective of the wish of the detained person. Such agreements, however, generally also contain a provision to the effect that consular officers from states of which a person is a political refugee are deprived of all rights in respect of the refugee, whether detained or otherwise.

Consular officers have the right to visit a national of the sending state who is in prison, custody or detention, to converse with him and to arrange for his legal representation (a consular officer, however, may take no action on his behalf which the national expressly opposes). This right, jealously guarded by consular officers, tends to be accorded unwillingly and hesitatingly by the authorities of the sending state. Although to be exercised "in conformity with the laws and regulations of the receiving state", this is subject to the provision that "the said laws and regulations must enable full effect to be given to the purposes for which the right is intended".

Communications between the consular post and the sending state
The consular post may communicate with its government, diplomatic missions and other consular posts "wherever situated". The receiving state undertakes to "permit and protect" such communications. All appropriate means may be used, including diplomatic and consular couriers, diplomatic and consular bags, and messages in code and cipher. Wireless transmitters may be installed only with the receiving state's consent. The rules governing the consular courier are identical to those relating to the diplomatic, except that the authorities of the receiving state may request that the consular bag be opened in their presence if they have "serious reasons to believe" that it contains something other than official correspondence or articles intended exclusively for official use. This request may be refused, but in that case the bag must be returned to its place of origin.

CONSULAR PREMISES
The buildings and land, irrespective of ownership, used exclusively for the purposes of the consular post constitute the "consular premises". They are inviolable except

(*a*) where it is necessary to expropriate them for purposes of national defence or public utility, in which case prompt, adequate and effective compensation is to be paid, and all possible steps (including assistance in finding new premises) taken to avoid impending the performance of the mission; and

(*b*) in case of fire or other disaster requiring prompt protective action.

In all other cases agents of the receiving state are forbidden to enter any part of the premises used exclusively for the work of the consular post, except with the express consent of the head of the consular post, or the head of the diplomatic mission.

CONSULAR ARCHIVES
Consular archives include "all the papers, documents, correspondence, books, films, tapes and registers of the consular post, together with the ciphers and codes, the card-indexes and any article of furniture intended for their protection or safekeeping". They are at all times inviolable, wherever they may be.

CONSULAR PERSONNEL

Head of the consular post
There are four classes of head of consular post to correspond with

the four classes of consular post, namely consuls-general, consuls, vice-consuls and consular agents. In appointing a head of consular post the sending state must send, through the diplomatic channel, to the receiving state a "commission" attesting his name, class, consular district and seat of the consular post. The authorisation of the receiving state admitting the head of post to the exercise of his functions takes the form of the grant of an "exequatur". The receiving state must then notify the competent authorities of the consular district.

Persona non grata

The receiving state may declare a consular officer *persona non grata* at any time without the need to give reasons. The sending state is then obliged to recall him or terminate his functions with the mission, failing which the receiving state may withdraw his exequatur (in the case of the head) or cease to consider him a member of the staff of the consular post (in the case of other consular officers).

Nationality of consular officers

Consular officers, that is to say, any member of the consular post entrusted with consular functions, ought in principle to have the nationality of the sending state. However, two states may appoint the same person as a consular officer in the receiving state, with its consent. In normal practice a substantial number of honorary consular officers are not nationals of the sending state.

"Honorary consular officers"

Career consular officers are regular members of the foreign service and may not carry on for personal profit any professional or commercial activity in the receiving state. They should be distinguished from "honorary consular officers" of whom there is no definition, but who are variously classed as being non-nationals of the sending state, not regularly salaried, authorised to engage in private gainful occupation, and permitted to perform only certain limited functions. Each state is free to decide whether it will receive or appoint honorary consular officers. They are, however, sufficiently numerous for the 1963 Vienna Convention to devote a whole chapter (Chapter III) to the regime applicable to them.

FACILITIES, PRIVILEGES AND IMMUNITIES RELATING TO CAREER CONSULAR OFFICERS

The Vienna Convention contains 18 Articles governing the status of career consular officers, dealing with the following matters.

Protection of the person of a consular officer

The receiving state should take "all appropriate steps" to prevent any attack on the person, freedom or dignity of a consular officer, who should be treated by the authorities with the respect due to his office and the inviolability of his person.

Immunity from criminal jurisdiction

A consular officer is not immune from the criminal jurisdiction of the receiving state. In the case of a grave crime there is an exception to the inviolability of his person and he may be arrested and detained pending trial, in which case the proceedings must be instituted with a minimum of delay. In other cases the consular officer may only be deprived of his personal freedom in execution of a judicial decision of final effect. The receiving state must notify the head of the consular post, or, as the case may be, the sending state through the diplomatic channel.

Immunity from civil (and administrative) jurisdiction

Consular officers are amenable to the jurisdiction of the civil and administrative authorities of the receiving state in respect of their private but not of their official acts. However, a civil action by a third party for damage arising out of an accident in the receiving state by a vehicle, vessel or aircraft, or arising out of a contract concluded by a consular officer "in which he did not contract expressly or impliedly as an agent of the sending state", are subject to the jurisdiction of the courts, whether or not considered as official acts, i.e. "acts performed in the exercise of consular functions".

An important question arises as to who, in other cases, is to say when an act is "performed in the exercise of consular functions". The scope of the function is the result of agreement between the two states and not the individual. The fact that immunity has been claimed proves that the sending state considers the act in question to have been in performance of those functions, and also, since immunity has not been waived, that it is "a proper case". To permit a national court complete discretion to decide whether the case falls within its jurisdiction in these circumstances would jeopardise the careful balance between the interests of the sending and the receiving states which had been worked out by international agreement.

Two decisions of French courts illustrate the dilemma. In *Zizianoff* v. *Kahn et Bigelow* (Tribunal Correctionnel de la Seine, 1927), a consul refused to issue the plaintiff with a visa, and asked by certain journalists why he had acted so, replied in terms alleged to be defamatory of the plaintiff (that she was a spy!). The court held that although the act of refusing a visa was an official act, the subsequent publication to third parties of the reasons was not. The correct approach, it is thought, is to be seen in the later case of *Boyer et al.* v. *Aldréte* (Tribunal Civil de Marseilles, 1956), also involving alleged defamatory statements, in which it was decided that evidence of a consul's intent to act in an official capacity even if in fact *ultra vires* serves to remove the action from local jurisdiction.

Duration of privileges and immunities

A member of the consular post enjoys his privileges and immunities from the moment of entering the territory of the receiving state on proceeding to take up his post, and ceases to do so when, his functions having come to an end, he leaves the territory, or on the expiry of a reasonable period in which he might have done so. Immunity from jurisdiction for acts performed in the exercise of consular functions continues to exist without limitation of time.

VI. ARMED FORCES

There is no rule of international law requiring states to maintain any armed forces, any more than there is a rule forbidding them to do so. However, certain exiguous states apart, all states, except Japan whose present constitution forbids it, do in fact maintain some armed forces, their purpose being as much internal as external; as much, that is, to ensure the ability of the government to impose its will on the population in times of civil disturbance or insurgency, as to ensure the defence, and thereby maintain the independence, of the state in its relations with other states. The best example of this duality of function is the French "gendarme" who, contrary to popular belief, is a member of the French armed forces, not a mere policeman.

DEFINITION OF "ARMED FORCES"

It does not appear that any definition of "armed forces" exists in international law. It is sufficient for our purpose to note that the regular armed forces will comprise any body of men under military discipline. This will serve to distinguish those parts of the police-forces whose duties are restricted to the maintenance of internal order within the state. The Geneva Convention of 1949 on the treatment of prisoners-of-war distinguishes between members of regular armed forces and members of militia, volunteer corps and "organised resistance movements operating in or outside their own territory, even when that territory is occupied." Entitlement to treatment as prisoners-of-war will depend upon fulfilment of the four following conditions:

(a) that they are commanded by a person responsible for his subordinates;

(b) that they have a distinctive sign recognisable at a distance;

(c) that they carry arms openly;

(d) that they conduct military operations in accordance with the laws and customs of war.

ARMED FORCES AS AN ORGAN OF THE STATE

So long as they remain under its control the armed forces are considered in international law as an organ of the state. This applies as much in time of peace as of war. Conversely, bodies of men under arms cannot constitute an "armed force" unless they accept allegiance to some state. Thus, the acts of an independent organised guerrilla force operating, with its consent, from the territory of one state against another, will not be considered in international law as acts of the state from which the guerrillas operate. Such acts, however, are imputable to that state for the purpose of responsibility and of the use of force as a reprisal.

ARMED FORCES IN TIME OF PEACE

Normally, the armed forces remain within their state, and thus outside the ambit of international law. Exceptionally, however, part of the forces of one state may be stationed within the territory of another, while remaining under the control and military discipline of their own state, or else falling to a greater or lesser degree under a joint command. Such cases are governed by special agreements between the states concerned. The mere entry, for whatever purpose, of armed forces of one state into the territory of another requires the prior permission of the latter. This may be given subject to any conditions the territorial state may impose. Permission may be withdrawn at any time, subject to any treaty rules which may apply if the permission and conditions of its grant are incorporated in a written agreement.

WARSHIPS

The above does not apply to warships. The law applying to warships is of customary origin. It contrasts with the rules applicable to other armed forces in that prior permission need not be sought before a warship enters the territory (the water territory) of another state. However, in other respects their position is the same, in that a state retains the right to exclude warships at least from internal waters, and it may, so long as the special status of the warship is respected, subject their entry to any conditions it thinks fit. Thus, a warship is expected to comply with the laws and regulations of the littoral state in regard to order in the port, the place for casting anchor, sanitation, quarantine, customs and other similar matters. If it does not do so, the consent of the littoral state to its presence within its territory can be withdrawn and it will be required to leave.

Status of a warship in the territory of a foreign state

Neither the jurisdiction nor the law of a foreign state extend to warships on the high seas. Once within its territory, the warship is immune from the jurisdiction of the littoral state, whether exercised through its courts or in any other way. No legal proceedings can be taken against the ship whether for damages or collision, for salvage, reward, or for any other cause. In *The Schooner Exchange* v. *Mcfaddon* (United States Supreme Court, 1812) proceedings were brought in the United States for recovery of possession of a ship which had been a merchant ship, but which had been captured by the French and fitted out as a warship. This case is always considered, but wrongly so, as laying the foundations of the law on state immunity. It did, on the contrary, provide the first example of an attempt to subject a foreign warship to the jurisdiction of the courts of the littoral state. The Supreme Court held that the ship, being now a warship, was immune from the jurisdiction of the court.

Although immune from its jurisdiction, the law of the littoral state does nevertheless apply to acts taking place on board warships although to what extent is doubtful. For example, when immunity from jurisdiction is waived, a killing on board could properly be considered as a "murder" according to the law of the littoral state. In the case of *Chung Chi Cheung* v. *The King* (Judicial Committee of the Privy Council, 1939), a British court decided that a waiver of immunity could be implied from the failure of the authorities of the nationality of the warship to take the proper steps to secure the surrender of the accused who escaped into port after a killing on board. He was found guilty by the local court of murder. In principle, however, waiver ought to be express.

Crew of a warship ashore

State practice with respect to the position of crew members ashore is uncertain. The principle would appear to be that the littoral state is prepared not to enforce its jurisdiction against persons going ashore for purposes connected with the ship, for so long as they remain under military discipline. Persons going ashore on leave and for purposes unconnected with the ship fall under the exclusive jurisdiction of the littoral state (except to the extent that military police are permitted to co-operated with the port police for the maintenance of order). However, a member of the crew on leave who commits a crime (for example against another member of the crew) may, as a matter of courtesy, be handed over to the authorities of the warship.

Whether a crime committed by a crew member ashore for purposes connected with the ship and under military discipline is within the jurisdiction of the littoral state is uncertain. It clearly falls outside the jurisdiction of the courts if the act constituting the crime is classed as an "act of state" (an act for the commission of which the state subsequently assumes full responsibility). In the *McLeod Incident* in 1840 a member of a British expeditionary force in Canada was sent by ship across one of the Great Lakes into United States territory to destroy and sink the *Caroline*. The *Caroline* was duly sunk, causing the death of certain persons on board. The raid was a reprisal, and was part of a military operation, McLeod thus being throughout under military discipline. He later came into the United States as a private citizen, was arrested and tried by the New York State Court for the "murder" of one of the persons killed. The United Kingdom protested, and the United States Secretary of State subsequently disavowed the action of the court. He "entertained no doubt that after the avowal of the transaction as a public transaction, authorised and undertaken by the British authorities, individuals concerned in it ought not ... to be holden responsible in the ordinary tribunals for their participation in it." In all other cases it is thought the criminal jurisdiction of the littoral state is not displaced.

VII. TRADE DELEGATIONS, INFORMATION CENTRES, ETC.

The distinguishing feature of all trade delegations, information centres, tourist offices and other such officials or offices as are sent, or maintained abroad by one state in the territory of a foreign state, is that all are "agents" or "agencies" of the state, to which have been delegated the performance of certain specific and limited functions. They are not state organs.

LEGAL STATUS OF STATE AGENCIES AND AGENTS ABROAD

Since an agent, unlike an organ, is not part of the state, the first point to consider is whether, and if so to what extent, a state agency or agent does act for or on behalf of the state. Only if this is the case is there any need to enquire whether the entity or person is entitled to the protection accorded to his state abroad. Moreover, such protection can only exist to the extent that the agent or entity acts in the performance of his or its functions. Other acts are subject to no protection of any sort. This immediately distinguishes the position of state agents and agencies and persons in their employ from that of state organs and officials and persons in their employ.

The protection afforded in relation to acts in the performance of the function depends upon the law of "state immunity". Thus, once it is established that the body or person sued was, in respect of the subject-matter of the proceedings, acting for or on behalf of the foreign state as its agency or agent, the court is obliged to treat the case as if the defendant was the state itself, and bring into play its rules on state immunity. The same applies in respect of suits *in rem* with regard to merchant ships, and to any other property to which the foreign state asserts title, possession or control. As to the nature and extent of this immunity, *see* section VIII.

VIII. STATE IMMUNITY

In addition to the protection given abroad to its organs, protection is accorded to the "state" itself. The term state immunity refers to the immunity accorded by one state through its courts to another state against which it is sought to entertain proceedings, attach property, or execute judgments. Developed almost exclusively through the decisions of national courts, the basis, nature and scope of state immunity are all uncertain. The following paragraphs are no more than a statement of the lowest common denominator of immunity actually granted and claimed by all states.

THE "STATE" FOR THE PURPOSES OF THE GRANT OF IMMUNITY

There is no definition of state in international law. Nor as it seems, does any state define itself for the general purposes of its own law. It is not surprising, therefore, that there is no definition of a foreign "state" for the purposes of according it immunity.

It is, however, *the state as a subject of international law* which is entitled to immunity. But this is not as helpful a guide as might appear, since in proceedings before a national court, and this is where the matter comes to be decided, the "state" appears as a subject of the national law applied by that court. It does, however, mean that the individual states of a federal state are not entitled to immunity unless (and then only to the extent that) they are endowed with a measure of international personality; nor can the administrative subdivisions, regions, departments, and individual cities and towns of a state claim any immunity whatsoever.

STATE AGENCIES

State agencies established or operating abroad are not part of the state as an international person. They do not need to obtain the permission of the state of the forum before being established within its territory, but may on the contrary be set up and operate in the same conditions as any other foreign corporate entity. Accordingly, they are entitled to no immunity. However, to the extent that, in the subject matter of the proceedings, an agency was acting for or on behalf of the state (i.e. in performing the role that an "agent" normally performs for his "principal"), the agency can nevertheless benefit from state immunity if the state itself might have benefited therefrom had the proceedings been introduced directly against it.

The acts of an agency operating in the state's own territory might give rise to proceedings before a foreign court either because a particular transaction was concluded abroad, or because proceedings are brought abroad although the act giving rise to the dispute occurred within the state's own territory. In either case, the fact that the agency has been set up with a distinct legal personality under the foreign state's *own* law is of no influence on the question whether it is to be considered part of the state as an international person: for the internal organisation of one state is of no concern to other states. A national bank, for example, has a separate personality, but will nevertheless be entitled to immunity in relation to its functions as the authority which issues bank-notes, etc. Moreover, in some states, as for example France and the United Kingdom, certain government ministries and departments of the central government are, exceptionally, endowed with a separate legal personality for their own administrative convenience.

IMMUNITY

Basis

In international law all states are sovereign and they must therefore deal with each other on a basis of equality. When the courts of one state are confronted with the person, or the acts, of another state, this equality must be respected. A state, but no one else, may freely choose whether to act on the level of international law, or by reference to some system of national law (generally its own). If it chooses the latter it cannot subsequently claim a status or protection to which it would only have been entitled had it chosen the former. It is part of the very sovereignty of a state that it may choose to act as a subject of some national law. When it does so, it is entitled to no immunity, for the immunity, as already stated, belongs to the state as a subject of international law.

Nature: waiver

It is by no means certain whether the protection given to a state is in the nature of an immunity from the law (so that, if waived, the law would apply) or a non-liability, in which case, strictly speaking, no immunity would be necessary. The great weight of authority and precedent support the former theory: however, it is noticeable that the closer a state approaches to the minimum level of immunity for foreign states, the more hesitant courts and commentators become as to whether the foreign state can waive what is left of it. The question is of theoretical interest only as it is generally inconceivable that a foreign state would waive immunity in relation to an exercise of its public authority.

Ratione personae, or ratione materiae?

Those states whose courts still follow the theory of absolute immunity do so on the basis that this immunity attaches to the person of the defendant and his property. Proceedings between private persons may also be stayed if the state demonstrates a sufficient legal interest in the property in dispute. States whose courts apply a relative immunity attach importance to the subject-matter of the proceedings. Immunity will only lie where the act (or property) in dispute was performed (or acquired) *jure imperii,* that is to say, in the exercise of its sovereign capacity.

Extent

Whenever the party being sued before a court of one state is a foreign state, the defendant will be entitled to immunity from the jurisdiction of that court so soon as it appears that the proceedings could not go to judgment without the court pronouncing upon the validity of an act (or some right or interest in property) which could only have been performed (or acquired) by an entity endowed with sovereignty. We shall deal successively with immunity arising from the state's external sovereignty, and internal sovereignty.

In respect of acts performed within the territory of state of the forum

When a state performs an act in the territory of another state in its capacity as a subject of international law, the question arises whether it did so with that state's consent. If it was performed with consent the state is entitled to immunity, for two public authorities cannot operate under the law of one of them. As already noted, whenever an organ of one state is permitted to perform a public function or carry out an act of public authority within the territory of another, the corollary is the grant of an equal measure of immunity. If this applies to an organ of the state it must apply *a fortiori* to the state itself. When consent has not been given, the acting state has, through its agent, committed a breach of international law in violation of the territorial sovereignty of the state of the forum. The act in question then lies outside the competence of a national court, and can be judged only by a court having international jurisdiction.

In respect of acts performed by a state within its own territory

The sovereignty of a state is manifested both externally in its relations with other states, and internally in respect of persons and things present within its territory. Acts there performed, or rights or interests in property there acquired by the state occasionally become relevant to the resolution of a dispute before a foreign court. In such cases, whether the foreign state is a party to the proceedings is not immediately relevant. All such cases bring into operation the rules of international law (conflict of laws) of the state of the forum, the court generally applying the *lex loci* — the law of the place where the act was performed or where the right or interest was vested — or, in other words, the law of the state performing the act or acquiring the property. Through the operation of the conflict rules, states normally do in fact *recognise* the legal effects of acts performed by foreign states within their own territory. However, no state is obliged to do so by any rule of public international law. It is thus the public policy of the state of the forum which is the determining factor. If the policy behind the act is abhorrent or politically unacceptable to that state, the courts may refuse recognition. For example, a decree of nationalisation or confiscation of the property of the nationals of a certain state might very well not be recognised within the territory and before the courts of the state being discriminated against. The original owners might therefore reclaim the property on the ground that the present owners have no right or title to it, and where the defendant is some private party to which the property has subsequently been sold by the confiscating state no question of state immunity can arise so that the case can be decided in this way.

It should be added that the courts of some states have refused recognition in this type of case, not on the ground of the public policy of their own state, but by deciding that the act of the foreign state was contrary to international law. Any such pretension is in itself a breach of the principle of the equality of states, for to allow national courts to decide which acts of foreign states are, and which are not, in accordance with international law is to bring the law into disrepute and rob it of its international character. Only international courts, that is to say courts endowed with international jurisdiction, have the authority validly to interpret and apply rules of international law.

Where in this type of case the confiscating state is also a party to the proceedings, the position is slightly different. Where the state is plaintiff its act or acquisition of property will be judged by reference to its own law. Although the legal effects of the act will be recognised, the law will never be enforced. Proceedings brought to enforce a foreign state's criminal law, or its fiscal laws or generally any public law, will be dismissed. Where the state is defendant, it will be entitled to immunity from the jurisdiction wherever the proceedings relate to an act performed or property acquired by the state within its own territory by the operation of its public law or its particular position as a sovereign authority. Such immunity, which is a reflection of the defendant state's own internal sovereignty, also avoids the embarrassment of a court of one state being obliged to apply to a foreign state the public law of that foreign state.

From execution of judgment

The order by which a court enforces its judgment in the face of an unwilling or uncooperative judgment debtor is, obviously, a direct exercise of sovereignty. To employ it against a recalcitrant foreign state, whatever may be the merits or the justice of the situation, would be to cause an affront to its dignity, and be likely to give rise to international friction. Hardly any state today permits execution of judgment against foreign states. Only Greece and Switzerland permit it in all cases; Italy does so subject to the *fiat* of the Ministry of Justice; there is one case of an inferior court in Belgium and some recent decisions of the courts of the Federal Republic of Germany. The exercise of this power always gives rise to protests from the states against which it is exercised. Execution against a foreign state is contrary to international law, except perhaps in relation to immoveable property within the territory of the state of the forum. But this immunity may be waived in cases where it would in no way interfere with the purposes for which the immunity was given.

An interesting new approach to this problem is to be found in the European Convention on State Immunity of 1974, under the provisions of which each contracting party undertakes to "comply" with judgments given against it by the courts of other contracting states.

CHAPTER SIX

The Law of Treaties

The Vienna Convention on the Law of Treaties was concluded on 23rd May 1969. The preamble states that it is to be considered as a "codification and progressive development of the law of treaties", the rules of customary law continuing to govern questions not regulated by the convention. This Treaty entered into force in February 1980 after ratification by the 35th state, and will apply to treaties concluded thereafter. The convention applies only to treaties concluded between states, including treaties which are the constituent instruments of international organisations, and those adopted within such organisations subject to any relevant rules of the organisation. The rules of the law of treaties which exist independently of the Vienna Convention continue to apply to treaties to which the parties, or some of them, are not states. Subject to these conditions and limitations the Vienna Convention sets out, in 85 articles, a comprehensive code of rules governing the law of treaties. References are made to the relevant articles throughout.

I. THE NATURE AND FORMATION OF A TREATY

NATURE OF A TREATY

The rule "pacta sunt servanda"
Pacta sunt servanda (agreements are to be observed) is a rule which predates international law. It applies to all agreements made within the framework of the international legal system, and is the basis of the law of treaties.

The observance of treaties
Once in force, treaties are binding upon the parties to them and must be performed in good faith. A state may not, in particular, justify non-observance by reference to any impediment of its municipal law.

Definition

A treaty is "an agreement between subjects of international law in written form and governed by international law" (Article 2 (1) (a), adapted to take account of the fact that the Vienna Convention applies only to treaties between states).

Agreements not in written form

The capacity to make oral and other informal agreements is an exercise of state sovereignty. By virtue of the rule *pacta sunt servanda* such agreements are, moreover, binding under international law. For an example, see the discussion of the Ihlen declaration dealt with below, though such agreements are not treaties.

Agreements governed by international law

The law of treaties is concerned only with agreements governed by international law. These are sometimes referred to as "international agreements". States may, however, make agreements between themselves which are subject to some national law and not to international law. It is convenient to make agreements of this sort about, for example, the sale of commodities or arms, or the lease of property, when some third party not a subject of international law is closely involved in the transaction. Although such agreements are in a sense "international", they are not governed by international law, and are not treaties but state contracts.

"Offer" and "acceptance" in international law

A treaty need not consist of a single document setting down the terms accepted jointly by the parties. One common form of treaty consists of an exchange of diplomatic notes, or of letters, whereby the proposal or offer of one party is accepted by the other. The treaty then consists of the two texts read together.

Another form of offer and acceptance occurs in a more subtle way. A declaration, whether written or not, may be either a strictly unilateral act (in which case it is not binding, although it may become so if accepted and acted upon by another party in good faith), or a disguised "offer" or "acceptance". An interesting example occurred in the *Eastern Greenland Case* (P.C.I.J., 1933). During the course of a discussion with the Danish Minister accredited to Norway, in the context of the question of the extension of Danish influence in Greenland, the Foreign Minister of Norway, Mr Ihlen, declared that "the Norwegian Government would not make any difficulties in the settlement of this question." A note was made of this conversation, but was never shown to the Danish Minister, so that the case was treated as an oral declaration. This note makes it clear that the declaration, so far from being merely unilateral in intent, was made as an implicit *quid pro quo* for the Danish Government taking up a similarly reticent attitude in relation to the extension of Norwegian influence in Spitsbergen. Accordingly, the Permanent Court qualified this as an "undertaking" and concluded that, as the result of it, Norway was "under an obligation to refrain from contesting Danish sovereignty over Greenland."

Intention of the parties to enter into a legal relationship

An essential element of a treaty is the intention of the parties to enter into a legal relationship. Statesmen sometimes have occasion to issue a joint written statement of future intent — the Yalta Agreement is an example — which, whatever its political importance, is of no legal value since it is constitutive neither of rights nor of obligations under international law.

Another form of instrument which, while closely resembling it, may not be a treaty is an agreement to conclude an agreement. The test is again whether the parties intended to enter into a legal relationship, that is to say, to create rights and obligations between themselves. A mere statement of joint future intention expressed by both parties in the same terms in the same document will not constitute a treaty. Where, however, the first agreement is so drafted as to give rise to an obligation on the parties to enter into negotiations with a view to concluding the subsequent agreement, the first agreement, if in writing, is a treaty known as a *pactum de contrahendo*. Some writers reserve this term for the rarer case of agreements giving rise to an obligation actually to conclude a subsequent agreement.

Names given to treaties

Whether an international instrument is a treaty can be discovered only from its contents (and written form) and not from its name. A wide variety of names have been given to it, besides that of treaty, such as convention, agreement, declaration, protocol, act, final act or general act (terms used generally in the context of a diplomatic conference), exchange of notes, *modus vivendi*, arrangement (used mainly for inter-departmental treaties), pact, covenant, charter or statute. Agreements between the Pope and a head of state for the purpose of safeguarding the interests of the Roman Catholic Church are called "concordats".

Language in which the treaty is written

Treaties are frequently made in more than one language. In such cases, a provision of the treaty will decide which text is authentic. Where two or more texts are "equally authentic", the terms of the treaty are presumed to have the same meaning in each authentic text (Article 33).

STATE REPRESENTATIVES

In negotiating, adopting, authenticating, signing, ratifying or acceding to treaties, states are obliged to act through their representatives. The persons who represent the state are obliged to produce their credentials (usually referred to as "full powers") if asked to do so. Such a rule does not apply to heads of state, heads of government and ministers of foreign affairs. Heads of diplomatic missions are assumed to have full powers in relation to the adoption of the texts of treaties with the state to which they are accredited, as are representatives of states to international conferences or organisations in relation to the adoption of texts by or within the conferences or organisation.

A state may disavow the act of its representative expressing the state's consent to be bound, if it was given in circumstances demonstrating a "manifest" violation of the state's municipal law, even if the representative had full powers, or by reason of his office did not need them.

THE CAPACITY TO MAKE TREATIES

"Every sovereign state possesses the capacity to conclude treaties" (Article 6). All sovereign states possess this capacity in the fullest degree. Since, however, a state may voluntarily deprive itself of the right to make treaties in the future about certain matters and since international persons other than sovereign states have only a limited capacity to enter into treaties, states are expected, before concluding a treaty with other subjects of international law, whether states or not, to satisfy themselves of the international capacity of the other parties to conclude the agreement under consideration. States cannot subsequently allege the incapacity of the other party to conclude the treaty as a ground for themselves refusing to apply its terms.

THE CREATION OF A TREATY

The birth of a treaty involves various stages. The first is the stage of negotiation of the text by the negotiating states. At this point there is no international instrument, merely a draft. The next stage is the adoption of the text by the negotiating states: if adopted during an international conference it must be adopted by a two-thirds majority; if within an international organisation, by the majority laid down in the rules of that organisation; otherwise unanimously. Immediately following its adoption is the stage of authentication of the text of the treaty. Authentication is a formal act (the signature or initialling by the representatives of the negotiating states) expressing acceptance of the accuracy of the written text. Errors discovered in the text thereafter require to be corrected by formal rectification. After these three stages the treaty is "concluded". This does not mean that it has entered into force, merely that a new international instrument has come into existence.

THE RELATIONSHIP BETWEEN A TREATY AND A STATE

Distinct from the question of "conclusion" of the treaty is that of the relationship between the treaty and a state. The first stage in such a relationship once the treaty has been concluded is the act by which the state expresses its consent to be bound by the treaty. A state may express such consent either before or after the treaty has entered into force. If it does so before, it is called a "contracting state"; if after, a "party" to the treaty. A "third state" means a state not a party to the treaty (Article 2).

MODES OF EXPRESSING CONSENT TO BE BOUND BY A TREATY

A state may express its consent to be bound by a treaty by signature, by ratification or by accession. In the case of a treaty constituted by an exchange of notes or letters, the act of exchange may be accepted as the expression of consent.

Signature

The treaty itself will normally specify whether signature can have the effect of expressing the consent of the state to be bound. If the treaty does not provide that signature can have this effect, or, in the absence of any provision, if it can be established that the negotiating states were agreed that it might do so, the signature of a state's representative will have this effect so long as this is in accordance with his "full powers". But if either the treaty itself or the "full powers" of the state representative are made "subject to ratification", signature has the effect only of an intermediate state. A "signatory" state is under obligation to refrain from acts which would defeat the object or purpose of the treaty until it has made clear its intention whether to become a party to the treaty (Article 18).

Ratification

The treaty may itself specify that it is subject to ratification, or this may be established as the intention of the negotiating states. Alternatively, ratification may be required in relation to a given state either because the full powers of its representative so provides, or because he has signed the treaty subject to ratification. The interval between signature and ratification in these cases provides the state with the chance to verify that its representative has acted in accordance with his instructions, and to put in hand the measures necessary to satisfy any constitutional requirements as to the implementation of the treaty in national law before accepting its international obligations. The terms "acceptance" or "approval" are also occasionally used in this context: they have the same legal effect as the act of ratification.

Accession
States which for one reason or another do not qualify to become parties to a treaty by signature or ratification may be permitted to accede thereto. Accession is permitted when the treaty so provides, if it can be established that the negotiating states so intended, or if all the parties to the treaty subsequently agree. Accessions may be made conditional or unconditional.

ENTRY INTO FORCE
The entry into force of the treaty must be distinguished from the entry into force of the treaty in relation to a particular state. Both these questions relate exclusively to the legal effect of the treaty in international law.

Entry into force of the treaty
It is for the negotiating states to decide when a treaty shall enter into force. These provisions of the treaty relating to matters which must precede its entry into force apply as from the adoption of the text. These include the manner in which states may express their consent to be bound, the manner and date of the treaty's entry into force, the question of reservations and certain other matters. The treaty nearly always does contain a provision about entry into force. If it does not, and if the negotiating states have not agreed otherwise, the treaty will enter into force only after consent to be bound has been established for all the negotiating states. Perhaps the most common formula, at least with respect to multilateral treaties, is for the treaty to enter into force "three months — or thirty days — after the deposit of the . . . instrument of ratification".

Entry into force in relation to a state
If a treaty enters into force, as the Vienna Convention, "on the thirtieth day following the date of deposit of the thirty-fifth instrument of ratification or accession", the treaty will both enter into force and enter into force in relation to those thirty-five states, on that day. In relation to the thirty-sixth state, the treaty would normally provide that it would "enter into force on the (thirtieth) day after deposit by such state of its instrument of ratification or accession."

RESERVATIONS

A state may wish to become a party to a treaty with reservations, that is to accept to be bound by most, but not all, of the provisions of the treaty. The importance of the reservation will naturally depend on its scope and on the object and purpose of the treaty.

Legal effect of reservations

A state which has entered a reservation may not demand observance of the reserved provisions by the other parties. The effect of a reservation is therefore always reciprocal.

This being so, a reservation to a bilateral treaty (a treaty to which there are only two parties) has the same effect as an amendment (except that a reservation may be withdrawn at any time). In relation to a multilateral treaty the position is different. A treaty already in force between states A, B and C is unaffected, so far as the relations between these states are concerned, by the fact that state D becomes a party with reservations. It is only in the relations between states A–D, B–D and C–D that the reservation has any effect. If the reservation is accepted by state A, the result is to modify the provisions of the treaty to which the reservation relates to the extent of the reservation in the relations between states A–D. The same result occurs if state B objects to the reservation but accepts state D nevertheless as a party to the treaty. State C may object to the reservation and refuse to accept state D as a party to the treaty. In this case the treaty does not apply between states C–D (Article 21).

Prohibited reservations

In general, states are permitted to make reservations unless the treaty itself prohibits reservations (or reservations of a certain type). There is however one exception. As the court had occasion to observe in the case of *Reservations to the Convention on the Prevention and Punishment of the Crime of Genocide* (I.C.J., 1951), "a multilateral convention is the result of an agreement freely concluded and none of the contracting parties is entitled to frustrate or impair, by means of unilateral decisions . . . the object and purpose of the convention." A reservation is a unilateral decision and the rule enunciated in the *Genocide Case* finds confirmation in the Vienna Convention. Reservations which are "incompatible with the object and purpose of the treaty" are prohibited.

Negotiated reservations

A useful technique in the case of multilateral treaties which seek to achieve the greatest possible measure of agreement between the negotiating states, is for these states to decide, at the stage of the negotiations, on the precise text of reservations which will be permitted. It is even possible to go further and to permit only a named state to make a reservation. The reservations are then put into an appendix and the treaty provides that only these reservations will be permitted.

Acceptance and refusal of reservations

"No state may, in its treaty relations, be bound without its consent" (*Genocide Case*). A reservation formulated by a state wishing to become a party to a treaty must therefore be accepted or rejected by each state already party to the treaty. Reservations authorised by the treaty itself do not require acceptance.

Acceptance will be implied from failure to react over a certain period of time (in the Vienna Convention, twelve months). Objection, which must be express, can take two forms. It may involve denial of any treaty relationship between the objecting and reserving state, or it may involve acceptance of the treaty relationship as modified by the reservation. It is for the objecting state to make clear which effect is intended.

When an instrument of consent containing a reservation becomes effective

The expression of the reserving state's consent to be bound becomes effective if even one state accepts it. In the special case of treaties constituting the constituent instrument of international organisations it is the competent organ of the organisation which must accept the reserving state as a member of the organisation.

There is, however, one type of treaty where acceptance is required by all the parties before the reserving state's instrument of consent becomes effective. Whether a treaty is of this type can be seen only from the limited number of the parties to it and its object and purpose. The Treaty of Rome, constituting the European Economic Community, is a good example of such a treaty.

II. THE TREATY IN FORCE

AMENDMENT

The procedure for the formal amendment of a treaty is the same as that for the formation of the treaty, unless the treaty itself provides for some simplified form. Thus, all the parties to the treaty must agree on the text of the amendment, adopt and authenticate it, and each express its consent thereto. However, until the amended text has entered into force for all the parties to the original treaty, there are two international instruments in existence side by side. The amended treaty is in force only as between the parties to it: the original treaty remains in force both for the parties which have not yet become parties to the amended text, and in the relations between states which have and those which have not become parties to the amended text. This transitional stage can last a long time as the following example will show. The original text of the Convention for the Pacific Settlement of International Disputes was concluded in 1899. The United Kingdom became a party in 1900. An amended text was drawn up in 1907. The United Kingdom became a party thereto on 13th October 1970!

MODIFICATION

Some of the states party to a multilateral convention may wish to go further than the text provides. They may then conclude a supplementary agreement within the framework of the main treaty. Such a modification may be permitted by the treaty: if not, the parties wishing to modify must inform the other parties of their intention, to give them the opportunity either to join the negotiations or to object. An objection is only valid if the modification is "incompatible with the effective execution of the object and purpose of the treaty" or would affect the enjoyment by the other parties of their rights under the treaty (Article 41). The word "modification" is also used as a synonym for amendment.

APPLICATION

Treaties and third parties

Treaties apply only to the states party to them. A treaty cannot create rights or obligations for a third party without its consent. Obligations must be accepted expressly: acceptance of rights is presumed so long as the contrary is not indicated. The fact that a rule, already binding as a rule of customary international law, is set forth in a treaty, does not deprive it of its binding force *vis à vis* states not party to the convention.

Territorial application

Unless otherwise stated or implied, a treaty will apply to the entire territory of the state. The application of this principle in cases of state succession has already been considered. (*See* Chapter Three, section I: The principle of "movable treaty frontiers".)

Application in time

The provisions of a treaty will not apply to facts or situations anterior to the date of entry into force of the treaty with respect to the party concerned, unless a different intention is established.

INTERPRETATION

The proper interpretation of a treaty requires account to be taken of three points, namely the ordinary meaning of the terms used, the intention of the negotiating states, and the object and purpose of the treaty. What cannot be stated is the relative importance of these three elements. The matter was not much advanced by the Vienna Convention which enunciated a general rule of interpretation including all three elements. The rule is as follows: "A treaty shall be interpreted in good faith in accordance with the ordinary meaning be given to the terms of the treaty in their context and in the light of its object and purpose."

Ordinary meaning

The meaning given to terms in the ordinary use of language is the most likely meaning of any written text, whether a treaty or otherwise. The Vienna Convention cites certain cases where the ordinary meaning can be put aside: where a special meaning can be established from the intention of the parties, and where the ordinary meaning leaves the true meaning ambiguous or obscure, or leads to a result which is manifestly obscure or unreasonable.

Intention of the parties

What is in question is the intention of the negotiating states, and, moreover, their over-all intention rather than the particular intention of one or some amongst them. For this reason, it is not only the intention of those states which subsequently become parties to the convention which matters. The criterion is the intention of the negotiating states and not that of the parties to the treaty.

The Vienna Convention accords a somewhat less important place to intention that some publicists might have led one to expect: the treatment is, however, an accurate reflection of state practice on this matter.

The "context" of the treaty (*vide* the general rule), is stated to comprise, in addition to the text, its preamble and annexes (but not, apparently, the title), agreements between the parties relating to the treaty and drawn up in connection with its conclusion. Moreover, any subsequent agreement between the parties regarding the treaty's interpretation or application is to be taken into account together with the context.

The principal means of establishing the intention of the negotiating states is to resort to the preparatory work (*travaux préparatoires*). This is permitted only as a "supplementary" means of interpretation, and then only to "confirm" the meaning resulting from the application of the general rule. Only in cases where this, the general rule, leads to an ambiguous, obscure or absurd result, may the *travaux préparatoires* "determine" the meaning.

Object and purpose of the treaty

The inclusion of the "object and purpose" clause as one of the criteria of the "general rule" marks something of a triumph for common sense. States always have some principal object and purpose in mind in concluding a treaty. Where the result is some mere contractual arrangement, a bargain struck, the object was the bargain and one is little further advanced. The position is quite different where the text of the treaty creates not a static but a dynamic situation — where it establishes a body or an organisation which will then set to work on its own account. The Vienna Convention accordingly provides that "any subsequent practice" in the application of the treaty which established the agreement of the parties regarding its interpretation is to be taken into consideration. It should be noted that the subsequent practice is not necessarily that of the parties (it might be the practice of the body or organisation itself). Some cautionary remarks as to the scope of this rule in relation to treaties constituting the constituent instruments of international organisations have already been made. (*See* Chapter Three, section II: Interpretation of the powers of an international organisation.)

The surrounding circumstances

The Vienna Convention accords to the "circumstances of [the treaty's] conclusion" only the same place as that accorded to the *travaux préparatoires*. However, the inclusion of the "object and purpose" clause in the general rule would seem to warrant a more generous resort to such circumstances. The state of affairs which the treaty was designed to remedy, that is, its object, may well not appear expressly either in the text of the treaty or in the *travaux préparatoires*, since it was such common knowledge to the authors that they had no need to refer to it. The surrounding circumstances at the time of the treaty's conclusion will alone, in such a case, explain the true object of the treaty.

INVALIDITY

A treaty in force may nevertheless not be applicable because it is invalid. If the ground of invalidity is such that the treaty is void, it ceases to have any legal effect: if it is voidable, the treaty may become invalid with respect to a particular party or parties. Cases of invalidity must be distinguished from cases of termination or suspension of the operation of the treaty which will be dealt with subsequently. There are two grounds on which treaties become void:

(a) Conflict with jus cogens. A treaty in conflict with *jus cogens*, described in the Vienna Convention is a "peremptory norm of

general international law", is void. A peremptory norm is one from which no derogation is permitted.

(b) Coercion of a state by the threat or use of force. A treaty concluded under the threat or use of force in violation of the principles of international law embodied in the Charter of the United Nations is void. This rule, while an accurate reflection of states' views, is something of an innovation. A contrary rule existed before the First World War and perhaps also between the World Wars.

Invalidity of state's consent to be bound by a treaty
Fraud and the corruption or coercion of a state's representative are grounds of invalidity of the state's consent to be bound in all circumstances. Subject to certain limitations such invalidity may also be invoked through error, and through irregular or misguided conduct by the state representative.

Error
The error must relate to a fact or situation which the state assumed to exist which formed an essential basis of its consent to be bound by the treaty.

Irregular conduct of state representative
If the authority of the representative to express his state's consent to be bound has been made subject to a restriction which he has not observed, and if this has been known to the other parties, the state may invoke this as a ground of invalidity.

Misguided conduct
Persons who represent their state at the signing or ratification of treaties must be assumed to know the law of their own state, and in particular, any constitutional limitations there may be as to their binding the state. An expression of consent by a properly authorised representative in violation of such provisions of internal law is not a ground of invalidity, unless it was "manifest". It is manifest where it would have been "objectively evident to any state conducting itself in this matter in accordance with normal practice and good faith." This is one of the innovations in the Vienna Convention.

Consequences of invalidity of treaty
An invalid treaty is void. The provisions of a void treaty have no legal effect. The parties are under an obligation so far as possible to undo anything done under the treaty.

SUSPENSION
A treaty which is terminated cannot be revived whereas a treaty which is merely suspended may be, and generally will be revived when the circumstances leading to the suspension no longer apply.

Suspension by agreement

The operation of a treaty, or its operation with respect to one or more parties, may always be suspended if all the parties agree. Two or more parties may agree to a temporary suspension even without the consent of the other parties so long as this is not incompatible with the treaty's object and purpose, and so long as the rights of the other parties under the treaty are not adversely affected.

Subsequent agreement

Where the parties to a treaty conclude a later treaty relating to the same subject matter, the earlier treaty will be considered as suspended or terminated if it can be implied from the terms of the later treaty that that was the parties' intention, or if the provisions of the two treaties are so incompatible that they are incapable of being applied at the same time.

Breach

Only a "material" breach is sufficient justification for suspending or terminating the operation of a treaty. Any unjustified repudiation of the treaty, or any violation of a provision essential to the object and purpose of the treaty, will constitute a "material" breach.

TERMINATION

Supervening impossibility of performance

The permanent disappearance or destruction of an object indispensable for the execution of a treaty terminates the treaty. If the impossibility is temporary it may be invoked as a ground for suspending the treaty. However, a party cannot benefit from its own wrong, so that this ground cannot be invoked if the impossibility is the result of its own breach of any international obligation.

Fundamental change of circumstances

The rule *rebus sic stantibus* can apply so as to terminate or suspend the operation of a treaty in certain very narrowly defined circumstances. The change must be in regard to the circumstances which existed at the time of the conclusion of the treaty, and it must be one not foreseen by the parties. Not just any change of circumstances will do: on the contrary, the change must be in regard to circumstances the existence of which constitute an "essential basis" of the consent of the parties to be bound. Finally, the effect of the change must be "radically to transform the extent of the obligations still to be performed under the treaty."

A treaty constituting a boundary cannot be affected by any change of circumstances.

Withdrawal and denunciation

A treaty will often provide expressly that a party may withdraw from or denounce it, stating how much notice must be given for this to become effective. If the treaty makes no provision it may be possible to imply the right to withdraw from it from the nature of the treaty. Such a right could normally be implied in a political or military treaty. Otherwise a party may not denounce or withdraw at will unless it can be established that this was the intention of the negotiating states. The Vienna Convention sets the period of notice in such cases at "not less than twelve months". In such cases, the right to withdraw from a treaty can only arise in circumstances justifying the termination of the treaty.

Consequences of termination, withdrawal and denunciation

A party to a treaty which has terminated, or a party which has withdrawn from or denounced a treaty has no further obligation to perform under the treaty, but has no duty to undo anything done while the treaty was still in force. Withdrawal and denunciation take effect only at the expiry of the period of notice.

DEPOSITARY

It is common practice, in the case of multilateral treaties, for the negotiating states to designate a "depositary" for the treaty. This can be one of themselves, or an international organisation, or its chief administrative officer. The functions of the depositary, besides safeguarding the text of the treaty, generally include keeping a chart of the state of signature, ratification, entry into force, denunciation, etc., of the treaty; and communicating to all parties any act of consent of a new party, the text of any reservation, any special ratification to be made pursuant to the treaty. The functions of a depositary are international in character and there is a duty to act impartially in their performance.

REGISTRATION OF TREATIES

Every treaty entered into by any member of the United Nations after the entry into force of the Charter is to be registered with the Secretariat of the United Nations and published by it (Article 102 of the Charter and Article 80 of the Vienna Convention). These treaties are published in the *United Nations Treaty Series (U.N.T.S.)*.

CHAPTER SEVEN

Personal Jurisdiction of the State

I. STATE AUTHORITY

THE CONCEPTION OF STATE AUTHORITY

The very conception of a state implies a relationship between persons, territory and an organised authority. That authority is exercised alike over persons and territory. Indeed, the personal as well as the territorial jurisdiction of the state are derived from the same source, its sovereignty, and they are of equal legal importance.

THE CO-EXISTENCE OF PERSONAL AND TERRITORIAL JURISDICTION

A state exerts jurisdiction with respect to its nationals wherever they may be (personal jurisdiction), as well as over its territory and all persons and things upon it (territorial jurisdiction). The former is, however, largely obscured and overlaid by the latter.

Nationals residing within their own state

Most nationals live for most of the time within the territory of their own state, so that the exercise of territorial jurisdiction makes resort to personal jurisdiction unnecessary. Some laws, based on the nationality principle and applicable to nationals wherever they may be, clearly derive from the exercise of personal jurisdiction. The law of treason, which is based on the offender's allegiance to the state of his nationality, is of this kind. In the United Kingdom, murder and bigamy are also offences which nationals may commit anywhere. The Federal Republic of Germany, India and Korea apply the whole criminal code to the acts of nationals wherever committed abroad which are also criminal in the place of commission, or carry a penalty of a certain degree of severity, or are committed against co-nationals. As a corollary, such states normally refuse to extradite their nationals.

A national's obligation to perform military service is based on

151

personal jurisdiction, so that it arises and continues to subsist whatever the physical location of the national.

Nationals in the territory of foreign states

Nationals visiting or residing in the territory of a foreign state fall under its territorial jurisdiction. States must, however, in the exercise of their territorial jurisdiction, respect the personal jurisdiction which foreign states continue to exert over their own nationals. It is the latter which provides the legal basis for the diplomatic protection which a state asserts in relation to its citizens abroad. So as to identify such persons for the benefit of the authorities in foreign states, and thus for their own protection, each state issues its nationals with passports.

Allegiance and diplomatic protection are reverse sides of the same coin. Where the former would have been available, the latter can be demanded. Thus in *D.P.P.* v. *Joyce* (English House of Lords, 1946), an American national, who obtained by fraud and used a British passport, was found guilty of treason by a British court for making hostile wireless broadcasts for the enemy during the Second World War.

Allegiance can also be demanded of members of a state's armed forces whether or not they are nationals. Thus a South African court found guilty of treason a German national who, after having begun but not completed naturalisation proceedings in South Africa, joined the South African army, and subsequently aided the Germany army (*R.* v. *Neumann* (Supreme Court of South Africa, 1949)).

Taxation

Taxation is another area where some states assert personal jurisdiction, in particular the United States of America whose nationals are taxed on personal income wherever they may be. The application of this principle in the area of personal taxation is, however, regrettable, for it interferes with the application of those principles which otherwise govern taxation throughout the world. These are based not on nationality but on residence, and the state thus acts by reference to its territorial sovereignty. Nevertheless it is convenient to set these principles out here.

The first is that the individual is subject to taxation on his worldwide income within the state of his residence for the tax year in question. The second is that the authorities of the state in which any particular revenue has arisen within that year may tax him, but with respect to that revenue only. Broadly speaking, these two principles govern the whole field of personal taxation, and, with refinements, apply as much to corporations as to individuals.

To avoid double taxation based upon the joint application of these two principles is thus the main object of Double Taxation

Treaties, most of which also provide a series of criteria for determining in relation to any person in which state he is to be considered as resident for any particular tax year.

The generally favoured solution today is for a tax (sometimes called a "withholding tax") to be levied by the non-resident state in which the revenue has arisen, and for a corresponding tax-credit to be accorded in the state of residence. It must be stressed, however, that generalised as these principles are, their application in respect of avoidance of double taxation depends entirely upon treaties, all of which are bilateral; and the principles themselves are subject to exception in the case of states which for one reason or another do not levy taxes (or do so at exceptionally low rates), the so-called "tax havens".

It will be immediately apparent that the United State's solution renders the above system unworkable; nor do the authorities of that state suggest any other system which might be universally applicable. They merely rely on their economic and financial weight to negotiate individually with all other states a special regime in relation to their own nationals resident therein. The threat of wholesale withdrawal of American individuals, corporations and capital is generally sufficient to achieve an agreement permitting American nationals resident abroad to be placed in a more favourable position with regard to the tax obligation to the state of residence than anybody else, to the benefit of the tax authorities of the United States.

Nationals neither within their own territory nor in the territory of a foreign state

Although today the inhabited parts of the earth's land surface are all part of the territory of some state, miscellaneous situations do arise where persons carry on some activity but no territorial jurisdiction is in operation. In such cases the exercise by each state of personal jurisdiction over its nationals is in accordance with international law so long as, and to the extent that, the rights of other states are not infringed.

Thus on artificial islands attached to the sea-bed outside territorial waters (such as "Zealand" off the coast of the United Kingdom, or a pirate radio station off the coast of the Netherlands), the individuals on board have the nationality of some state, and the authorities of that state are entitled to interfere and assert sovereignty. The ludicrous situation has arisen of so-called "states" being set up by a handful of individuals on board a platform of infinitesimal proportions. Moreover, it is probably an act of treason, and is certainly a denial of allegiance, for an individual national to set himself up as a "head" of some so-called newly created "state", since the corollary is that he refuses any longer to recognise the personal jurisdiction of the state in relation to himself.

Ships and aircraft

The assignment to ships and aircraft of a fictive nationality solves most problems of jurisdiction with regard to crimes and other human actions which require regulation or surveillance. Article 6 of the High Seas Convention, 1958, stipulates that ships must sail under the flag of one state only, and that the flag state has a duty to exercise effective jurisdiction and control over such vessels as fly its flag on the high seas. Aircraft have the nationality of the state of registration, and while flying within airspace above the high seas and over unoccupied territory the jurisdiction of that state applies to actions taking place on board.

However, in the case of both ships and aircraft, the applicable jurisdiction is personal and not territorial. The theory once applied that vessels, or at least warships, were to be regarded as a piece of floating territory. The majority judgment in the *Lotus Case* (P.C.I.J., 1927), seems to have been given on this basis. This theory is today quite discredited. In the case of merchant ships and civil aircraft, in addition to the jurisdiction of the state of nationality (of the flag, or of registration) the state of the nationality of the victim or offender may also have jurisdiction over any offence committed on board to the extent that its nationals are involved. This is not so in the case of persons serving aboard warships, military aircraft and other vessels or planes in government non-commercial service who have a different nationality from that of the flag or state of registration, because their actions are performed in their capacity as agents of that state and not as private persons.

II. JURISDICTION

THE MEANING OF JURISDICTION

Jurisdiction means power, and, in relation to the state, the exercise of authority. This authority is manifested externally in the same manner as internally. It comprises the power to make the law and enforce it.

If the power to enforce the law outside the territorial limits of the state is called "coercive jurisdiction", and the power to make laws having an extraterritorial effect is called "legislative jurisdiction", it might be thought that a state's coercive jurisdiction is circumscribed by the application of territorial jurisdiction, while its legislative jurisdiction is co-extensive with personal jurisdiction.

Some writers, including the Austrian jurist, Kelsen, indeed define territorial jurisdiction by reference to the ability of a state to exercise coercion, from which it follows that they do not consider the state can do so elsewhere. However, as has already been seen, this is not so. Indeed, state practice does not today, and never has, reflected this theory.

The extent of coercive jurisdiction
Two rules are clear.

(*a*) A state has, within its territory, the power to exercise coercive jurisdiction.

(*b*) No state may exercise such power within the territory of any other state.

From these two rules it follows that a state has an *exclusive* power to exercise its coercive jurisdiction within its own territory.

In the *Lotus Case* (P.C.I.J., 1927) the court enunciated rule (*b*) above as follows: "the first . . . restriction imposed by international law upon a state is that — failing a permissive rule to the contrary — it may not exercise its power in any form in the territory of another state."

But the court then continued: "In this sense jurisdiction is . . . territorial: it cannot be exercised by a state outside its territory except by virtue of a permissive rule derived from international custom or from a convention." However, this last stated rule needs to be re-examined.

In the first place, *terra nullius* has, both historically and legally, been converted into part of the territory of a state through the prior, continuing, and effective exercise thereon of a state's coercive (and legislative) jurisdiction. Sometimes indeed, as in Eastern Greenland and in parts of Africa, two states have exercised such authority, each claiming for itself the exclusive right to do so.

Secondly, the *Lotus Case* concerned a collision between two vessels on the high seas. A state cannot exercise its coercive jurisdiction on the high seas because of the principle of the "freedom" of those seas. Indeed it may be said that the freedom of the high seas is freedom from the exercise of coercive jurisdiction by any state other than the state of the flag. (*See* the Geneva Convention on the High Seas: Reparation for Wrongful Visit.) In occupied territory, on artificial islands built on the bed of the sea, and in other miscellaneous situations, no such "freedom" exists. In such cases states may exercise a personal jurisdiction, and they may take measures to protect their nationals as well as their own interests, including the exercise of coercive jurisdiction, so long as and to the extent that they do not infringe the rights of other states.

It is thus not a case of seeking a permissive rule of customary or conventional international law before a state can exercise its coercive jurisdiction outside its own and any other state's territory, but rather of the creation of prohibitive rules.

The nature of legislative jurisdiction

The rules of public international law which prescribe the power of a state to apply its laws with extra-territorial effect are concerned solely and exclusively with its *public* laws. Entirely different considerations apply to its *private* laws, which are the concern of each state's rules of private international law, or, as it is called, the conflict of laws.

Whether in its municipal law a state makes a distinction between public and private laws, and if it does, whether each state makes the same distinction, is irrelevant: the distinction is made for its own purposes by public international law (and, it will be noticed, each state makes such a distinction for the purposes of its own system of conflict of laws).

The extent of legislative jurisdiction

Within its territory a state's legislative jurisdiction is complete; moreover, with three exceptions, it is exclusive. These exceptions are:

(*a*) acts with respect to which states have a universal jurisdiction;

(*b*) acts contrary to the security or public credit of a foreign state;

(*c*) situations involving foreign nationals subject to the law of their own state.

Outside the territory of any state, however, a state can exert a far more extensive legislative jurisdiction with respect to acts performed by and against nationals. Thus Danish law provides as follows:

"There fall within Danish jurisdiction, regardless of the perpetrator's nationality, acts committed abroad: . . . .

3. if committed outside . . . the territory of any state, if the act is committed to the injury of a Danish national . . . and is an act of such kind as to be punishable by a more severe penalty than Haepte (ordinary imprisonment)."

It must be stressed however that this jurisdiction would not be exclusive: it would operate with that of the state of the nationality of any "perpetrator" other than Danish. Subject to this proviso, such an extensive exercise of legislative jurisdiction is in accordance with international law. If other states do not exercise it this is through a voluntary limitation of their powers.

JURISDICTION BASED ON
THE UNIVERSALITY OF THE CRIME

States have under international law not only a right but also a duty to punish acts of piracy, and this irrespective of the nationality of the vessel or persons involved. Article 15 of the Convention on the High Seas defines piracy as:

"Any illegal acts of violence, detention or any act of depredation, *committed for private ends* by the crew or the passengers of a private ship or a private aircraft, and directed:

> *(a)* on the high seas, against any ship or aircraft, or against persons or property on board such ship or aircraft;
> *(b)* against a ship, aircraft, persons or property in a place outside the jurisdiction of any State."

The United Nations War Crimes Commission considers that "the right to punish war crimes is not confined to the state whose nationals have suffered or on whose territory the offence took place, but is possessed by any independent state, just as is the right to punish piracy."

The German Criminal Code states that, regardless of the place of the offence, it is applicable to crimes committed abroad by aliens if they are "major crimes employing explosives; traffic in women and children;... unauthorised traffic in narcotics; traffic in obscene publications."

ACTS CONTRARY TO THE SECURITY OR
PUBLIC CREDIT OF THE STATE

The protection of the state's own *persona* is the first and most evident example of the exercise of personal jurisdiction. No state can be prevented from regarding as criminal the acts of a revolutionary group which are directed at its own security, wherever and by whomsoever committed. The same applies to the counterfeiting of a state's currency or stamps.

If committed abroad, the acts in question are most unlikely to constitute penal offences in the state where they are committed, for each state considers it its duty to protect only its *own* security and public credit.

JURISDICTION OVER SITUATIONS INVOLVING NATIONALS IN FOREIGN STATES

The protective personality principle provides that a state may exercise legislative jurisdiction over situations involving nationals in foreign states where the "perpetrator" is a national, and where both the victim and the perpetrator are nationals. Can it do so where the victim alone is a national?

In 1886, Cutting, a United States national, was arrested in Mexico and charged with the offence of criminal libel. The victim of the libel was a Mexican living in Chihuahua, Mexico. However the offence with which Cutting was charged, and of which he was found guilty (*Cutting Case,* Chihuahua District Court, 1886) had apparently been committed in Texas. The United States issued a strong diplomatic protest. The prosecution amended the charge and made it depend upon the subsequent circulation of the libel in Mexico, to which no further objection was raised. Cutting was, however, released by decision of the Supreme Court of Chihuahua (*Cutting Incident*).

It is submitted that the application of this principle to acts taking place in the territory of foreign states is contrary to international law. Nationals do not carry with them into foreign states the protection of their own public laws. They merely remain themselves subject to certain obligations and certain of their laws.

JURISDICTION BASED ON THE EXTRA-TERRITORIAL APPLICATION OF (TRADE) LAWS

The United States applies certain of its trade laws to the acts of non-nationals abroad, including the acts of foreign corporations. It is submitted that such an extension of jurisdiction is contrary to international law to the extent that no distinction is made between acts taking place in the territory of foreign states, and those occurring outside the territory of any state.

The basis of jurisdiction in the case of the extra-territorial application of anti-trust law is the intention of the act or agreement to take effect in the United States, plus the fact that in the ordinary course of international trade it did take effect, and impliedly at least, that in the opinion of the United States this effect was deleterious to the economic interests of the United States, since if it had taken place in the United States, or been carried out by nationals of the United States, it would have been illegal.

Certain aspects of merchant shipping legislation are also given extra-territorial effect, and apply to ships and cargo destined for United States ports, whatever the nationality of the flag.

The reaction of several West European states to this assertion of extra-territorial jurisdiction was the passage of largely identical legislation making it a criminal offence for their nationals to comply with orders from American courts designed to implement such legislation, without obtaining prior authorisation from the government. A clearer example of "protest" in international law is difficult to envisage.

In *British Nylon Spinners* v. *I.C.I.* (English Court of Appeal, 1953) the court refused to recognise an order from an American court that the defendant, a British company, deal in a certain way with a patent it had obtained from the plaintiff, since the contract by which it had been acquired was concluded in Great Britain between two British companies and was subject to English law.

Part of the difficulty in defining the precise extent of application of trade laws in international commerce lies in the fact that they are neither public nor private laws but partake of aspects of both. However, unlike other public laws, trade laws are so designed as not only to benefit the legislating state but also in the context of international commerce to do so at the expense of other states.

CHAPTER EIGHT

State Territory and Territorial Sovereignty

The expression "state territory" refers to an area over which a state exercises a certain type of authority. The components of this area are treated in section I below, while the legal nature of the authority is treated in section II.

I. PARTS OF TERRITORY, DELIMITATION

There are three components of state territory: land, water and air. Of these the essential component is land, to which the other two are merely ancillary. Thus the internal waters, gulfs, bays and territorial waters of a state are only part of state territory because of the surrounding or contiguous land territory of the state; while the air space which falls within state territory is merely that which is super-adjacent to the area of land and water combined.

Thus an island, which is defined in Article 10 of the Geneva Convention on the Territorial Sea and the Contiguous Zone, 1958 (Art. 121, I.C.N.T.), as "a naturally formed area of land, surrounded by water, which is above water at high tide", will, if it forms part of the territory of a state, be surrounded by its own territorial sea; the air space above both island and territorial sea will also fall within state territory. On the other hand an artificial structure, whether fixed or floating in the seas, will give no right to a surrounding territorial sea or to super-adjacent air space. Thus installations built for the purpose of exploration or exploitation of the continental shelf are, by Article 5 of the Geneva Convention on the Continental Shelf (Art. 60(8), I.C.N.T.), merely accorded a "safety zone" of up to 500 metres. Paragraph 3 of that article states that "such installations do not possess the status of islands . . . have no territorial sea of their own."

Land is thus the essential ingredient of state territory.

FRONTIERS

The frontier is the outward limit of a state's territory. The land frontier is normally marked at ground level. Frontiers traversing a lake normally bisect the lake in a straight line; those following a river will either follow the middle, if non-navigable, or the *Talweg* (the middle of the deepest part), if navigable.

The sea frontier is at the outward edge of the territorial sea. This is still correct in spite of the recent developments in the law of the sea, under which the Coastal State is given "sovereign rights" over the Continental Shelf (that is the sea-bed and subsoil), up to 200 nautical miles from the baselines from which the territorial sea is measured, and over an exclusive economic zone of sea waters beyond and adjacent to the territorial sea up to the same limit. These are "frontiers", but are not territorial frontiers, these areas not being subject to the sovereignty of the state, and therefore not being part of its territory.

The "air frontier" is that which rises in a plane vertically from the land and water frontiers. Thus the frontier of a state territory is in reality not "an imaginary line on the surface of the earth" but a plane rising vertically into the air and descending into the centre of the earth from such an imaginary line.

Frontier zones and traffic

Frontier zones may serve several purposes. The smallest, of a few metres only, will be to mark the frontier, and will involve the destruction of all natural or artificial protrusions from the surface of the earth. Others may be of several kilometres width, and provide for a customs free zone, or, for example, that doctors and midwives may be permitted to practise their profession in the territory adjoining that of their own practice. Such zones are formed in the interests of the local populations on each side of the frontier, in an effort to palliate the disruptive effect of the political frontier. Certain categories of persons who live near and are often obliged to cross a frontier may be dispensed from frontier formalities, for example frontier workers, that is persons who live on one side of a frontier and work on the other.

"VOISINAGE"

The body of rules and practices which govern the conduct of neighbouring states are referred to as "relations of *voisinage*". This expresion refers to rules and practices which arise solely out of the contiguity of the two states. Thus the obligation to respect the frontier of a state, which is a general rule of international law and applies to every state, falls outside the scope of "relations of *voisinage*".

The duty to maintain frontier signs in good repair is a general rule of international law. States frequently provide for this by treaty, but the rule is independent of the treaty which merely regulates the details of its application. There is, however, no rule that a state must erect signs to mark out its frontier: the rule simply is that if it does erect them, it must maintain them in good repair.

Where the boundary line is a river, each state is obliged to maintain its own side of the river bank.

No state may change the natural flow or state of a frontier river or any water-course which flows from one state into another, in any manner which causes the other state damage (for example by the construction of canals, dams or large-scale irrigation works which reduce the water-level in the river).

Each state is obliged to prevent the pollution of water or air which will subsequently pass into the territory of another state. In the *Trail Smelter Arbitration* (1935) a privately owned factory in British Columbia, seven miles from the frontier between Canada and the United States, emitted sulphur dioxide fumes from its chimneys to the damage of crops in the United States. The arbitral tribunal set up by the two states to resolve the dispute, besides awarding damages for the loss caused, also stated that "no state has the right to make or permit the use of its territory in such a way as to allow fumes to cause damage to the territory of another state . . . if such use has serious consequences and if the damage caused is clearly and convincingly evidenced."

No state may use or allow the use of its territory in such a way as to endanger the lives of persons lawfully present in the adjoining territory of another state (*see* the case of the Cantons of *Soleure* v. *Argovie* (Swiss Federal Tribunal, 1900) which concerned the setting up of a rifle range in the Canton of Argovie, thus endangering the lives of persons within a portion of the Canton of Soleure).

Neighbouring states frequently establish a permanent bipartite commission to regulate all boundary questions. The United States and Mexico have had, since 1889, an international boundary commission, and with Canada the United States has an international joint commission.

THE SEA-BED AND SUBSOIL

The territory of a state includes the subsoil below the surface of land territory, internal waters and the territorial sea. By virtue of the Geneva Convention on the Continential Shelf, a state has "sovereign rights" over the sea-bed and the subsoil beneath the sea-bed of the continental shelf. Moreover that convention "shall not prejudice the right of the coastal State to exploit the subsoil by means of tunnelling irrespective of the depth of water above the subsoil."

The subsoil under the sea-bed of the high seas, apart from the continental shelf, is *res nullius.*

II. TERRITORIAL SOVEREIGNTY

The authority a state exercises over its territory is called territorial sovereignty.

TERRITORIAL JURISDICTION

The exercise of a state's authority or jurisdiction over the various parts of its territory is complete and exclusive. It is complete in that it extends to all parts of the territory of the state, and to all persons present upon it — irrespective of nationality. In stating that the territorial jurisdiction is exclusive what is meant is that no other state has the right to exert is coercive jurisdiction within that territory. So far as legislative jurisdiction is concerned, any attempt by another state to apply its own public law within the territory would be contrary to the *sovereignty* (i.e. the exclusiveness of the jurisdiction) of the territorial state. Thus an attempt to collect taxes, to arrest, to marry, to sign a register of birth, to make a will — all these acts can be carried out within the territory of another state only with the consent of that state. For these and other purposes, states are represented abroad by consular officers. Thus, the only public law in operation within the territory is that of the territorial state. Anyone present within the territory is subject to this law unless he is granted immunity therefrom, and then only to the extent of that immunity (*see* Chapter Five).

One consequence of its territorial sovereignty is that a state has no duty to admit a non-national into its territory. It may, for political reasons, refuse to admit the nationals of certain foreign states, or make the entry of such persons depend upon the prior issue of a visa. For the same reason, all persons are required to produce a passport at the point of entry. Nationals may then enter as of right. Stateless persons and refugees are subject to special rules.

On the other hand, a state may prevent a national from leaving the territory. Democratic states do not tolerate such a rule but many totalitarian states have to make use of it to avoid the danger of serious depopulation.

Once a foreign national is admitted the state has a duty to protect him in accordance with the rules of international responsibility.

States may, by treaty and on a basis of reciprocity, provide for an even higher standard of treatment of foreign nationals, i.e. the "most-favoured nation" treatment, or even national treatment. Bilateral treaties of friendship, commerce and navigation normally provide for at least the former of these two standards.

In addition, each state must respect the rights of other states, and must not knowingly allow its territory to be used for acts contrary to their rights. However, the rights in question are granted to the state and not to the government. Although governments have a natural tendency to desire to stay in office international law grants them no right to do so, so that for a neighbouring state to harbour rebels and grant them military training facilities with a view to their overthrowing the existing government and replacing it by another of their choice, is not *per se* contrary to international law. Only if the neighbouring state permits its own territory to be used for the actual hostilities, or the launching of a hostile operation, or encourages, whether openly or secretly, the participation of its own nationals in such hostilities, is it in violation of the political independence and territorial integrity of the other state. (*See* Chapter Three, section I: Non-intervention.)

LIMITATIONS UPON TERRITORIAL SOVEREIGNTY

A state exercises over its territory rights of *imperium* (or governance) and *dominium* (or ownership). Both are aspects of territorial sovereignty. Jurisdiction over territory and the territory itself can be ceded. Where the sovereignty itself is given up, we are in presence of a case of transfer of territory and of partial state succession (*see* Chapter Three: section I).

But while retaining the sovereignty, the state can yield up all or some of the rights of ownership over it. All such limitations upon territorial sovereignty are the result of a voluntary act on the part of the servient state.

Some limitations result in the territory in question being accorded a special status. Although established and set out in an agreement, the resulting status is impressed on the territory and does not depend upon the existence of the agreement. Accordingly, should the treaty come to an end because, for example, of the extinction of one of the parties to it, the status of the territory will not be affected. The new state can only inherit the rights which the former state retained over the territory.

Other limitations affect the territory, but do not impress it with a status: any limitation will result from and depend upon the agreement in which it was set out, and will automatically terminate on the extinction of the agreement.

While the first category of limitation is sometimes called "servitude" by analogy with the private law concept, it must be admitted that there does not exist in international law any clear guide as to which limitation belongs to one, and which to the other, category. Where the limitation has the legal effect of impressing the territory and outlasting the personality of the state, it may with propriety be called a servitude. But it is not possible to reverse the process and expect that by calling a specific agreement for limitation of sovereignty "a servitude", it will automatically have such a legal effect.

Clearly a lease of territory to another state to establish a military base is not "a servitude", but is personal to the parties to the agreement, and will depend entirely upon their political relationship to one another. On the other hand a right of passage between an enclave of territory belonging to one state, which is entirely surrounded by the territory of another state, will be servitude because the continued viability of the enclave is likely to depend upon it (*see Right of Passage (Portugal—India) Case* (I.C.J., 1960)).

CONCURRENT TERRITORIAL JURISDICTION AND EXTRA-TERRITORIALITY

Concurrent territorial jurisdiction
State practice shows examples of joint exercise of sovereignty over territory. This phenomenon is called a "condominium". The New Hebrides were the subject of a condominium between Great Britain and France. Other examples of this joint exercise of jurisdiction over territory occur where one state retains its sovereignty nominally, while permitting the territory to be jointly administered.

Where territory is leased as a military base it is not unusual for the lease agreement to provide for concurrent exercise of jurisdiction within the base area, military personnel falling under that of the leasing state, all other persons remaining under that of the territorial state. Special provision is then made for cases involving both military and civil personnel.

Extra-territoriality
Formerly the view was held that embassies and even warships were to be regarded as pertaining to the territory of the sending state. This view is now discredited; moreover it never reflected accurately the legal position. For were this to be true, it would not be that the embassy or warship in a foreign port was immune from the jurisdiction (the application of the law and its enforcement), but rather

that such jurisdiction, being territorial, did not apply to the "territory" of another state. The matter was, however, always treated as one of immunity which could be waived. Although still used, surprisingly, in some recent headquarters agreements, the term is now outmoded and its use likely to lead only to misunderstanding.

III. ACQUISITION AND TRANSFER
OF STATE TERRITORY

Title to territory is either original or derivative.

ORIGINAL TITLE

Original title can arise as a result of geophysical changes, or through the acquisition of *terra nullius* (i.e. territory which was not formerly under the sovereignty of any state).

Title by accretion

This mode of acquisition of territory occurs through natural geophysical changes. Thus an island may appear in the territorial waters of a state. It will then automatically belong to the coastal state. Thus ownership of a sandspit of less than 2 square miles which has recently formed in the Bay of Bengal is claimed by both India and Bangladesh, since although the island is considered worthless, any new boundaries that arise from determination of its ownership could give title to thousands of square miles of ocean floor.

Changes in the course of boundary rivers may, if produced by natural causes, result in a change in the boundary but this will depend upon whether the river formed the boundary, or merely marked it. Thus the main channel of the Hariabhange River that flows between India and Bangladesh continually shifts course in the swampy estuary that marks its entrance into the Bay of Bengal. But it is not possible that the boundary should also constantly change. The solution here seems to be that in one position the river merely marks the boundary.

Title by peaceful occupation

Land territory which was formerly unoccupied *(terra nullius)* may become part of state territory through occupation. Discovery alone is not enough; discovery plus a formal declaration of occupancy in the name of a state will form the starting point of a claim to title, but unless followed up by effective occupation the claim will remain inchoate. A state must "administer", that is to say, be in a position to exert authority over the territory. Thus in respect to New Moore Island, the subject of dispute between India and Bangladesh referred to above, India landed a force of men on the island and hoisted the Indian flag in an attempt to establish title.

The extent of the authority and scope of the administration vary according to circumstances. In an area such as Eastern Greenland where there is a sparse population scattered along the coast and a vast unpopulated hinterland, the administration may be small in numbers and primitive in extent, and yet be "effective". (*See* the *Eastern Greeland Case* (P.C.I.J., 1933).)

Sovereignty over the area brings duties as well as rights: not until a state can fulfil its duty of protection towards other states and their nationals will the administration be effective enough to confer title (*see* the *Palmas Island Arbitration* (1928)).

Arctic. Most of the Arctic regions are frozen ice and thus part of the high seas. The sovereignty of certain states over land areas in the Arctic Circle has been extended on the basis of "sectors" drawn on the map from meridian lines. There has been, however, no common agreement to recognise these titles.

Antarctic. By the Convention on Peaceful Co-operation in the Antarctic of 1st December 1959, the legal situation in the area was "frozen". While no state has renounced its existing territorial claims in the area, all have agreed not to make any new claims; and the claimant states have further agreed not to attach any legal significance to their subsequent activities in the area with respect either to the consolidation of existing or to the assertion of new claims.

DERIVATIVE TITLE
A state may obtain or lose title to territory formerly belonging to another state through cession, secession, subjugation or prescription, or "constitutively".

Cession
Cession may be defined as the transfer from one state to another of sovereignty over a definite territory. Cession occurs at the moment of effective transfer of authority to the cessionary state, which assumes all rights and obligations attaching to the territory. Cession may be by purchase (as the United States purchased Alaska), by exchange, as a result of a treaty of peace following a war, or through any lesser use or threat of force.

Nevertheless, the essence of cession is that, in form at least, the transfer was by agreement as the result of a voluntary act.

Secession
A state may lose territory by revolt followed by secession, i.e. the formation of a new state.

In a case of cession the legal title depends upon the agreement of the two or more states concerned; in a case of secession, the new state's title to territory will be the result of its own act, and will depend upon its recognition by other states as a "state" in international law.

Subjugation (or conquest)

Formerly conquest followed by annexation gave a title to territory. The prohibition of the threat or use of force in Article 2 (4) of the Charter of the United Nations has meant that subjugation can no longer be considered as a legal method of acquisition of title to property.

Israel's claim to recognition of title over the regions conquered in the Six Day War has been expressly repudiated by a Security Council resolution.

Prescription

That the passage of time may by itself be the root of title to property is a general principle of law in all civilised legal systems. However the *imperium* which a state exercises over its territory is different from the *dominium* which an owner possesses over his property. State practice evidences no case of acquisition of title to territory by prescription. Prescription requires a *de facto* exercise of sovereignty over a portion of territory under the *bona fide* but mistaken belief that it was a part of the territory. This implies a total absence of effective exercise of authority by the state to which it actually belongs. It was strongly suggested in the *Palmas Island Arbitration* that just as effective occupation may create a title of sovereignty, so subsequent ineffectiveness may *deprive* the state of that title. This seems sound as a matter of principle, for the state would no longer be in a position to fulfill the duties of territorial sovereignty. The title to property might therefore arise by novation, as the result of the loss of title by the original state through ineffective exercise of authority, and substitution of the title of the occupying state. The essence of this mode is, however, the *bona fide* belief of the acquiring state, and a long period of undisturbed possession. Where the original occupation occurred by force a title by prescription can *never* arise.

"Constitutive" title or title to territory as the result of the creation of a new state

Where several states agree together by treaty to create a new state out of the territory of one or more of their number, and to guarantee its independence (*see* the creation of Belgium as the result of the Treaty of London of 15th November 1831, read together with the

Treaty of London of 19th April 1839), that state's title to its territory is constitutive, that is to say that the title is to be found in the same legal act as created the state. This is not a case of cession, since there was no state to whom the territory could be transferred, nor of secession, since states created constitutionally do not owe their creation to their own efforts.

Former colonial territories which obtained independence through peaceful evolution acquired title to their territory in a manner which falls between the constitutive mode and simple cession. In theory at least, cession requires the transfer of territory between two existing states. As a matter of logic, a thing cannot be transferred except to an entity which already exists at the moment of transfer. However, most colonial transfers involved a transfer of full powers to an existing administration, over an already defined territory, and this had, in practice, all the characteristics of a cession.

CHAPTER NINE

Seas and Waterways

I. INTRODUCTION

SEAS AND WATERWAYS

This chapter deals with the international regime of the water. The distinction between "seas" and "waterways" is not clear-cut: "internal waters" include elements of both, while if international "straits" are part of the seas, their legal regime is closer to that of a waterway.

The "seas" may be broadly divided into the "high seas", the "exclusive economic zone" and the "territorial sea". "Bays and gulfs", which are treated as being identical, will be part of the high seas, the territorial seas, enclosed or semi-enclosed seas or internal waters, depending on their size and shape; while "inland seas" are, in spite of their name, not treated as sea but as part of a state's internal waters.

Waterways are either natural or artificial. The law on waterways is not codified, the status of each canal and river having been separately regulated. Nevertheless, the very characterisation of a waterway as international implies a right of unimpeded passage for the ships of all nations, this rule being a rule of custom. Only such rivers and canals as are international in character are of direct concern to international law.

INTERNAL WATERS

The internal waters of a state comprise: all parts of the sea landwards of the base-lines from which the territorial sea is measured; ports and anchorages; river-mouths; the water-courses of national rivers; bays and gulfs or parts of them; inland seas; lakes and land-locked seas or parts of them.

The state possesses full rights of sovereignty over its internal waters. Some writers have defined internal waters as being "waters, including parts of the sea, which are under the full sovereignty of the state." There is accordingly no right of entry or passage for foreign ships. Only in the case of areas which had formerly been territorial sea or parts of the high sea but which are now enclosed as internal waters as the result of being landward of a straight base-line is the right of "innocent passage" preserved.

The territorial state has a monopoly in the carrying of goods and passengers, and enjoys the exclusive right to exploit the natural resources of the sea. Merchant ships are subject to the regulations of the territorial state but, by courtesy, the consul of the flag state is normally contacted before any regulation is enforced. Warships are immune from such jurisdiction.

THE LAW OF THE SEA

No other area of international law is today subject to such extensive change as the law of the sea. Indeed, the Third U.N. Conference on the Law of the Sea has met annually since 1973, sometimes holding two sessions a year, with no less than 137 states represented. It can be said that the work of codification and the progressive develop-ment that has been achieved — somewhat modestly set out in a text entitled "Informal Composite Negotiating Text" (U.N. Document *A/CONF.* 62/W.P. 10 and *ADD.* 1) — constitutes a most substantial contribution to international law.

Before the convocation of this Conference, the law of the sea had been set out in four separate conventions, drawn up in Geneva in 1958, and known as the "Geneva Conventions on the Law of the Sea". Of these, one dealt with the high seas, one with the territorial sea and contiguous zone, one with the continental shelf and one with fishing and the conservation of living resources.

These attempts to regulate the law of the sea, the sea-bed and subsoil, were only partially successful, as witness the *North Sea Continental Shelf Case* (I.C.J., 1969) in which one of the argu-ments put forward by Denmark and the Netherlands was that the rule set out in Article 6 of the Continental Shelf Convention (the equidistance method for delimitation of the shelf) was binding upon the Federal Republic of Germany, not a party to that Convention, because the provisions merely stated an existing rule of customary international law. The court found that this was not so and that the Federal Republic was not so bound.

THE I.C.N.T.

While the "Informal Composite Negotiating Text" (I.C.N.T.) is not yet an international instrument, it is "composite" in the sense that it sets out the whole law previously to be found in the four Geneva

Conventions, with significant changes, and thus is destined, although the text carefully avoids saying so, to supplant and replace those conventions by a single "text".

The I.C.N.T. contains 303 Articles and 7 Annexes. The main text is divided into 16 parts. The part concerning settlement of disputes and those Annexes dealing with conciliation and arbitration will be treated in Chapter Twelve: Settlement of Disputes. The final clauses of the I.C.N.T. make the Annexes an integral part of the text, while Part One contains some definitions of terms used including those of "pollution of the marine environment" and "dumping".

The statement of the law set out below in this Chapter is largely based on the remaining parts of the I.C.N.T., since its provisions may be expected with the passage of time to exert an increasing and eventually preponderant influence on state practice. However, only in respect of Sections II, V, VI, VII and VIII of the I.C.N.T. (corresponding to the same Sections in this Chapter) can it clearly be asserted that the rules set in them constitute for the most part, existing rules of customary international law.

II. TERRITORIAL SEA AND CONTIGUOUS ZONE

DESCRIPTION AND BREADTH OF THE TERRITORIAL SEA

The sovereignty of a coastal state extends beyond its land territory and internal waters and in the case of an archipelagic state, its archipelagic waters, over an adjacent belt of sea described as the territorial sea. This sovereignty extends to the air space over the territorial sea as well as to its bed and subsoil. Every state has the right to establish the breadth of its territorial sea up to a limit not exceeding twelve nautical miles, measured from baselines.

BASELINES

The baselines are the sea frontier of a coastal state. Any waters on the landward side of the baseline form internal waters over which the coastal state exercises full and complete sovereignty; while any waters on the seaward side constitute, according to their distance from the baseline, the territorial sea, (twelve nautical miles) the contiguous zone (twenty-four nautical miles), the exclusive economic zone (two hundred miles), or the high seas. The legal regime of the sea-bed is similarly measured from the line of contact of the baseline on the bed of the sea. Seawards, it constitutes the bed of the territorial sea (twelve nautical miles), the Continental shelf (two hundred nautical miles), or the bed of the sea or ocean under the high seas. The regime of the subsoil follows that of the sea-bed.

The importance now attached to the manner in which baselines are to be drawn can, thus, hardly be over-estimated.

DELIMITATIONS OF BASELINES

The normal baseline is the low-water line along the coast, as marked on large-scale charts officially recognised by the coastal state.

However, in localities where the coastline is deeply indented, or if there is a fringe of islands along the coast in its immediate vicinity, the method of straight baselines joining appropriate points may be employed in drawing the baseline from which the breadth of the territorial sea is measured.

Where because of the presence of a delta, bay or other natural condition the coastline is highly unstable, the appropriate points may be selected along the furthest seaward extent of the low-water line.

The drawing of such baselines may not depart to any appreciable extent from the general direction of the coast, and the sea areas lying within the lines must be sufficiently closely linked to the land domain to be subject to the regime of internal waters.

The system of straight baselines may not be applied by a state in such a manner as to cut off from the high seas or the exclusive economic zones the territorial sea of another state.

Where the method of straight baselines is applicable, account may be taken, in determining particular baselines, of economic interests peculiar to the region concerned, the reality and importance of which are clearly evidenced by a long usage.

LOW-TIDE ELEVATIONS

A low-tide elevation is a naturally formed area of land which is surrounded by and above water at low-tide but submerged at high-tide. Where a low-tide elevation is situated wholly or partly at a distance not exceeding the breadth of the territorial sea from the mainland or an island, the low-water line on that elevation may be used as the baseline, on condition that lighthouses or similar installations which are permanently above sea level have been built on them.

BAYS

A bay is a well-marked indentation whose penetration is in such proportion to the width of its mouth as to contain land-locked waters and constitute more than a mere curvature of the coast. An indentation may only be regarded as a bay if its area is as large as, or larger than, that of a semi-circle whose diameter is a line drawn across the mouth of that indentation.

If the distance between the low water marks of the natural

entrance points of a bay does not exceed twenty-four miles a closing line may be drawn, and the waters enclosed thereby may be considered as internal waters; if the distance is more than twenty-four miles, a straight baseline of twenty-four miles may be drawn within the bay in such a manner as to enclose the maximum area of water possible.

These rules do not apply to "historic" bays, or to bays with respect to which straight baselines may be drawn. On the other hand, such rules apply only to bays the entire coasts of which form part of the same state.

DELIMITATION OF THE TERRITORIAL SEA BETWEEN STATES WITH OPPOSITE OR ADJACENT COASTS

The sea-frontier between states with opposite or adjacent coasts is the median line every point of which is equidistant from the nearest points on the baseline from which the breadth of the territorial sea is measured, save in cases of historic title, or by reason of other special circumstances, which may have the effect of such frontier being drawn in a manner at variance with this rule.

PORTS

The outermost permanent harbour works which form an integral part of the harbour systems shall be regarded, for the purpose of delimiting the territorial sea, as forming part of the coast. However neither off-shore installations nor artificial islands shall be considered as permanent harbour works.

ROADSTEADS

Roadsteads which are normally used for the loading, unloading and anchoring of ships, and which would otherwise be situated wholly or partly outside the outer limit of the territorial sea, are included in the territorial sea.

INNOCENT PASSAGE IN THE TERRITORIAL SEA

Rules applicable to all ships

Ships of all states, whether coastal or land-locked, enjoy the right of innocent passage through the territorial sea.

"Passage" means navigation through the territorial sea for the purpose either of traversing that sea without entering internal waters, or calling at a roadstead or port facility outside internal waters, or of proceeding to or from internal waters, or of calling at such roadstead or port facility.

Passage shall be continuous and expeditious; however, passage includes stopping and anchoring but only in so far as this is incidental to ordinary navigation or necessary by reason of *force majeure* or distress or rendering assistance to persons, ships or aircraft in danger or distress.

"Innocent passage" means passage which is not prejudicial to the peace, good order, or security of the coastal state. Any activity engaged in by ships not having a direct bearing on passage shall be considered as prejudicial, including fishing, research or survey, interference with the coastal state's systems of communications, any wilful or serious pollution, any embarking or disembarking of persons, commodities or currency contrary to the immigration, sanitary, customs or fiscal regulations of the state, as well as any more evidently aggressive act, such as exercise with weapons, launching, landing or taking on board of military devices, or any threat or use of force.

Submarines and other underwater vehicles are required in the territorial sea to navigate on the surface and to show their flag.

Regulation of passage by appropriate regulations made by the coastal state is permitted with respect to the following matters: safety of navigation; protection of navigational aids; protection of cables and pipelines; conservation of the living resources of the sea; enforcement of fisheries regulations; prevention of pollution, control of research and hydrographic surveys and enforcement of immigration, sanitary, customs and fiscal regulations. No such regulations, however, may apply to the design, construction, manning or equipment of foreign ships unless giving effect to generally accepted international rules or standards.

In general, the coastal state may not hamper innocent passage, and in particular it may neither impose requirements on foreign ships which have the practical effect of denying or impeding the right of innocent passage, nor discriminate in form or in fact against ships or cargoes of or destined for any particular foreign state or states.

Suspension of the right of innocent passage is only permissible if essential for the protection of the coastal state's security, and then may only be temporary, may be effective in specified areas only, and must apply without discrimination amongst foreign ships.

Rules applicable to warships

If a warship does not comply with the laws and regulations of the coastal state concerning passage through the territorial sea and disregards any request for compliance which is made to it, the coastal state may require it to leave the territorial sea immediately. The flag state shall bear international responsibility for loss or damage to the coastal state resulting from such non-compliance.

A "warship" means a ship belonging to the armed forces of a state bearing the external marks distinguishing such ships of its nationality, under the command of an officer duly commissioned by the government of the state and whose name appears in the appropriate service list, and manned by a crew under regular armed forces discipline.

Since a warship is immune from criminal or civil jurisdiction even within the internal waters of a state, it is evident that such immunity extends, *a fortiori*, to the warship in territorial waters.

Rules applicable to merchant ships

The coastal state is expected to exercise some voluntary limitation on the extent to which it exercises its criminal and civil jurisdiction with respect to foreign merchant ships exercising their right of innocent passage. Thus, *criminal jurisdiction* should not be exercised on board a foreign ship passing through the territorial sea to arrest any person or to conduct any investigation in connexion with any crime committed on board the ship *during its passage* unless:

(a) the consequences of the crime extend to the coastal state;

(b) the crime is of a kind to disturb the peace of the country, or the good order of the territorial sea;

(c) the assistance of the local authorities has been requested by the captain of the ship or by the diplomatic agent or consular officer of the flag state;

(d) such measures are necessary for the suppression of illicit traffic in narcotic drugs or psychotropic substances.

Where, however, the foreign ship is passing through the territorial sea after leaving internal waters, this voluntary limitation no longer applies.

In any case where criminal jurisdiction is nevertheless exercised in the territorial sea, the coastal state is under a duty to advise the diplomatic agent or consular officer of the flag state before taking any measure, save in cases of emergency, in which case the notification may be made while the measures are being taken.

Where the crime was committed on board the ship *before she entered territorial waters*, and the ship has not visited internal waters, no criminal jurisdiction may be exercised at all, save with respect to violations of laws and regulations enacted with respect to the exclusive economic zone, or with respect to pollution and dumping.

With respect to *civil jurisdiction*, a distinction is made between the exercise of jurisdiction in relation to persons on board, which ought not to be exercised in any circumstances, and an exercise of jurisdiction against the ship itself, the arrest of which or the levying of execution against which should only be entertained when the ship is in the territorial sea after leaving internal waters, or when in respect of obligations or liabilities assumed or incurred by the ship itself in the course of, or for the purpose of, its voyage through the waters of the coastal state.

Rules applicable to government ships
A distinction is made between government ships operated for commercial purposes, and government ships operated for non-commercial purposes. The, former are assimilated in all respects to merchant ships. The latter are assimilated for most purposes to warships, save that the rule concerning non-compliance with laws and regulations concerning passage through the territorial sea set out above, as presently drafted, applies only to warships and not to government ships operated for non-commercial purposes (Article 30 of the I.C.N.T.). Moreover, the scale of immunities of warships at harbour or in internal waters is, under customary rules of international law, wider than that accorded to other government ships.

CONTIGUOUS ZONE
In a zone contiguous to its territorial sea, described as the contiguous zone, the coastal state may exercise the control necessary to:

(a) prevent infringements of its customs, fiscal, immigration or sanitary regulations within its territory or territorial sea; or

(b) punish infringements of the above regulations committed within its territory or territorial sea.

The contiguous zone may not extend beyond twenty-four nautical miles from the sea-frontier of a state.

III. STRAITS USED FOR INTERNATIONAL NAVIGATION
The effect of the extension of the breadth of the territorial sea to twelve nautical miles from the baselines has had the effect of closing off areas of water between two states which previously constituted high seas. This is true, in the first place, of the English Channel between the United Kingdom and France, which is at its narrowest some twenty-one nautical miles wide. It was consequently found necessary to create a right of passage for international navigation by ships and aircraft as follows.

TRANSIT PASSAGE
This is the exercise of the freedom of navigation and overflight solely for the purpose of continuous and expeditious transit of the strait between one part of the high seas (or exclusive economic zone) and another. Passage for the purpose of entering or leaving a state

bordering the strait is assimilated to transit for the above purposes.

States bordering straits shall not hamper transit passage and shall give appropriate publicity to any danger to navigation or overflight within or over the strait of which it has knowledge. There shall be no suspension of transit passage.

The above rules do not apply to straits in which passage is regulated in whole or in part by long-standing international conventions in force specifically relating to such straits.

DUTIES OF SHIPS AND AIRCRAFT DURING PASSAGE

Ships and aircraft shall proceed without delay through or over the strait; they shall refrain from any threat or use of force and from any activity other than those incident to their normal modes of continuous and expeditious transit unless rendered necessary by *force majeure* or by distress. Ships shall comply with the International Regulations for Preventing Collisions at Sea and other generally accepted international regulations.

Aircraft shall comply with rules of the air established by the International Civil Aviation Organisation and at all times monitor the radio frequency assigned by the appropriate internationally designated air traffic control authority or the appropriate international distress radio frequency.

SEA-LANES AND TRAFFIC SEPARATION SCHEMES

The regime of transit passage shall not in other respects affect the status of waters forming such straits or the exercise by the states bordering the straits of their sovereignty and jurisdiction over such waters and their air-space, bed and subsoil.

In particular, states bordering straits may designate sea-lanes and prescribe traffic separation schemes for navigation in straights where necessary to promote the safe passage of ships; and, where circumstances require, and after due publicity, substitute other lanes or schemes. Such lanes and schemes shall be referred, before adoption, to the competent international organisation with a view to their adoption, after which states may bring them into force. Where such schemes are proposed through the waters of two or more states, the states concerned shall co-operate in formulating proposals in consultation with the organisation.

LAWS AND REGULATIONS RELATING TO
TRANSIT PASSAGE

States bordering straits may make such laws and regulations with respect to the following matters: safety of navigation and regulation of marine traffic, pollution, fishing, "the taking on board or putting overboard of any commodity, currency or person in contravention of the customs, fiscal, immigration or sanitary regulations".

But such laws and regulations must not discriminate in form or in fact amongst foreign ships; nor in their application have the practical effect of denying, hampering or impairing the right of transit passage.

IV. ARCHIPELAGIC STATE

An "archipelago" means a group of islands, or parts of islands, interconnecting waters and other natural features which are so closely interrelated that such islands, waters and other natural features form an intrinsic geographical, economic and political entity or which historically have been regarded as such.

An "archipelagic state" is a state constituted by one or more archipelagos, whether wholly or in conjunction with other islands.

Such a state may draw straight baselines joining the outermost islands and drying reefs of the archipelago provided that within such baselines are included the main islands and an area in which the ratio of the area of the water to the area of the land, including atolls, is between 1:1 and 9:1. The length of such baselines shall not exceed one hundred nautical miles, except that up to three per cent of the total number of baselines may exceed that length to a maximum of one hundred and twenty-five nautical miles.

However the drawing of such baselines shall not be done in such a manner as to cut off the territorial sea of another state from the high seas or the exclusive economic zone.

Where certain parts of the waters of an archipelagic state lie between two parts of an immediately adjacent state, existing rights, whether customary or by treaty, and other legitimate interests which the latter state has traditionally exercised or protected in such waters, shall continue to be respected.

The sovereignty of an archipelagic state extends to the waters enclosed by the baselines, described as archipelagic waters, regardless of their depth or distance from the coast, to the air space over such waters, to the bed and subsoil thereof, and to the resources contained therein.

With respect to the mouths of rivers, bays and ports, an archipelagic state may draw closing lines marking internal waters in the same manner as other states. Otherwise an archipelagic state does not have internal waters, even with respect to waters landwards of straight baselines.

There is, on the contrary, a right of innocent passage through archipelagic waters, which may only be suspended by the archipelagic state where such suspension is "essential for the protection of its security".

Submarine cables passing through archipelagic waters shall be respected and permission given for their maintenance and repair. Traditional fishing rights shall also be respected as shall "other legitimate activities" of immediately adjacent states.

An archipelagic state may designate sea-lanes and air routes suitable for the safe, continuous and expeditious passage of foreign ships and aircraft through or over its archipelagic waters and the adjacent territorial sea. The right to such sea-lane passage shall be enjoyed by the ships and aircraft of all states.

Archipelagic sea-lane passage is the exercise in accordance with the present convention of the rights of navigation and overflight in the normal mode solely for the purpose of continuous, expeditous and unobstructed transit between one part of the high seas or exclusive economic zone, and another part of such seas or zone.

Where an archipelagic state makes use of this right to designate such lanes or air routes, these shall include all normal passage routes used for international navigation or overflight through such waters or within such routes. Should such a route pass through narrow channels, the archipelagic state may prescribe traffic separation schemes. All such sea-lanes and traffic separation schemes shall conform to generally accepted international regulations. If an archipelagic state does not designate sea-lanes or air routes, the right of an archipelagic sea-lanes passage may be exercised through routes normally used for international navigation.

V. EXCLUSIVE ECONOMIC ZONE

The exclusive economic zone is an area beyond and adjacent to the territorial sea, which may extend up to two hundred nautical miles from the baselines, and which is subject to a specific legal regime under which the rights and jurisdictions of the coastal state and the rights and freedoms of other states are assigned in the manner set out below.

RIGHTS AND JURISDICTION OF COASTAL STATE

In the exclusive economic zone, the coastal state has "sovereign rights" for the purpose of exploring and exploiting, conserving and managing natural resources of the sea-bed and subsoil, and of the superjacent waters, and for the purpose of other economic activities such as the production of energy from the water, currents and winds.

The state also has jurisdiction with regard to:

(a) the establishment and use of artificial islands, installa:ions and structures;

(b) marine scientific research;

(c) the preservation of the marine environment.

The state also has other rights and duties as set out elsew˥ere in the convention.

RIGHTS AND FREEDOMS OF OTHER STATES
All states enjoy the freedoms of navigation and overflight, of the laying of submarine cables and pipelines, and "other internationelly lawful uses of the sea related to these freedoms".

ARTIFICIAL ISLANDS, INSTALLATIONS AND STRUCTURES
The coastal state has the exclusive right to construct and to authorsse and regulate the construction, operation and use of all artificsal islands, as well as any installation or structure which may interfe˥e with the exercise of the rights of the coastal state in the zone. T˥e coastal state also has exclusive jurisdiction over such islands, installations and structures.

Such artificial structures shall not be constructed before du꞊ notice has been given and adequate warning of their presence pu˥ in place. Disused or abandoned structures must be entirely removed. Reasonable safety zones may be established by the coastal state no꞊ exceeding a distance of five hundred metres around them, such zone꞊ to be respected by the ships of all states, it being understood that these shall not be established in such a manner as to interfere with the use of recognised sea-lanes essential to international navigation.

LIVING RESOURCES

Conservation
The coastal state shall determine the allowable catch of the living resources in its exclusive economic zone, and shall take measures to maintain or restore populations of harvested species at levels which can produce the maximum sustainable yield.

Utilisation
Without prejudice to the above principles concerning conservation, the coastal state shall promote the objective of optimum utilisation of the living resources in the exclusive economic zone.

The I.C.N.T. sets out detailed rules for permitting the nationals of other states to fish where the coastal state considers that its own capacity to harvest living resources would not cover the entire allowable catch, for the case where stocks occur within the exclusive economic zone of two or more states, for migratory species, and for marine mammals, etc:

VI. CONTINENTAL SHELF

The continental shelf of a coastal state comprises the sea-bed and subsoil of the submarine areas that extend beyond its territorial sea throughout the natural prolongation of its land territory to the outer edge of the continental margin, or to a distance of two hundred nautical miles from the baselines from which the breadth of the territorial sea is measured where the outer edge of the continental margin does not extend up to that distance.

RIGHTS OF THE COASTAL STATE

The coastal state exercises "sovereign rights" over the continental shelf for the purpose of its exploration and the exploitation of its natural resources. *Natural resources* consist of mineral and other non-living resources of the sea-bed and subsoil together with living organisms belonging to sedentary species. These rights are exclusive in the sense that no other state or person may undertake these activities without the coastal state's express consent. They do not depend upon occupation, effective or notional, nor upon any express proclamation. The existence of such sovereign rights does not, however, affect the legal status of the superjacent waters, or the air space above those waters.

Drilling, tunnelling, the construction of artificial islands, installations and structures all fall within the exclusive jurisdiction of the coastal state.

However, all states have the right to lay submarine cables and pipelines and the coastal state may only take such steps to control the laying or maintenance of such cables and pipelines as may be necessary for the prevention, reduction and control of pollution. The I.C.N.T. provides for payments or contributions in kind to the international authority to be established for the area with respect to the exploitation of the shelf beyond two hundred nautical miles. It remains to be seen whether agreement will be reached with respect to this revolutionary proposal.

VII. HIGH SEAS

The high seas includes all parts of the sea that are not included in the exclusive economic zone, in the territorial sea, in the internal waters of a state, or in the archipelagic waters of an archipelagic state.

FREEDOM OF THE HIGH SEAS

The high seas are open to all states, whether coastal or land-locked. Freedom of the high seas comprises, *inter alia*, both for coastal and land-locked states:

(a) freedom of navigation;
(b) freedom of overflight;
(c) freedom to lay submarine cables and pipelines;
(d) freedom to construct artificial islands and other installations permitted under international law;
(e) freedom of fishing;
(f) freedom of scientific research.

It follows that no part of the high seas may be the subject of a claim to sovereignty by any state. The I.C.N.T. also states that "the high seas shall be reserved for peaceful purposes."

FREEDOM OF NAVIGATION

Every state, whether coastal or land-locked has the right to sail ships under its flag on the high seas. States shall fix the conditions under which ships may be granted its nationality, be registered in its territory, and have the right to fly its flag. Ships have the nationality of the state whose flag they are entitled to fly, and of none other. There must exist a genuine link between the state and the ship. Where a state has entitled a ship to fly its flag, it shall issue it with documents to that effect.

Ships shall fly the flag of one state only, and shall be subject to the exclusive jurisdiction of that state while upon the high seas, save in exceptional cases expressly provided for in international treaties or in the I.C.N.T. Only in cases of real transfer of ownership or change of registry may a ship be entitled to change its flag during a voyage or in a port of call. Any ship sailing under the flags of two or more states, using them according to convenience, may be assimilated by third states to a ship without any nationality.

DUTIES OF FLAG STATE

Every state is under the duty effectively to exercise its jurisdiction and control in administrative, social and technical matters over ships flying its flag, and shall in particular maintain a register of shipping and ensure safety at sea for all ships flying its flag.

In case of a marine casualty or incident of shipping, either the flag state or the state whose nationals have suffered loss of life, or whose property has suffered serious damage, shall cause an inquiry to be held before a suitably qualified person.

Warships on the high seas have complete immunity from the jurisdiction of any state other than the flag state. Ships used only on governmental non-commercial service have, on the high seas, a similar immunity.

Penal jurisdiction in matters of collision or any other incident of navigation concerning a ship on the high seas, involving the responsibility of the master or other person in the service of the ship shall remain exclusively with the flag state, save that each state may institute penal proceedings in such circumstances against its own nationals. No arrest or detention of the ship of any sort may be ordered by any authorities other than those of the flag state.

DUTY TO RENDER ASSISTANCE

Save where to do so would cause serious damage to the ship, the master of every ship shall be enjoined by the flag state:

(a) to render assistance to any person found at sea in danger of being lost;

(b) to proceed with all possible speed to the rescue of persons in distress;

(c) after a collision, to render assistance to the other ship, its crew and passengers.

PIRACY

Any of the following acts constitute piracy:

(a) all illegal acts of violence detention or depredation committed for private ends by the crew or passengers of a private ship or aircraft and directed, on the high seas, against persons or property on board, or against a ship or aircraft, persons or property in any place outside the jurisdiction of any state;

(b) any act of voluntary participation in the operation of a ship or aircraft with knowledge of the facts making it a pirate;

(c) any act of inciting or of intentionally facilitating any act of piracy.

Assimilated to a private ship is any warship or government-owned ship or aircraft the crew of which has mutinied and taken control. Any ship or aircraft under the "dominant control" of persons who intend to use it for the purpose of committing an act of piracy, or who have so used it, shall be considered a pirate ship or aircraft, for so long as it remains under their control. All states shall co-operate to the fullest extent possible in the suppression of piracy, and on the high sea or in any place outside the jurisdiction of any state any and every state may seize a pirate ship or aircraft, arrest the persons on board and seize all property. The courts of the state which carried out the seizure may decide upon the penalties to be imposed, and the action to be taken with regard to the ship, aircraft or property, subject to the rights of third parties acting in good faith. Such seizure may only be carried out by warships or military aircraft, or ships or aircraft clearly identifiable as being on government service. Seizure without adequate grounds shall give rise to the international responsibility of the seizing state for any loss or damage caused by the seizure.

TRANSPORT OF SLAVES

Any slave taking refuge on board any ship whatever its flag shall, *ipso facto*, be free. Every state shall adopt effective measures to prevent and punish the transport of slaves.

ILLICIT TRAFFIC IN NARCOTIC DRUGS

All states shall co-operate in the suppression of illicit traffic in narcotic drugs.

UNAUTHORISED BROADCASTING

Unauthorised broadcasting means the transmission of sound radio or television broadcasts from a ship or installation on the high seas intended for reception by the general public contrary to international regulations.

Any person engaged in unauthorised broadcasting from the high seas may be prosecuted before the courts of any of the following states:

(a) the flag state of the vessel;
(b) the place of registry of the installation;
(c) the state of which the person is a national;
(d) the state from any part of the territory of which the broadcast can be heard;
(e) the state whose authorised broadcasts are suffering interference.

All states shall co-operate in the suppression of unauthorised broadcasting from the high seas.

RIGHT OF VISIT

A warship which, on the high seas, encounters a foreign ship other than a ship entitled to a complete immunity may board her if there is a "reasonable ground for suspecting":

(a) that the ship is a pirate;
(b) that the ship is engaged in slave trade;
(c) that the ship is engaged in unauthorised broadcasting;
(d) that the ship is without any nationality, or that, although flying a foreign flag, it is in reality of the same nationality as the warship.

Similar provisions apply to military aircraft, and to ships and aircraft clearly marked and identifiable as being on government service.

RIGHT OF HOT PURSUIT

When the competent authorities of the coastal state have "good reason to believe" that a ship has violated its laws or regulations, hot pursuit may be undertaken, so long as the ship or one of its boats is still within the internal waters, or the territorial sea, and may only be pursued beyond these waters or sea if the pursuit is uninterrupted.

Where the ship or boat is still within or overlying

(a) the contiguous zone, or
(b) the exclusive economic zone, or
(c) the continental shelf, or
(d) the safety zones around installations erected upon the continental shelf,

a right of hot pursuit shall exist, but only if the suspected violation is in respect of one of the rights for the protection of which the zone or shelf was established.

Pursuit may only begin after a visual or auditory signal has been given at a distance which enables it to be seen or heard by the foreign ship. Compensation shall be paid to any ship stopped or arrested in circumstances which do not justify exercising the right of hot pursuit.

SUBMARINE CABLES AND PIPELINES

All states may lay submarine cables and pipelines on the bed of the high seas beyond the continental shelf, subject to not interfering with those already in position, the possibilities of repair and maintenance of which must not be prejudiced. Any ship cutting, breaking, interrupting or obstructing such a cable or pipeline commits under the law of the flag state a punishable offence and every state shall take the necessary legislative measures so to provide. Where such damage is caused by the owner, such legislation shall ensure that the owner shall bear the full cost of repair.

RIGHT TO FISH

All states have the right to permit their nationals to fish upon the high seas subject to their treaty obligations, and the rights, duties and interests of other states in those special cases where the same stock or associated species occur both within the high seas and within the exclusive economic zone of a coastal state.

However, states shall adopt for their nationals such measures as may be necessary for the conservation of the living resources of the high seas and shall co-operate with other states concerning the management and conservation of living resources in the area of the high seas.

VIII. ISLANDS

An island is a naturally formed area of land surrounded by water, which is above water at high tide.

Rocks which cannot sustain human habitation or economic life of their own have no exclusive economic zone or continental shelf, but have a territorial sea and contiguous zone. This case apart, an island has a territorial sea, a contiguous zone, an exclusive economic zone and a continental shelf as determined in accordance with the I.C.N.T. text.

IX. ENCLOSED OR SEMI-ENCLOSED SEAS

An "enclosed" or "semi-enclosed sea" means a gulf, basin or sea surrounded by two or more states and connected to the open seas by a narrow outlet, or consisting entirely or primarily of the territorial seas and exclusive economic zone of two or more coastal states.

States bordering such seas have a duty to co-operate in particular with respect to the exploitation of living resources, the preservation of the marine environment, and scientific research programmes.

X. ACCESS OF LAND-LOCKED STATES

Land-locked states, that is states without a sea coast, have a right of access to and from the sea for the purpose of exercising the rights provided in the I.C.N.T. text including those relating to the freedom of the high seas and the common heritage of mankind. To this end land-locked states enjoy freedom of transit through the territory of transit states by all means of transport.

Traffic in transit shall not be subject to any customs duties, taxes or other charges except charges levied for specific services rendered in connection with such traffic. Free zones or other customs facilities may be provided at ports of entry. Ships flying the flag of land-locked states enjoy treatment equal to that accorded to other foreign ships in maritime ports.

XI. THE AREA AND THE AUTHORITY

The "Area" means the sea-bed and ocean floor and subsoil thereof beyond the limits of national jurisdiction.

The Area and its resources are the common heritage of mankind. Activities in the Area are to be carried out for the benefit of mankind as a whole irrespective of the geographical location of the states and taking into consideration the interests and needs of developing countries. All rights in the resources of the Area are vested in mankind as a whole, on whose behalf the "Authority" shall act. Such resources are not subject to alienation. The minerals derived from the Area may only be alienated in accordance with the provisions of the I.C.N.T. text.

The "Authority" (the "International Sea-bed Authority") is established with an Assembly, a Council and a Secretariat: all states are *ipso facto* members of the Authority. There is also established "an Enterprise", the organ through which the Authority shall directly carry out activities in the Area. The essential aim of the Authority is to establish a system for the equitable sharing of benefits derived from the Area, such benefits to be derived from charging a levy upon, and limiting production of, the mining of minerals and in particular nickel.

This ambitious part of the proposed convention has not yet received sufficient support for it to be possible to state whether these provisions will become part of the new international legal order.

XII. PROTECTION AND PRESERVATION OF THE MARINE ENVIRONMENT

States have a duty to protect and preserve the marine environment, and their sovereign right to exploit their natural resources shall be exercised subject to this right.

The I.C.N.T. then lists a series of measures to be taken to reduce and control pollution of the marine environment, including a prohibition of dumping, and a series of Articles under which states accept the obligation to adopt necessary enforcement measures.

XIII. MARINE SCIENTIFIC RESEARCH

Irrespective of their geographical location, states have the right to conduct marine scientific research subject to the rights of other states pursuant to the I.C.N.T. text. Such research shall not, however, form the legal basis of any claim to any part of the marine environment or its resources. Research may only be carried out in the exclusive economic zone with the consent of the coastal state.

XIV. RIVERS

For the purpose of international law, rivers are divided into two types, national and international rivers.

NATIONAL RIVERS

A national river is one of which the banks and mouth lie entirely within the territory of one state. In this case the river is itself part of the territory of the state, and is subject to its complete sovereignty.

INTERNATIONAL RIVERS

International rivers flow through or between the territory of two or more states. In this case each of the riparian states exercises sovereignty over the part of the river flowing through its territory, but the sovereignty of the riparian state is subject to the duty to permit the navigation of foreign merchant ships and to the right of such ships to trade throughout the whole navigable length of the river.

A boundary river is an international river which in itself forms the boundary between two states. If the river should happen to change its course through natural causes, the boundary between the two states will also change. The two riparian states exercise complete sovereignty over the river, the boundary between them normally being the centre line of the river.

"INTERNATIONALISED" RIVERS

Certain international rivers have been made the subject of a special legal status, and in some cases a permanent commission has been established to administer them. Some examples of commissions of this kind are: the Central Commission for the Navigation of the Rhine, established by the Convention of Mannheim in 1868; the Danube Commission, established by the Belgrade Convention of 1948; and the Special Commission for the Niger River, established by the Convention on Navigation and Economic Co-operation between the States of the River Niger of 1963. In south-east Asia the Mekong, in North America the Colorado, Rio Grande and St Lawrence, and in South America the Amazon, are among the principal international rivers which have been internationalised as a result of an agreement between the riparian states or concessions granted by them. Only in the case of the Rhine have non-riparian states been admitted to participate in the administration of the river.

UTILISATION OF THE FLOW OF RIVERS

The rule is that riparian states have a duty, in the case of boundary and international rivers, to use river waters in a manner which is not detrimental to the interests of other riparian states. Water utilisation is governed by agreement in the case of the Nile (between the Sudan and the United Arab Republic), the Indus (between India and Pakistan), and the Drava (between Yugoslavia and Austria).

The emerging principle seems to be that of the equal rights of *all* riparian states to the utilisation of river waters.

XV. CANALS

As with straits, international law is only concerned with international canals, that is to say, artificial waterways connecting two parts of the high seas.

In contemporary international law the three most important international canals, Suez, Panama and Kiel, are all under the sovereignty of the territorial states, namely the United Arab Republic (formerly Egypt), Panama, and the Federal Republic of Germany respectively. In each case, however, the original status of the canal was governed by treaty and was not under the sovereignty of the territorial state. The three treaties were the Convention of Constantinople, 1888 (Suez); the Hay-Pauncefote Treaty, 1901 (Panama); the Treaty of Versailles, 1919 (Kiel). Each of these treaties provided for free navigation of the ships of all nations, at least in time of peace. Each of them has been repudiated or terminated, but in affirming or re-affirming its sovereignty, the territorial state has been careful to uphold the principle of free navigation.

The United Arab Republic formerly defended its prohibition of access to the Suez Canal of ships flying the flag of Israel on the ground that it had not yet recognised that state.

The Corinth Canal has always been under the sovereignty and control of Greece.

CHAPTER TEN

The Air Space, Outer Space, Telecommunications

I. THE LEGAL REGIME OF THE AIR

The legal regime of the air reflects that of the underlying land and water. It consists either of "air territory" or of "open skies".

AIR TERRITORY

State sovereignty over air territory

"Every state has complete and exclusive sovereignty over the air space above its territory" including its territorial waters (Article 1 of the Chicago Convention on International Civil Aviation, 1944, which entered into force on 4th April 1947). The territory of a state thus includes, besides its land and water territory, a layer of "air territory". In principle, therefore, and apart from treaty provisions, no aircraft may fly into the "air territory" of a foreign state unless that state's permission has been obtained in advance. The Chicago Convention affirmed that "no *state* aircraft of a contracting state shall fly over the territory of another state or land thereon without authorisation by special agreement."

Delimitation of air territory

There is no agreement as to the breadth of the layer of air comprised within air territory. It is only with the exploration of outer space and the formation of a different legal regime to apply to it, that the question of the boundary between air and outer space has become of legal importance.

"OPEN SKIES"

The regime of the high seas applies to the air space above it. The freedom of the seas comprises the "freedom to fly over the high seas" (Article 2(4) of the High Seas Convention). This freedom exists also with respect to the air space above territory not subject to the sovereignty of any state (such as the Antarctic and the Arctic). But the open skies principle is subject to exception in the interests of air safety. The speed at which modern aircraft fly has made it necessary in some cases for states to extend their regulations for the control of air traffic beyond the borders of their own territories out across the sea. For the same reason six states in Western Europe have banded together to create, in "Eurocontrol", a single authority to govern air flight over their combined territories.

JURISDICTION OVER AIRCRAFT
States exercise over aircraft both personal and territorial jurisdiction.

Personal jurisdiction
The principle is that the state's personal jurisdiction extends to any person (or thing) having its nationality wherever it may be. An aircraft has the nationality of the state in which it is registered. This state therefore has the power, but not the duty, to extend both its criminal and civil jurisdiction to acts taking place on board the aircraft wherever it may be.

Aircraft in the "open skies"
While flying in the open skies or over unoccupied territory, the law and jurisdiction of the state of registration will thus be the only one applicable to the aircraft.

Territorial jurisdiction
While in its "air territory", however, the territorial state has jurisdiction to apply its law to acts taking place on board the aircraft. Thus an infringement of its customs regulations may be complete so soon as the aircraft enters "air territory" and not merely upon its landing and undergoing customs inspection.

Concurrence of personal and territorial jurisdiction
Treaty provisions apart, no territorial state would seem to be obliged, with respect to an aircraft present within its territory, at least in penal matters, to recognise the concurrent (but personal) jurisdiction of the state of registration, and it is certainly not obliged to recognise it in priority to its own. Thus where an "offence" was alleged by state A to have been committed in an aircraft of its nationality while flying in the air territory of state B, the latter state might refuse to recognise that any "offence" had been committed under the law of state A such as to justify a demand for extradition on the ground that the act in question had been committed within its own territory. If the act constituted an offence under its own laws, state B might prosecute the case itself. Thus everything depends upon

where the aircraft was situated when the act occurred. This is obviously unsatisfactory in modern conditions.

Criminal jurisdiction under the "Tokyo" Convention

The Convention on Offences and Certain Other Acts Committed on board Aircraft concluded at Tokyo on 14th September 1963 endeavoured to provide a legal regime more suited to the realities of air travel than that outlined above. For the states which are party to that Convention the legal regime with respect to criminal jurisdiction is as follows: "The state of registration of the aircraft is competent to exercise jurisdiction over offences and acts committed on board." Such jurisdiction, however, is not to exclude "any criminal jurisdiction exercised in accordance with national law". A state other than the state of registration may not interfere with an aircraft *in flight* over its air territory in order to exercise its criminal jurisdiction over an offence committed on board, except in the five following cases:

(a) when the offence has an effect on the territorial state; or

(b) when an offence has been committed by or against a national or a permanent resident of that state; or

(c) when an offence has been committed against its security; or

(d) when an offence is a violation of the flight navigation laws of that state; or

(e) when interference is necessary to ensure observance of any obligation of such state under a multilateral international agreement.

"Certain other acts"

The convention applies not only to offences against penal laws, but also to acts which jeopardise the safety of the aircraft or of persons or property on board. The commander of the aircraft is given certain powers of restraint, in particular in relation to these "other acts", and may deliver into the hands of the authorities of the state where the aircraft lands, any person he has "reasonable grounds to believe" has committed a serious offence according to the law of the state of registration.

Hijacking of aircraft

Any unlawful act of interference, seizure or other wrongful exercise of control of an aircraft in flight obliges the state in which the aircraft subsequently lands *(a)* to permit its passengers and crew to continue their journey and *(b)* to return the aircraft and its cargo to the persons lawfully entitled to possession. The treaty says nothing as to the treatment to be accorded to the wrongdoer.

To fill this gap two further treaties have been concluded recently under the auspices of I.C.A.O., namely the Convention for the Suppression of Unlawful Seizure of Aircraft, signed at the Hague on 16th December 1970, and the Convention for the Suppression of Unlawful Acts against the Safety of Civil Aircraft, concluded at Montreal on 23rd September 1971.

The Hague Convention makes it an "offence" for any person on board an aircraft unlawfully, by force or threat of force, or by any other form of intimidation, to seize or exercise control of the aircraft or to attempt to do so (Article 1). The contracting parties undertake to make the offence punishable by "severe penalties". Moreover, the contracting state in the territory of which the alleged offender is found shall be obliged either to extradite him or to submit his case for prosecution within its own territory.

The Montreal Convention completes the definition of "offence" given in the Hague Convention in respect of persons committing any act of violence against a person on board an aircraft in flight which is likely to endanger its safety, or places an object on board an aircraft which is likely to destroy or damage it while in flight, or even communicates information which he knows to be false thereby endangering the safety of the aircraft in flight. Contracting states' obligations as to the punishment of offenders are identical to those under the Hague Convention.

II. AIR NAVIGATION

THE LAW CONCERNING AIR NAVIGATION
Air navigation law is exclusively governed by treaties. There are no customary rules in this area except that of prohibition of flight in air territory without permission. "Air navigation" is the subject of Part 1 of the Chicago Convention.

Classification of aircraft for navigation purposes
A distinction is made, for the purposes of the Chicago Convention, between "state aircraft" and "civil aircraft". The convention applies only to the latter. The term "state aircraft" comprises "aircraft used for military, customs and police services". Thus, an aircraft is not to be considered a "state aircraft" merely because it is owned by a state or operated by a state airline.

Airworthiness of aircraft
No aircraft may fly without a certificate of airworthiness issued by the state of nationality, in conformity with international standards.

NATIONAL NAVIGATION OR "CABOTAGE"
The privilege of carrying traffic between two points in the same state

may be reserved exclusively for aircraft of the territorial state, but if it is not it must not be granted to any other state on an exclusive basis.

INTERNATIONAL NAVIGATION
The rules differ sharply depending upon whether the flight is non-scheduled or scheduled.

"Non-scheduled flight"
Aircraft not engaged in scheduled international air services have the right to make flights into the territory of another contracting state and to make stops for non-traffic purposes (or to pass in transit non-stop across its territory) without the necessity of obtaining prior permission and have the privilege of taking on or discharging passengers, cargo or mail, for remuneration or hire, subject to the right of the territorial state to impose such regulations, conditions, or limitations as it thinks fit.

Scheduled flight
"No scheduled international air service may be operated over or into the territory of a contracting state except with the special permission or authorisation of that state."

Definition of "scheduled international air service"
An "air service" is one "performed by aircraft for the public transport of passengers mail or cargo." An "international air service" is an air service which passes through the air space over the territory of more than one state. A "scheduled international air service" is an international air service performed for remuneration, in such a manner that each flight is open to use by the public, and operated to serve traffic between fixed points according to a published time-table (or so regularly or frequently that the flights constitute a recognisably systematic series).

Transit rights: the "two freedoms"
By the International Air Services Transit Agreement each contracting state granted to each of the others the freedom to fly across its territory without landing, and the freedom to land for non-traffic purposes.

Traffic rights: the third, fourth and fifth freedoms
Before scheduled international air services can operate, however, the three following freedoms have also to be acquired through the conclusion of a network of bilateral agreements: the freedom to put down passengers, mail and cargo taken on in the territory of the state of the aircraft's nationality; to take on passengers, mail and

cargo destined for the territory of that state; and to take on passengers, mail and cargo destined for the territory of any other contracting state and the privilege to put down passengers, mail and cargo coming from such territory.

The model for most such bilateral agreements is the Bermuda Agreement of 11th February 1946 between the United States and the United Kingdom, concluded on the basis of ensuring a fair and equal opportunity for the carriers of the two nations by the provision of services giving a carrying capacity adequate for but not in excess of traffic demands and requirements. It was agreed that traffic rates were to be fixed internationally by the International Air Transport Association.

The International Civil Aviation Organisation (I.C.A.O.) was established by Part 2 of the Chicago Convention. The Council of the I.C.A.O. is to adopt international standards and recommend practices which are to be added as annexes to the convention and amended from time to time. States agree to collaborate in securing the highest practicable degree of uniformity in these matters, and to notify the I.C.A.O. of any differences between its own regulations and those laid down by the Council. However, "over the high seas, the rules in force shall be those established under this Convention."

III. OUTER SPACE

The basic principles of the law of outer space are still to be found in the Treaty on Principles Governing the Activities of States in the Exploration and Use of Outer Space, including the Moon and other Celestial Bodies, concluded in 1966. But already in January 1962, the General Assembly of the United Nations had declared, by Resolution 1721 (XVI), that "international law, including the Charter of the United Nations, applies to outer space and celestial bodies."

Since that time the following treaties have been concluded by the United Nations General Assembly in the form of annexes to resolutions:

Resolution 2345 (XXII): Agreement on the Rescue of Astronauts, and the Return of Objects Launched into Outer Space (December 1967);

Resolution 2777 (XXVI): Convention on International Liability for Damage Caused by Space Objects (December 1971);

Resolution 3235 (XXIX): Convention on Registration of Objects Launched into Outer Space (November 1974);

Resolution 34/68: Agreement Governing the Activities of States on the Moon and other Celestial Bodies (December 1979).

SCOPE AND DELIMITATION

The expression "outer space" is now taken to include "the Moon and other celestial bodies", and not just the "space" between them. Delimitation of the outer limit is both unnecessary and impossible (in the present state of knowledge). It is, however, both necessary and possible to delimit the inner limit of outer space, and, consequently, the upper limit of "air space". However, no such frontier has been agreed upon by states. It may be noted that aircraft cannot fly in space, and it would seem reasonable to provide that the legal regime of the air should apply wherever aircraft can fly, however high that may be. Spacecraft while in air space seem to be exempt from the rules of air law.

LEGAL REGIME OF OUTER SPACE

"Outer space . . . shall be the province of all mankind (and) is not subject to national appropriation by claim of sovereignty . . There shall be: freedom of access to all areas of celestial bodies; freedom of scientific investigation; and freedom of exploration and use, save that it shall be used by all states . . . exclusively for peaceful purposes."

These statements of principle have been incorporated into the Agreement Governing the Activities of States on the Moon and other Celestial Bodies, which adds the following: that the Moon and its natural resources are "the common heritage of mankind; [and that] neither the surface nor the sub-surface . . . shall become the property of any states . . . or person." States shall however, exercise "jurisdiction and control over their personnel, space vehicles, facilities, stations and installations" on the Moon and other celestial bodies.

RESPONSIBILITY OF STATES OVER ACTIVITIES IN OUTER SPACE

Activities in space are the responsibility of states. They are internationally responsible for the activities of both governmental and non-government entities in outer space; non-governmental entities "shall require authorisation and continuing supervision by the appropriate state." When an activity is carried on by an international organisation, both it and the member states remain responsible for compliance with this treaty.

Military and nuclear activities

States "undertake" not to send nuclear weapons into outer space, not to install military bases and not to test any type of weapons on celestial bodies. But the use of military personnel for any peaceful purposes, or of (military) equipment necessary for peaceful exploration, is not prohibited.

SPACE CRAFT OR SPACE OBJECT

"A state . . . on whose registry an object launched into outer space is carried, shall retain jurisdiction and control over such object and over the personnel thereof . . . Ownership of (spacecraft) and of all objects carried on board or installated (on a celestial body) is unaffected by their presence in outer space . . . If found beyond the territory of the state of registry such objects are to be returned to that state."

The 1974 Covention adds that when a space craft is launched into earth orbit or beyond, the launching state shall register the object . . . and shall supply the Secretary General of the United Nations with the following information: the name of the launching state; an appropriate designation of the object; the date and location of the launch; certain basic orbital parameters, including the nodal period, inclination, apogee and perigee; and the general function of the object.

The expression " 'launching state' is to be taken to apply to any intergovernmental organisation which conducts space activities if the organisation declares its acceptance of the rights and obligations of the 1974 Convention and if a majority of the states members of the organisation are parties to that convention and to the basic 1966 Treaty." These conditions having been met, the European Space Agency has become an "accepting party" to the 1974 Convention.

ASTRONAUTS

Astronauts are to be regarded as "envoys of mankind in outer space", and states shall render them all possible assistance in the event of accident, distress or emergency landing on the territory of any state, or on the high seas, and shall return them promptly and safely to the state of registry of the spacecraft.

These statements of principles are reproduced and expanded in the 1967 Agreement which will enter into force only after ratification by five states including the United Kingdom, United States and the U.S.S.R. The European Space Agency has become an accepting party in the same conditions as above.

LIABILITY FOR DAMAGE

Damage caused by a spacecraft or its component parts to a "state or its natural or juridicial persons" shall involve the absolute liability of the state of registry and, should this be different, of the state from whose territory the spacecraft was launched. This applies wherever the damage occurs, whether "on Earth, in air space or in outer space".

The 1971 Convention, while citing the principles of absolute liability of the launching states, defines and limits this liability in the following respects: there shall be no liability whatsoever where the damage results from activities of the state suffering damage which were not in themselves in conformity with international law; or where such damage is the result, in whole or in part, of a serious fault or an act or omission done with the intention of causing damage. On the other hand, the obligation to make reparation does not apply at all to the state with respect to damage caused to its own nationals; or to non-nationals who participate in the operation of the spacecraft at the invitation of the launching state.

The claim for reparation may be made by the state suffering damage or whose nationals suffer damage in the traditional manner by the diplomatic channel, but it is specified, in Article XI, that there is no need to exhaust local remedies. The convention also provides for compulsory settlement by a Commission for Settlement of Claims if no agreement is reached within one year from the date on which the injured state has presented evidence of its loss to the defendant state.

IV. TELECOMMUNICATIONS

It is convenient, but not entirely logical, to treat the law of tele-communication under the heading air space and outer space, because radio waves travel through air and space. Moreover the law of tele-communications ignores the fact that separate legal regimes apply to the air and to outer space.

The principal forms of telecommunication are telegraph, tele-phone, radio and television. Telecommunications are defined in the Montreux Convention, 1965, as "any transmission emission or reception of signs, writing, images and sounds or of intelligence of any nature by wire, radio, optical or other electromagnetic systems". "Radio" is a general term applied to the use of the radio waves, and thus includes television.

INTERNATIONAL TELECOMMUNICATIONS
International law is only concerned with international telecom-munications, that is "telecommunications between offices or

stations of any nature which are in different countries or are subject to [the control of] different countries".

The International Telecommunications Union (I.T.U.)

A framework for continuous international co-operation in telecommunications is provided by the I.T.U., which is set up on a permanent basis with an international secretariat. The I.T.U. is the oldest truly international organisation, and practically every state in the world is a member of it. Its statute was last revised in 1965, and is set out in the International Telecommunications Convention, concluded at Montreux in that year. Regulations adopted within the I.T.U. are detailed, complex and comprehensive; in no other field has international regulation of the international community been so successful.

The objects of the I.T.U.

The I.T.U. was set up to harmonise the actions of states and increase their co-operation so as to improve and rationalise the use of telecommunications, increase their efficiency, and so far as possible make them generally available to the public.

THE BASIS AND PRINCIPLES OF INTERNATIONAL CO-OPERATION

Reciprocity

Each state has the sovereign right to regulate its telecommunications. Any international telecommunication service thus requires the agreement of at least two states — the state of emission and the state of reception. If the communication "passes" through any third state, that state's agreement is also required. The basis of international co-operation is reciprocity of treatment: each state agrees to receive or allow transit for such other states as may agree to receive or allow transit of communications sent from its own territory.

The financial consequences of reciprocity

Although this does not appear at first sight, the principle of reciprocity has important consequences for the level of rates and the national financing of telecommunications. If one state fixes rates so high as to make a commerical profit while another holds them so low as to operate at a loss, the "cost of the service" that one state supplies to the other would no longer be reciprocal even if the use of the service remains unaffected. In fact, however, the "use of the service" would probably increase in the state where rates are cheap, thus increasing the burden on other states. Article 4 (2) (c) of the Montreux Convention accordingly lays down as one of the specific aims of the I.T.U. that it "foster collaboration among its members . . .

with a view to the establishment of rates at levels as low as possible consistent with an efficient service and taking into account the necessity for maintaining independent financial administration of telecommunication on a sound basis." In other words, states must aim to make neither a profit nor a loss, thus ensuring that the basis of reciprocity is not upset by unequal financial treatment and aims.

Use by the public
The second principle of inter-state co-operation is that international telecommunications should be for the benefit, not of states, but of the general public. Each member of the I.T.U. "recognises the right of the public to correspond by means of the international services of public correspondence." States retain the right to stop the transmission of any private telegram or cut off any private telephone or telegraph communication which may appear "dangerous to the security of the state, contrary to their laws, public morals or decency". States may also suspend the international telecommunications service for an indefinite time, provided they immediately notify all other members. States all retain the faculty of giving priority to government telegrams and, if need be, to telephone calls, over all other users.

Prohibition of discrimination
"Services, charges and safeguards shall be the same for all users in each category of correspondence without any priority or preference." Any attempt, therefore, to discriminate on the basis, for example, of nationality or of residence, is prohibited since it would undermine the reciprocity and detract from the generality of user by the public.

Humanitarian considerations
International telecommunication services and radio stations must accord absolute priority to telecommunication concerning safety of life at sea, on land or in the air, and to distress calls or messages regardless of their origin.

ALLOCATION OF THE RADIO-FREQUENCY SPECTRUM
The "radio waves" are a precious but limited commodity which are also totally independent of political boundaries. Their importance is increasing with the opening up of space travel. Without agreement between states they would nevertheless be almost worthless, since the unregulated operation of radio stations in different territories would inevitably lead to so much harmful interference that the result, for the broadcasting public, would be intolerable. The original cause (and still the greatest achievement) of the I.T.U. was the division of the radio-frequency spectrum between states. Each state

was allocated bands of the spectrum at different wavelengths in proportion to its size and its population. Each state undertakes to ensure that all stations on its territory operate in such a manner as not to result in harmful interference to the radio services of other members. A permanent organ of the I.T.U., the International Frequency Registration Board, keeps this allocation under continuous review, advises states on the more effective use of their own allocation of the spectrum, and seeks to eliminate any harmful interference which may occur from time to time.

BROADCASTING STATIONS

Every broadcasting station (that is a station broadcasting to the general public) must be authorised by the state, and must operate on a radio frequency allocated by the I.T.U. to that state. The state must, in its turn, register every new registration with the International Frequency Registration Board which will authorise it or not, after examination of the extent to which it is capable of causing harmful interference. The operation of a broadcasting service by mobile stations at sea or over the sea is, for the same motive (avoidance of the possibility of harmful interference) prohibited. It is evident that "pirate" or unauthorised stations jeopardise the basis of the whole system. By the European Agreement for the Prevention of Broadcasts transmitted from Stations outside National Territories, 1965, each contracting party has made it a punishable offence to aid or abet in its territory the operation of "pirate" radio stations by selling, advertising or supplying provisions.

CHAPTER ELEVEN

Responsibility

I. GENERAL

THE NATURE OF INTERNATIONAL RESPONSIBILITY
Whenever the breach of any obligation under international law causes damage, a new legal relationship arises between the party committing the illegal act and the part injured thereby. The former becomes "responsible" to the latter.

There are thus only three elements involved: an illegal act, injury or damage, and a link of causation between the act and the damage.

Contractual and delictual responsibility
The concept of international responsibility is, however, *sui generis*. It is directly analogous neither with contractual nor with delictual liability in municipal law. In the *Russian Indemnity Case* (1912), the court rejected any notion that there might be a difference between liability arising out of obligations *ex contractu* and that arising *ex delictu*: ". . . all liability whatever may be its origin is finally estimated in money terms and transferred into obligations to pay. . . . It is not possible for the Tribunal to perceive essential differences between various responsibilities." In particular it should be stressed that "fault" or *culpa* is not an essential ingredient in the notion of international responsibility. It is true that there are some situations resulting in damage where the question of whether a breach of international law has taken place will depend in the circumstances upon whether the responsible entity exercised a sufficient degree of control, or whether its agents had failed to perform some act. That this was through ignorance, carelessness or negligence is however not important, for the standard is objective: has a breach of international law been committed, and has it resulted in damage? Thus in *The Jessie* (Mixed Claims Commission, United Kingdom and United States, 1921), American naval officers interfered with the sealing operations of British vessels in the *bona fide* belief that this action was justified by joint regulations adopted by

the two states. They were mistaken and their action was taken to involve the international responsibility of the United States.

Civil and criminal responsibility

International responsibility is civil rather than criminal. Although the criminal responsibility of individuals is established in international law, no case has occurred of the condemnation of an international person for an international crime. Moreover, in no case has a tribunal awarded exemplary damages as a means of punishing the responsible entity for the gravity of the illegal act.

THE CONSEQUENCE OF RESPONSIBILITY

"It is a principle of international law ... that any breach of an engagement involves an obligation to make reparation" (*Chorzow Factory (Merits) Case* (P.C.I.J., 1928)). "It follows from the establisment of responsibility that compensation is due" (*Corfu Channel (Compensation) Case* (I.C.J., 1949)).

THE ILLEGAL ACT

International responsibility can only arise as the result of the breach of an international obligation, whether of treaty, customary international law or general principles of law. The abuse of a right is to be assimilated to the breach of an obligation for this purpose.

The "compulsory" jurisdiction of the International Court of Justice extends to all legal disputes concerning *inter alia* "the existence of any fact which, if established, would constitute a breach of an international obligation"; and "the nature and extent of the reparation to be made for breach of an international obligation" (Statute of the International Court of Justice, Article 38).

Omissions

Inaction in situations in which the responsible entity ought to have acted is assimilated to positive action. Thus in the *Corfu Channel (Merits) Case* (I.C.J., 1949), Albania's responsibility was the result of an omission to act in that its officials had failed to inform shipping of the existence of a mine-field in her territorial waters, with the result that British warships were sunk.

Municipal law no defence

If an act is in breach of international law, the fact that it may be in accordance with municipal law is no defence. Thus in the *Alabama Arbitration* (1872), a vessel constructed in a British port to the order of the Confederate States was permitted to sail. This was in breach of Great Britain's duties of neutrality. The British Government would have liked to prevent it sailing, but it had no power to do so under British law! This was held by the arbitrators to be no defence. It would be more correct to say that municipal law is irrelevant in the context of international responsibility except where it may be relevant as an element of fact.

DAMAGE

Breach of an international obligation, without more, does not give rise to responsibility: it must result in "damage". However, although not all damage is occasioned by illegal acts, it would appear from the international case law that all illegal acts give rise to some damage.

So long as it has been caused by the commission of an illegal act or an illegal omission, an international person is entitled to reparation for any form of damage, whether material or moral, to itself, or to those it is entitled to protect or persons claiming through them.

But the converse of this rule also applies: any form of damage incurred either by an international person or those it is entitled to protect will be *damnum sine injuria* if the court finds in the circumstances that there was no breach of an international obligation. This is the case with damaged suffered in a civil war and also with damage resulting from mob violence if the government exercised "due diligence". In the *Home Missionary Society Case* (1920) the imposition of an unpopular tax caused a riot by the native population of a West African colony during which as many white people as could be found were slaughtered. The United States presented a claim arising out of the death of American missionaries. It was held that no state can be found liable for damage resulting from riotous acts against its own policy when, as in this case, it was not itself guilty of any lack of foresight in their prediction or of due diligence in their suppression.

CAUSATION

The link of causation between the illegal act and the damage is inherent in the concept of responsibility. It is satisfied so soon as it can be shown that if the act had not occurred the damage would not have taken place. Thus, it is not only the direct, but also the indirect, or secondary, consequences of the act that give rise to a claim to reparation.

II. STATE RESPONSIBILITY

THE ELEMENTS OF STATE RESPONSIBILITY

To complete the elements involved in a case of *state* responsibility it is only necessary to add to those already given that the illegal act must be imputable to the defendant state; and that the damage must have been caused to the claimant state.

Before examining these two elements it is necessary to consider the different forms of state responsibility, since both the imputability and the damage caused differ according to the form involved.

THE FORMS OF STATE RESPONSIBILITY
Since the illegal act can be either directly or indirectly illegal, and the claimant state can be injured either directly or indirectly, there are four forms of state responsibility.

Direct-direct claim
An example of a *direct-direct* claim would occur where agents of the defendant state cause damage to the property of the claimant state. Thus in the *Arbitration between Portugal and Germany* (1930), German troops attacked Portuguese colonial territory prior to Portugal's entry into the First World War. Portugal was awarded damages in respect of destruction of roads, damage to fortifications and loss of beasts of burden.

Direct-indirect claim
A *direct-indirect* claim would occur where agents of the defendant state injure a national of the claimant state. Thus in the *De Falcon Case* (United States–Mexico Claims Commission, 1926), Mexican soldiers shot and killed a United States national bathing in the Rio Grande because they thought, erroneously, that he was a smuggler. The Commission awarded damages against Mexico.

Indirect-direct claim
An *indirect-direct* claim would involve private individuals within the defendant state causing damage to the claimant state's agents or property, as, for example, where a rebellious mob attacks a foreign consulate and burns it to the ground.

Indirect-indirect claim
Finally, an *indirect-indirect* claim would occur where private individuals within the defendant state injure nationals of the claimant state. Thus in *Janes' Claim* (United States–Mexico Claims Commission, 1926) Janes, a United States citizen, was a mining engineer in Mexico. He was shot dead by C, a Mexican, in front of many witnesses. The police were informed but did nothing, although it was well known that C was at a ranch only six miles away for at least a week after the shooting. Only when the mining company offered a reward did the police take action. However, C was never apprehended. Damages were awarded against Mexico.

IMPUTABILITY

The state, not being a natural person, cannot itself act. Like all legal persons it can act only through others. A state can "act" through its organs, its officials or its agents. Before the actor can involve the state's responsibility, two questions have to be answered in the affirmative: can the act or omission of the organ, official or agent be considered, in the circumstances, *as if it were* the act of the state; and would this act be illegal in international law *if it had been* committed by the state? It is the first of these which poses the question of imputability; the second, that of responsibility.

The imputability of the acts of the organs, officials and agents of the state (referred to collectively as "state agents"), and of private individuals and revolutionary or insurgent bands, will now be considered in that order.

The acts of state agents

The rules given below, governing the imputability to the state of the acts of its agents, are not the same as those applicable in its municipal law.

The act of a state agent may be imputable to the state under international law although the act was *ultra vires,* and even though it is the exact opposite of the action ordered. Thus in *Youman's Claim* (United States–Mexico Claims Commission, 1926), Youman and other American citizens became involved in a riot in a Mexican town. The militia, summoned by the mayor to disperse the mob and protect the threatened Americans, instead joined with the mob and helped to bring about the death of the Americans. This action was imputed to Mexico which was found responsible.

Acts of the legislature, the judicature and the executive (or administration) are imputable to the state under the following circumstances.

The Legislature. Acts of the parliament, for example the enactment of legislation, are in all cases attributed to the state, any constitutional inability notwithstanding, for the state cannot shelter behind the inadequacy of its own law.

The Judicature. Acts of the courts and judges are imputable to the state where municipal law makes the attribution or where the court or judge was acting within the scope of apparent authority.

The Executive. Acts of the government are always imputable to the state, as are also the acts of individual ministers so far as they concern their own ministry. On the other hand, acts of the administration performed by state officials or agents are only imputable: where municipal law makes the attribution; where the official or agent was acting without authorisation but within the scope of his apparent authority; or where the performance of the act was made possible by means put at the disposal of the official by the state as in *Youman's Claim*. The last case is subject to exception where the lack of authority was so apparent that the person injured ought to have been able to realise this and avoid the damage.

In addition to the above, an act is imputable to the state wherever and whenever the state subsequently ratifies the unauthorised acts of its agents or nationals. Acts of state agents not imputable to the state are assimilated to the acts of private individuals.

The acts of private individuals
The acts of private persons within its territory are not imputable to the state, which can thus never be directly responsible for such acts.

State responsibility may, however, arise from the omission of the state's agents to react to such acts. It is then the omission which is imputed to the state. An omission to act can only be established if there is, in the circumstances, a duty to act. Thus the question of the imputability of the act to the state and the question whether that act involved a breach of an international obligation, become one and the same. This may be illustrated by considering the following examples.

(a) A rebellious mob attacks a foreign consulate and burns it to the ground. Every state has a duty within its territory to protect the rights of all other states. There is a special duty to protect those officials and agents of a foreign state that are permitted to enter the territory and perform there foreign public functions. The burning down of a consulate by a mob would constitute at least a *prima facie* case of an omission by the defendant state to provide effective protection, an omission which will be imputed to the state, and involve its international responsibility.

(b) *Janes' Claim*. When in the territory of a state one individual shoots and kills another, a killing or murder has been committed under municipal law. No illegality of any sort has been committed under international law. In the circumstances of Janes' claim, the subsequent conduct of the police amounted to a failure by the state to live up to its international duty of protection of aliens, an omission to act which was imputed to the state.

However, the converse of this is also true: where there is no duty to act, the acts of private persons never involve the state's responsibility. This applies not only within its own territory, but in respect of acts committed by its nationals acting in a private capacity within the territory of foreign states. A state has no duty to control such acts, since any attempt to do so would constitute, in the absence of prior consent, a breach of the territorial sovereignty of the other state. However, in the *Zafiro Case* (1925), it was held that acts of looting committed ashore by the crew of a naval vessel were to be treated as the acts of private individuals but that they nevertheless involved the responsibility of the state for failure to take effective preventative measures, in that the crew was permitted to go ashore uncontrolled in circumstances in which looting might have been foreseen!

The acts of revolutionaries and insurgents

The acts of revolutionary groups or insurgents may be distinguished from those of a mere mob by reference to the object of the use of violence. Only where this is directed at the overthrow of the existing government will the actors quality as revolutionaries or insurgents.

It is evident that an act aimed at the destruction of a government cannot be imputed to the state while it is internationally represented by that government. For this reason damage caused by insurgent bands does not involve the responsibility of the state, unless and until the government is overthrown; but should it be replaced by the insurgents, their acts are *retroactively imputed* to the state, which thereupon becomes responsible for the damage caused.

"DIRECT DAMAGE" TO STATE PROPERTY

Very few cases involving damage caused directly to the claimant state have been adjudicated before international tribunals. Cases involving injury to state agents or property which was caused within the territory of another state are normally the subject of direct diplomatic settlement. Nor is there any need to resort to the courts of the territorial state where the damage is caused by an act imputable to that state (*par in parem non habet imperium*). The small amount of property which a state owns abroad probably accounts for the dearth of cases involving damage caused to it by the acts of private individuals. It is likely, however, that, with the increasing intervention of the state in industrial, commercial and financial matters, this form of state responsibility may become more common.

Damage to a foreign state's property or injury to its agents within the territory of the defendant state will involve the responsibility of that state only where knowledge of the illegal act could be imputed to it. "Every state has a duty not to allow *knowingly* its territory to be used for acts contrary to the rights of other states." Yet, "it cannot be concluded from the mere fact of a state's control over its territory and waters that that state knew or ought to have known of any unlawful act perpetrated therein" (*Corfu Channel* (*Merits*)

Case (I.C.J., 1949)). In that case the court considered that the Albanian Government must, in the circumstances, be assumed to have had knowledge of the laying of mines by the agents of a foreign state within her territorial waters. Albania was thus held responsible, and ordered to make reparation for the damage to British public ships and for the cost to the United Kingdom of the pensions paid to the families of the sailors who had been killed.

NON-MATERIAL DAMAGE TO THE STATE

In the same case, the International Court of Justice upheld Albania's counter-claim that the re-entry of British vessels into her territorial waters to carry out a mine-sweeping operation constituted a violation of her territorial sovereignty; but state that "this declaration . . . constitutes in itself appropriate satisfaction."

In *The Carthage Case* (1913), France claimed, in addition to substantial damages for injuries to her nationals, 1 franc as non-material reparation for an offence to the French flag, and 100,000 francs as exemplary damages or "sanction" for political and *non-material* damage arising out of Italy's violations of her treaty obligations. The court said: "If a power should fail to fulfil its obligations . . . to award, constitutes in itself a serious sanction."

In the *"I'm Alone" Case* (Special Commission, 1935), however, the arbitrators recommended that $25,000 should be paid to Canada by the United States on account of the wrong done to her through the sinking of a vessel on the high seas which flew her flag, although neither the owners of the ship nor those of the cargo were Canadian nationals. This appears to be the only case in which material damages were awarded for non-material (or "moral") damage. The case can moreover, be distinguished in that it was not an award, but a mere recommendation.

INJURY TO A STATE'S NATIONALS ABROAD, OR "INDIRECT DAMAGE"

The vast majority of claims before international tribunals have concerned injury done to the nationals of the claimant state. Indeed, much of the nineteenth century theory and practice were not so much concerned with the law of state responsibility as with the diplomatic protection of aliens abroad.

The damage suffered by the state

Just as, in feudal times, the allegiance owed by a subject to his lord found its corollary in the lord's protection of his subject, so today a subject owes allegiance to his state wherever he may be, and the state correspondingly exerts a right of universal protection over its subject. The state exerts over its subject abroad a right of personal jurisdiction. Any lack of respect to, or improper treatment of a subject abroad by a foreign state is therefore *a violation of the personal sovereignty of the claimant state*. "By taking up the case of one of its subjects and resorting to diplomatic action or international judicial proceedings on his behalf, a state is in reality asserting its own rights, its right to ensure, in the person of its subjects, respect for the rules of international law (*Mavrommatis Palestine Concessions Case (Jurisdiction)* (P.C.I.J., 1924)). For this reason the dispute, which arose out of an alleged injury to a Greek national by the United Kingdom which held the mandate for Palestine, was held to be a dispute between two states. However,

"rights or interests of an individual the violation of which cause damage are always on a different plane to rights belonging to a state, which rights may also be infringed by the same act. The damage suffered by the individual is never therefore identical with that which will be suffered by a state; it can only afford a convenient scale for the calculation of the reparation due to the state" (*Chorzow Factory (Merits) Case* (P.C.I.J., 1928)).

In that case, the owners of the factory were pursuing a parallel claim before a special international tribunal to which private claimants had been given access by treaty.

The damage suffered by the individual
The type of damage for which a state may claim on behalf of its injured nationals includes virtually all rights and interests recognised in municipal law. It includes non-material as well as material damage. Thus in the *Janes' Claim* an award was made on behalf of the widow and children of Janes by taking into account the individual grief of the claimants, the indignity done to them by the non-punishment of the culprit, and the mistrust and lack of safety resulting from the Mexican Government's attitude of indifference to the outrage.

CASES INVOLVING BOTH DIRECT AND INDIRECT DAMAGE – "THE PREPONDERANT RULE"
In the *Interhandel Case* (I.C.J., 1959), Switzerland sought not only diplomatic protection for the owners of the company "Interhandel" but also a declaration from the court that the United States had a treaty obligation to submit to arbitration the question whether the company was owned by Swiss (neutral) or German (enemy) nationals, the assets of the company having been confiscated by an order

made under the Trading with the Enemy Act. The court considered that the satisfaction of the first claim (whether by pursuing a "local remedy before American Courts or by an international tribunal") would "remove the cause" for the other, both applications arising out of the same dispute.

It would seem that whenever in the same proceedings claims are made for damage suffered both by the state directly and also indirectly through its nationals, the court will be obliged to proceed only with that which is, in the circumstances, the preponderant claim.

ACTS INVOLVING THE RESPONSIBILITY OF THE STATE

The duty of protection

"Territorial sovereignty . . . involves the exclusive right to display the activities of a state. This right has as its corollary a duty; the duty to protect within the territory the rights of other states, together with the rights which each state may claim for its nationals in foreign territory" (Judge Huber, *Palmas Islands Arbitration*).

The government must therefore so organise its territory as to make it safe for those who are not members of the body politic to live therein. Failure to accord this protection in any particular case will involve the international responsibility of the state. This does not mean that there is no duty also to make it safe for its own nationals: on the contrary, this is the government's primary duty, but it is a purely national constitutional duty. As such it is outside the purview of international law which is concerned (the law of human rights apart) only with the situation of other international persons, and their nationals.

The distinction between acts directly, and indirectly, illegal in international law

Some acts causing damage to foreign nationals are directly illegal in international law: for example, any act in breach of a treaty obligation; or a law which discriminates against aliens or certain class of aliens; or a law expropriating property without compensation; or the act of a minister in annulling a government contract or concession with an alien in an arbitrary manner. However, in most cases in which foreign nationals are concerned, the breaches of international law which a state must rely upon in making a diplomatic claim are a failure of the municipal law or the municipal courts to comply with the international obligations of the state. The act causing damage to the individual is thus only indirectly illegal in international law.

The international minimum standard

The duty of protection requires that each state within its territory protects the lives, liberty and property of the nationals of every other state. The standard of protection offered is called the "international minimum standard" which may be described as a universal minimal municipal law. This may be, according to circumstances, a higher or a lower standard than the municipal law of the state in question. Moreover it is not just the standard of the law but the standard of its enforcement — the effective protection. It is of course only by resorting to the local law and its remedies that it can be discovered whether the minimum standard has been met, for a state is not expected to prevent damage happening to foreigners any more than it can prevent damage to its nationals. It is on the contrary expected to provide an effective civil remedy, and/or criminal sanction when such damage or injury occurs, and it is international law which defines what is "effective". Where it is not, the state is in breach of its international obligation of minimal protection of all foreign nationals. It follows that the argument that "foreigners are entitled to no better treatment than nationals" is misconceived.

Denial of justice

It is sometimes said that wherever there is a failure to live up to the international minimum standard there is a "denial of justice". An example of this may be seen in the quotation given below ("the Calvo Clause"). However, it seems better to reserve this term for a specific example of that failure (*see* below: Judicial acts).

Discriminatory acts always illegal

Any act of a state which on the face of it discriminates against aliens in general or the nationals of one state in particular and which thereby causes them damage, is contrary to international law.

Thus to deprive persons of Asian descent living in an African state of their licence to trade (and therefore of their livelihood) because they had exercised their option to retain a foreign nationality rather than acquire the nationality of the African state, appears to be discriminatory and is for that reason directly illegal in international law.

This general category apart, it is clearly not possible to list every example of an illegal act. Some of the main cases are given below (legislative, judicial and executive acts).

LEGISLATIVE ACTS

A state can incur international responsibility either "as the result of the enactment of legislation incompatible with its international obligations" or "of the non-enactment of legislation necessary for carrying out those obligations" (Hague Codification Conference,

1930), unless the obligation is carried out through some other means.

It is sometimes difficult to establish the moment at which the state's responsibility is engaged. Thus, in the *Phosphates in Morocco Case* (P.C.I.J., 1938), Italy alleged that France had infringed its treaty rights. The court found that "the situation which the Italian Government denounce[d] as unlawful [was] the legal position resulting from the legislation of 1920", not the subsequent acts of the Moroccan officials in application of that legislation.

Where, however, the claim arises out of injury to a national, the state's responsibility will arise only on the enforcement of the legislation. Thus in the *Mariposa Development Company* (General Claims Commission, 1933), Panama enacted legislation expropriating property without compensation. It was held that it was only the enforcement of that legislation against the foreign company which gave rise to the claim.

JUDICIAL ACTS

Although independent of the government the judiciary is not independent of the state and is as much a part of the latter for international purposes as is the executive. Judicial acts can accordingly give rise to international responsibility. This may arise "from a judicial decision which is not subject to appeal and which is clearly incompatible with the international obligations of the state" (Hague Codification Conference (1930)).

Denial of justice in the strict sense

Denial of justice means refusal by a state to give foreigners access to the national courts for the protection of their rights; unreasonable delay in the administration of justice (*Fabian Claim* (1896)); or refusal to implement a decision in favour of a foreign national.

In 1895, Brown, a United States national, attempted to secure an order from a court in the South African Republic recognising his title to mining rights in a certain area. His efforts were met by the resistance of both the Government and the Parliament. After two abortive judicial proceedings his claim for damages in the High Court was lost only after the Chief Justice had been dismissed by the President of the Republic and the court had been packed. As the arbitral tribunal said: "All three branches of the state conspired to ruin his enterprise. We are persuaded that . . . a definite denial of justice took place" (*Robert E. Brown Claim* (1923)).

Injustice

An "unjust" decision may involve the responsibility of the state if it is manifest, discriminatory, motivated by bad faith, or due to outside pressure.

Denial of fair hearing

"Manifest" denial of a fair hearing will involving the responsibility of the state. Advance information of the charge, time to prepare the case, and the services of a lawyer are the principal safeguards, although each case would have to be judged in the light of surrounding circumstances.

EXECUTIVE ACTS

Governmental or administrative acts will involve the state's responsibility in the following cases.

(a) When an alien is wrongfully arrested or detained.

(b) When it shows a lack of due diligence in protecting aliens (*Janes' Claim*).

(c) When an alien's property is deliberately destroyed or damaged, except in case of compelling necessity, or where justified by reasons of public order or health. Where property is destroyed as a military necessity in case of war, whether international or civil, the alien must suffer his loss with no greater expectation or recompense than a national of the territorial state (*Rosa Gelbtrunk's Claim* (1902)).

(d) When an alien's property is taken or he is deprived of its use or enjoyment, except where this is for a public purpose, in which case prompt payment should be made. Expropriation, or nationalisation of property, including the property of foreigners, is not in itself contrary to international law. A taking which is not discriminatory and for a public rather than a private purpose gives rise, in the case of a foreign national, to a right to compensation rather than to a right to damages. Where the property is taken in pursuance of an act of nationalisation of property, the measure of compensation demanded by international law is not the full market value, but a "fair value", striking a balance between the social and egalitarian purposes of the act of nationalisation, and the economic interests of the foreign national. Such compensation is only "fair" if it is "prompt, adequate and effective". The promptness of payment needs little comment, compensation being due as from the date of the taking, lateness of payment involving the duty to revise upward any amount due so as to preserve the value if in the meantime inflation has reduced the value of the currency. "Adequacy" has tended to be in practice something between 50 per cent and 70 per cent of value. In the case of shares in companies the value seems to be market value where there is a market, uninfluenced by government measures, and where government interference with the company has not been such as to influence the results in any significant respect; where there is no market, or where there has been significant government interference, then value of the assets must be compensated, due account being taken of future profitability. "Effective" compensation requires that the form in which the state issues compensation (in Government bonds for example), shall be such as to be freely convertible into cash, the word "freely" implying that the conversion is not to attract taxation.

(e) When it constitutes an arbitrary violation of a contract or concession between the government of the state, and an alien. A contract is normally governed solely by municipal law. This has not prevented international tribunals pronouncing upon the question whether there has been a breach of that law (*see the Serbian Loans issued in France* (P.C.I.J., 1929)). An arbitrary breach is one in which an organ of the state has interfered with the law governing or the very terms and effect of the contract to which it is itself a party, to its own benefit or the alien's loss. The issue of public bonds by a state and claims arising thereon by foreign nationals follow similar principles.

The Calvo Clause. In the nineteenth and early twentieth centuries it was a common practice for contracts granted by the governments of Central and South American states to foreign companies to contain a "Calvo Clause". That used in the leading case, the *North American Dredging Company of Texas Case* (1926) read as follows:

> "The contractor, and all persons . . . engaged in the execution of the work under this contract . . . , shall be considered as Mexican nationals in all matters . . . concerning . . . the fulfilment of this contract. They shall not . . . have . . . any other rights . . . than those granted by the laws of Mexico to Mexicans. . . . They are consequently deprived of any rights as aliens, and under no circumstances shall the intervention .of foreign diplomatic agents be permitted in any matter related to the contract."

The case-law has not been entirely consistent as to the effect of such clauses, but it is submitted that the position is the following: the clause is effective on the level of national law (first sentence) including the rules of conflict of laws so as to exclude the application of any other municipal law (second sentence); but ineffective on the level of public international law (first and third sentences). The right of diplomatic protection is the right of the state, not of the national who thus has no power to renounce it either in a contract or at all. As the tribunal said in that case, in upholding the validity of the clause:

> "this provision did not deprive the company of its undoubted right to apply to its own Government for protection if its resort

to Mexican tribunals ... resulted in a denial of justice.... In such a case the company's complaint would be not that the contract was violated but that it had been denied justice."

This, argued the tribunal, is not a "matter related to the contract". But the question whether the Calvo Clause can have any effect on the law of diplomatic protection is not one which depends upon the wording of the clause of the contract. A contract governed by municipal law can never, under any circumstances, have a direct effect on a rule of international law, for in the eyes of international law municipal laws and instruments made under them are purely facts.

ACTS OF PRIVATE INDIVIDUALS

The responsibility of the state can arise only from the acts or omissions of its own organs, officials or agents. Where acts of private individuals, whether singly or in groups, occasion damage to foreign nationals, responsibility can arise only from an omission of the state through its agents, to take "such measures as in the circumstances should normally have been taken to prevent, redress, or inflict punishment for the acts causing the damage."

But a state cannot be "the insurer of lives and property". In particular "it cannot be held responsible for the acts of rebellious bodies of men committed in violation of its authority where it is itself guilty of ... no negligence in suppressing insurrection" (*Home Missionary Society Case*, 1920). However, "if the state is not responsible for the insurrectionary activities themselves, it may nevertheless be responsible for the steps taken or not taken by its own authorities in seeking so far as possible to guard against their consequences" (*Spanish Zone of Morocco Claims* (1925)).

Responsibility will also be incurred if the connivance of the authorities can be established, or, it seems, if the outbreak of violence was directed against the nationals of a particular state, for in such a case the authorities ought to have been aware of the state of feeling and taken special measures to guard against it.

FACTORS EXCLUDING RESPONSIBILITY

Self-defence

A state may resort to force in self-defence against an illegal use of armed force, but not against other violations of law. Some writers consider that force can also be used in self-defence against "economic or ideological aggression".

United Nations sanctions

The United Nations is authorised to apply certain preventative or enforcement measures against states not acting in conformity with the provisions of the Charter. There will be no responsibility for resulting loss or damage.

Reprisals

A state is not responsible for loss or damage caused if it proves that it acted in circumstances justifying the exercise of reprisals. Reprisals can only be resorted to after redress has been unsuccessfully demanded; and they must be proportionate to the loss suffered by the injured state.

An act of reprisal is one which would, in other circumstances, be unlawful, but which is justified in the particular circumstances, since its object is to ensure respect by the delinquent state for the rule or rules of international law which the delinquent state has violated.

Necessity

It is sometimes alleged that a state does not incur responsibility when, out of necessity, it takes action to avert some grave or imminent danger to itself, and in so doing violates the rights of another state. In the *Corfu Channel (Merits) Case* (I.C.J., 1949) the court rejected this theory: "The alleged right of intervention cannot find a place in international law ... from the nature of things it would be reserved for the most powerful states and might easily lead to perverting the administration of international justice itself."

However, necessity may, for humanitarian reasons, justify an otherwise illegal act; for example, a foreign ship carrying provisions as cargo may be detained in port and its food cargo expropriated, if there is a famine in the country (*The Neptune* (1797)). In all such cases, however, adequate compensation must be paid.

Force majeure

Examples have occurred of illegal acts taking place in the territory of a state and causing loss or damage which was beyond the control of that state. It is a general principle of law that a state cannot incur responsibility for damage occurring independently of its will. To impute the damage to the state in such circumstances would be to replace the concept of responsibility by that of absolute liability.

REPARATION

The nature and extent of reparation

"Reparation must so far as possible wipe out all the consequences of the illegal act and re-establish the situation which would, in all probability, have existed if that act had not been committed" (*Chorzow Factory (Merits) Case* (P.C.I.J., 1928)).

Reparation may consist of restitution, indemnity or satisfaction.

Restitution (restitutio in integrum)

Restitution in kind is designed to re-establish the situation which would have existed if the act had not taken place. It is the normal form of reparation, indemnity or satisfaction only taking its place if restitution in kind is not possible.

Restitution may be materially or legally impossible. In federal states, for example, the central government may be powerless to revoke an illegal act of one of the federal states; or the illegal act may be the result of a judicial decision which cannot be revoked.

Examples of restitution are the redistribution of unlawfully collected taxes, and the annulment of obligations arising out of court decisions.

Indemnity

Indemnity is compensation measured in money terms. It requires "payment of a sum corresponding to the value which a restitution in kind would bear." An indemnity may consist of the following:

(*a*) Replacement cost at the time of the decision, even if this would be higher than its value at the time of the illegal act. "The [unlawful] dispossession of an industrial undertaking ... involves the obligation to restore it, and, if this is not possible, to pay its value at the time of the indemnification, which value is designed to take the place of restitution which has become impossible" (*Chorzow Factory (Merits) Case* (P.C.I.J., 1928)).

(*b*) Indirect damages, so long as these are in a direct chain of causality with the illegal act, unless the conduct of the victim was such as to exacerbate the damage (*Arbitration between Portugal and Germany* (1930)).

(*c*) Lost profits, so long as the profit would have been possible in the normal development of the undertaking. In the *Chorzow Factory (Merits) Case* the Permanent Court of International Justice took into account the loss of profits to be anticipated in the normal development of the undertaking.

(*d*) The payment of interest-damages whether in compensation for the loss of the use of the sum due during the period within which payment is withheld, or for the injury suffered by the creditor (*Russian Indemnity Case* (1912)).

Satisfaction

This form of reparation is appropriate only in cases on non-material damage or moral injury to the personality of the state. The presentation of official regrets, punishment of guilty officials and the formal acknowledgment of the unlawful character of the act, are in modern times the more usual forms of satisfaction.

In the *Corfu Channel (Merits) Case* (I.C.J., 1949) the court stated that "the action of the British Navy [in entering Albanian territorial waters without permission] constituted a violation of Albanian sovereignty. This declaration is in accordance with the request made by Albania through her counsel, and is in itself appropriate satisfaction."

PROCEDURE

The international claim
The procedure by which the injured state presents its claim for reparation differs according to whether the damage was suffered by it directly or indirectly. Where the state suffers damage directly, either through injury to a state agent or official, or through damage to state property, the claim may be served immediately through the diplomatic channel on the delinquent state. Where the state suffers damage indirectly through injury to its nationals or their property certain preliminary conditions need to be fulfilled.

The rule of nationality of claims
For a state to prove that it has been injured through injury to a private person or his property, some connection must be established between the individual and the state. This "connecting link" is, generally speaking, the possession by the individual of the nationality of the injured state.

This rule is, however, subject both to qualifications and to exceptions.

Qualifications to the rule of nationality of claims
Possession of bare nationality is not enough: there must be a genuine link, a "real and effective" nationality. Such a rule applies to all persons who acquired nationality by naturalisation. The reason is that such an acquisition, which is an act of will on the part of the individual, may be obtained either for genuine or for improper motives. A genuine motive for acquiring the nationality of a state would include a feeling that the state in question was the motherland or fatherland, the state with which the person had the closest and most intimate connection. As the court said in the *Nottebohm Case* (I.C.J., 1955), "the habitual residence of the individual, the centre of his interests, his participation in public life, attachment shown to a certain country and inculcated in his children" — all these are signs that the motive for seeking naturalisation was genuine,

and that the resulting nationality was "real and effective" for the purpose of that state's acquiring the capacity to protect him in international law.

However, nationality acquired by birth, according to the principle either of the *jus soli* or the *jus sanguinis* is sufficient in itself to give the state a title to protection.

In rare cases, something short of nationality has been considered sufficient. Thus in the *Koszta Case* (1853) the Austrian Government acquiesced in the claim of the United States to protect the Magyar rebel leader on the ground that he was a "declarant alien", an immigrant foreign national who had filed preliminary notice of intention to apply for naturalisation. In *Falla-Nataf* v. *Germany* (Franco–German Mixed Arbitral Tribunal, 1927), the tribunal held that the term "ressortisant" included a French protégé who was not a French national.

Although the grant of nationality is within the *domaine réservé* of states, proof that a claimant under a treaty provision has the nationality of a particular state must be sufficiently clear to satisfy the tribunal: the mere assurance of the authorities of the state in question is not enough. Failure to prove this point will deprive the state of its right to protect the national under the treaty provision in question (*Flegenheimer Case* (U.S.A.–Italy Mixed Claims Commission, 1958)).

Exceptions to the rule of nationality of claims

A state may not protect a national against another state of which he is also a national.

The nationality of a merchant vessel invests the state of the nationality with power to protect the interests of the owners of the ship and of the cargo whatever their nationality (*The Wimbledon* (P.C.I.J., 1923)).

That a corporation has the nationality of a state is not the sole ground for presenting a claim for protection. In the *Agency of Canadian Car and Foundry Company Case* (American–German Mixed Claims Commission, 1939) a Canadian-owned firm was protected by the United States on the ground that it was incorporated in the United States, it employed American labour, and that it traded in the United States. Where the nationality of a corporation is acquired by mere incorporation, a substantial share-holding vested in nationals has been required to justify a state protecting its "national". In such cases, however, the state may also protect the non-national section of the shareholders.

The person on whose behalf the state is intervening must have possessed that nationality from the time of the injury until the moment of the judgment, or perhaps only until the moment of institution of proceedings. Where the individual possesses the nationality of state A at the time of injury, but of state B at the moment of the institution of proceedings, state practice permits and pursues claims jointly presented by states A and B.

The exhaustion of local remedies

Where an act is committed against the nationals of another state which involves the direct responsibility of the delinquent state, no claim can be presented on the international level until a local remedy has been sought. A "local" remedy, as the name implies, is one obtainable under the law of the locality where the act was committed. This law is national rather than international.

That local remedies be "exhausted" means that a failed claim before a lower court must be followed by an appeal to a higher court; that administrative procedures be engaged; that a petition for clemency be presented if it could be shown that there was a reasonable hope of it being successful. Any "remedy" whatsoever, whether ordinary or extraordinary, must be tried and exhausted before a successful international claim can be presented. However, the reverse of this also applies: no procedure need be pursued which evidently would not provide a "remedy" for the wrong committed. Thus, recourse to the courts is clearly not a remedy if the illegal act is incorporated in a law framed in unambiguous terms which is binding on the courts.

A state is not expected to exercise such a degree of care and control over those who act in its name or with its authority, that no acts directly engaging its international responsibility are ever committed. It is expected, however, to provide an adequate remedy for persons injured by such illegal acts. That this remedy is of municipal law, while the act complained of was illegal under international law, is of no importance, since the concept of responsibility merely requires that the harm done shall be repaired! The justification for the rule is merely that the alleged wrongdoer must first be given a chance to put the matter right before resort is had to the international judicial process.

Extent of the local remedies rule

The local remedies rule applies only to the state injured indirectly through its nationals. Where the state is damaged directly, either through injury to one of its agents or officials or to state property, the rule does not apply; nor does the rule apply where the act which forms the basis of the claim to responsibility is only indirectly unlawful. In these cases it is the absence of any remedy which constitutes the act for which the state is internationally liable. For the local remedies rule to apply there must already be, on the level of international law, something to "remedy". The local law might or might not provide such a remedy: if it does not do so, the claim may proceed before an international tribunal.

The rule applies only where the injured national has by some voluntary act established a connection with the foreign state whose legal remedies are to be resorted to. Thus injury to its nationals on its own territory dispenses the claimant state and the persons involved from resorting to any "local" tribunals; a civilian aircraft shot down while flying over the territory of a foreign state would not involve the occupants or their heirs resorting to the courts of the territory in question (*Aerial Incident of 27 July 1955, Israel* v. *Bulgaria* (I.C.J. pleadings, 1959)). Ships voluntarily seeking port in a state would, however, be enough to establish the connection (*Ambatielos Claim* (Award of the Commission of Arbitration, 1956)).

III. RESPONSIBILITY OF INTERNATIONAL ORGANISATIONS

THE CAPACITY OF AN INTERNATIONAL ORGANISATION TO PRESENT A CLAIM

Any international organisation which has some measure of international personality and is consequently capable of possessing international rights and duties, will have the capacity to maintain those rights by bringing international claims. This capacity may be exercised whenever necessitated by the discharge of its functions. Whether such claims may be brought against a non-member state would appear to depend upon the objective or subjective nature of this international personality. The United Nations, at any rate, may pursue such claims against non-member states. Thus in the *Reparations for Injuries suffered in the Service of the United Nations Case* (I.C.J., 1949) the court advised that the United Nations could pursue a claim against Israel, before the latter had become a member of the United Nations, in respect of the killing by terrorists of certain members of the Peace Keeping Force within that territory.

CLAIMS AGAINST INTERNATIONAL ORGANISATIONS

It is not possible to answer with certainty the question whether a claim may be brought by a state against an international organisation. Should a state decide, for example, to present a claim on behalf of one of its nationals against an international organisation on the ground of his wrongful dismissal, it would seem in principle that the state must be considered to have the *capacity* to present such a claim, although there may well be a good defence. The need for the official first to pursue the claim before the appropriate administrative tribunal set up by the organisation would be an application of the requirement of exhaustion of local remedies.

In the *Effect of Awards made by the United Nations Administrative Tribunal* (I.C.J., 1954) the court advised that the General Assembly, as an organ of the United Nations, was obliged to give effect to such an award which gave substantial compensation to certain officials, who were United States Nationals, on the ground of their unjust dismissal.

THE NATURE OF THE PROTECTION AFFORDED BY AN INTERNATIONAL ORGANISATION

An international organisation, like a state, can present a claim in respect of an injury suffered by itself. But an international organisation may, according to circumstances, also present a claim in respect of damage caused to its officials or agents or to persons claiming through them. The basis of this claim is the need to provide *functional protection*. Functional protection differs from diplomatic protection in that it does not depend upon the link of nationality; it depends solely upon the establishment of a functional link between the victim and the organisation. Where the victim has a nationality, the claim of the state of his nationality is not barred solely by reason of the exercise by an organisation of a claim to exercise functional protection. Both claims continue to subsist: however, it may be doubted whether the defendant state would be condemned in damages twice over in respect of the same international delinquency. The claim of the state of the nationality would have to overcome the defence that the victim was not admitted into the territory of the defendant state in his capacity as a private individual of the state of his nationality.

REPARATION AND THE MEASURE OF DAMAGES

It is thought that the rules on these questions would be similiar to those in cases of state responsibility.

CHAPTER TWELVE

Pacific Settlement of Disputes

Once a dispute has arisen, there are only two methods by which it may be settled: force and reason. The progress of a legal system may be measured by the extent that reason is substituted for force in the settlement of disputes. The "pacific" settlement of disputes has therefore been a constant and abiding preoccupation of the system of international law and of those required to work within its limitations. "Pacific" in this context means settlement without resort to force or threat of force. Before "war" was outlawed (the Pact of Paris, or Kellog-Briand Pact of 1928) and before Article 2(4) of the Charter of the United Nations required all members "to refrain . . . from the threat or use of force" in their international relations, states were, consistently with the requirements of international law, presented with a choice for the settlement of their international disputes — pacific settlement, or settlement through force.

Today, Article 33 of the Charter of the United Nations lays down a new rule: the parties to any dispute, the continuance of which is likely to endanger the maintenance of international peace and security, shall, *first of all*, seek a solution by peaceful means. The Security Council shall, when it deems necessary, call upon the parties to settle their dispute by such means. Article 37 provides that should the parties to such a dispute fail to settle it by the means indicated in Article 33, they shall refer it to the Security Council. If the Security Council deems that the continuance of the dispute is in fact likely to endanger the maintenance of international peace and security, it shall decide whether to take action under Article 36 or to recommend such terms of settlement as it deems appropriate. (Article 36 states that the Security Council may, at any stage of a dispute of the nature referred to in Article 33, recommend appropriate procedures or methods of settlement.)

This new rule applies not only to the members of the United Nations, but to *all* parties to a dispute "the continuance of which is likely to endanger international peace and security." It should be recalled that Article 2(6) requires "The organisation [to] ensure that states which are not members of the United Nations act in accordance with these principles [the 'principles' set out in the five previous sub-paragraphs of Article 2] so far as may be necessary for the maintenance of international peace and security." That is why, in addition to the obligations laid on the parties to the dispute, it is also provided by Article 34 that the Security Council "may investigate any dispute . . . in order to determine whether [its] continuance is likely to endanger the maintenance of [such] peace and security."

While a member of the United Nations "may bring any dispute . . . to the attention of the Security Council" (Article 35(1)) whether or not it is a party thereto, "a state which is not a member . . . may bring to the attention of the Security Council . . . any dispute to which it is a party if it accepts in advance, for the purposes of the dispute, the obligations of pacific settlement provided in the present Charter" (Article 35(2)).

There are thus two categories of dispute; those the continuance of which is likely to endanger international peace and security, and those whose continuance is not. It is open to either of the parties, or to the Security Council, to consider a dispute to be of the first category.

I. INTERNATIONAL DISPUTES

SITUATIONS AND DISPUTES

Situations which might lead to international friction or give rise to a dispute (Article 34) are to be distinguished from disputes. To be a dispute, a situation must have crystallised into a "disagreement on a point of law or fact, a conflict of legal views or interests between *two persons*" (author's italics). This definition occurred in the *Mavrommatis Palestine Concessions Case (Jurisdiction)* (P.C.I.J., 1924), in which the Greek Government demanded compensation for the loss caused to Mr Mavrommatis, a Greek national, arising out of the fact that the Government of Palestine, of which the mandatory power was the United Kingdom, had rendered further exploitation of his concessions impossible. The United Kingdom challenged the jurisdiction of the court on the ground that the conditions set out in Article 26 of the mandate had not been observed. The relevant part of Article 26 reads as follows: "The mandatory agrees that, if any dispute whatever should arise between the mandatory and another member of the League of Nations relating to . . . the mandate, such dispute, if it cannot be settled by negotiation, shall be submitted to the P.C.I.J."

The United Kingdom argued that there was no dispute or that, if there was one, it was between the Government of Palestine and Mr Mavrommatis. The court said: "It is true that the dispute was at first between a private person and a state. . . . Subsequently, the Greek Government took up the case. The dispute then entered upon a new phase; it entered the domain of international law, and became a dispute between two states." This case also serves therefore to illustrate the difference between disputes which are within the domain of international law and those that are not.

POLITICAL AND LEGAL DISPUTES

Reason, as applied to the settlement of disputes, may take a political or a legal form. In the context of international disputes the pacific settlement of disputes through political means takes place through "diplomacy". Disputes are frequently categorised as "political" or "legal", depending on whether they appear to be more amenable to political or to legal settlement. However, since the same dispute may, at various stages of evolution, pass from one mode of settlement to the other with no change of its basic character, it must not be thought that some disputes are by their very nature political, and others legal. All that is needed to convert a political into a legal dispute is a change of heart, or of interests, by the parties to it. Conversely, a dispute which could easily be settled by legal means may remain unsettled and "political", because one of the parties refuses to submit to arbitration or judicial settlement. From this it may be concluded that whether a dispute is to be categorised as legal or political depends on the attitude the parties take to it at the time.

On the other hand, since the principal concern of international law is the maintenance of peace, it contains procedures capable of settling any dispute at any time, whether classified as legal or political. We shall deal first with diplomatic and then with judicial modes of settlement.

II. DIPLOMATIC SETTLEMENT

NEGOTIATION

The simplest and most direct form of diplomatic action designed to settle a dispute is negotiation between the parties. Unlike all other diplomatic modes of settlement, no third party is involved, negotiation being restricted to the protagonists, the "parties" to the dispute.

Whether or not it is provided, as in Article 26 of the Palestine mandate quoted above, that it is only disputes which cannot be settled by negotiation that are to be submitted to judicial settlement, such a proviso obviously applies in practice, if only for the reason that "before a dispute can be made the subject of an action at law, its subject matter should have been clearly defined by means of diplomatic negotiations" (*Mavrommatis Palestine Concessions Case (Jurisdiction)* (P.C.I.J., 1924)). In the case of disputes likely to endanger peace, the parties are, under Article 33 of the Charter, under a duty to attempt to settle it by negotiation.

GOOD OFFICES AND MEDIATION
Unlike negotiations, good offices and mediation involve the intrusion of a third party. This may be a state, a group of states, or even (if permitted by treaty) a private citizen.

Good offices
A third party offers his good offices when the object of his intervention is to induce both parties to open negotiations. Such offers are not generally made public, so that it is difficult to be certain about recent diplomatic episodes. It is probable that the negotiations opened in Paris between North Vietnam and the United States were brought about through the good offices of France. One well established example is the successful intervention in 1906 by the President of the United States, leading to the opening of the negotiations by which the 1904 war between Russia and Japan was brought to an end.

Mediation
A third party opens negotiations with each of the parties to the dispute separately, with the object of getting each of them to agree to his final proposals. The mediator's task is "to reconcile the opposing claims and appease the feelings of resentment which may have arisen between the parties." His functions are at an end "as soon as one of the parties to the dispute declares, or the mediator himself realises, that the terms of his proposed settlement are not acceptable." The mediator may be either a state or an individual. There have been several recent examples of mediators appointed to mediate between Israel and the neighbouring Arab states.

Much of the law governing these two topics is set out in The Hague Convention No. I of 1899, as amended by the text of 1907. The official title of this is the "Convention pour le Réglement Pacifique des Conflits Internationaux" concluded at The Hague on 29th July 1899 (the text is in French only). The two quotations given in the previous paragraph are from Articles 4 and 5. Article 6 states that: "Good offices and mediation are exclusively concerned with the giving of advice and are never of binding force."

According to Article 3, states "not involved in the dispute have the right to offer good offices and mediation, even during hostilities . . . the exercise of the right can [thus] never be regarded as an unfriendly act." However, "acceptance of mediation shall not have the effect of interrupting . . . measures preparatory to war, or if accepted after the opening of hostilities, military operations in progress, unless it shall be otherwise agreed between the parties to the dispute" (Article 7).

These rules may be regarded as part of customary law. In addition, for the parties to The Hague Convention No. I (by 1st January 1971 sixty-four states were party to this treaty), there is the treaty obligation "in case of . . . dispute, to have recourse, as far as circumstances permit, to the good offices or mediation of one or more friendly powers, before resorting to arms" — an obligation which must now be read in the light of the Charter of the United Nations.

ENQUIRY

The contracting parties to The Hague Convention No. I also deemed it "expedient and desirable, . . . in the case of international disputes involving neither the honour nor the vital interests of the parties and which arose out of a difference of opinion on matters of fact, that the parties should . . . institute an International Commission of Enquiry . . . to elucidate the facts by means of an impartial and conscientious investigation" (Article 9). They are to be constituted by special agreement between the parties to the dispute (Article 10). The 1907 text contains twenty-five articles on the object, composition and procedure and costs of commissions.

In the *Dogger Bank Incident* (1904), Russian naval vessels opened fire on British fishing boats, believing, as it was alleged, that they were Japanese torpedo boats (Japan then being at war with Russia). An International Enquiry Commission was formed pursuant to The Hague Convention No. I, and its report contributed to the settlement of the dispute. In that case, the commission was asked, in addition to its investigation into the facts, to state where responsibility lay and the degree of blame attaching to the individuals concerned.

The Security Council (by Article 36(1)) and the General Assembly (by Articles 10, 11 and 14) are empowered to recommend acceptance by the parties or themselves to establish International Enquiry Commissions as a basis on which to recommend appropriate methods of settlement. The members of the commissions are in principle individuals, not representatives of states.

CONCILIATION

The law concerning conciliation is still very largely that set out in Chapter 1 of the treaty entitled "Pacific Settlement of International Disputes (General Act)", signed in Geneva on 26th September 1928. As stated by Article 15 "the task of the Conciliation Commission shall be to elucidate the questions in dispute, to collect . . . all necessary information by means of enquiry or otherwise, and to endeavour to bring the parties to an agreement."

The parties (on 1st January 1981, twenty-two states were parties to this treaty) undertook to submit "disputes of every kind . . . which it has not been possible to settle by diplomacy" to the procedure of conciliation. This obligation was, however, subject to any or all of the following reservations: that it should not apply to disputes arising out of facts prior to the accession of the parties; nor to disputes concerning questions which by international law are solely within the domestic jurisdiction of states; to disputes concerning particular cases, or clearly specified subject-matters, such as territorial status, or clearly defined catgeories (Article 39).

Conciliation commissions consisting of five persons, one appointed by each of the parties to the dispute, the three others appointed by agreement from amongst the nationals of third powers, were to be set up either permanently, or as a case arose. Their proceedings were not to be conducted in public (unless so decided with the consent of the parties) and were to be terminated within six months. At the close of the proceedings, the commission was to draw up a procès-verbal stating either that the parties had come to an agreement or that it had been impossible to effect a settlement.

Conciliation is most appropriate in the case of disputes of a mixed nature, containing both legal and political elements. It is impartial, discrete, rapid and informal.

The Security Council and the General Assembly both have power to constitute conciliation commissions. The General Assembly established by Resolution 268 (III) of 28th April 1949 a panel of persons considered suitable for selection by the parties as members of enquiry or conciliation commissions.

III. JUDICIAL SETTLEMENT

ARBITRATION

Arbitration differs from conciliation, enquiry and mediation in that that "award" of the arbitrator is final and binding on the parties to the dispute. An arbitration award has the force of *res judicata*. In this essential respect arbitration resembles judicial settlement.

Arbitration differs from judicial settlement in that the parties to an arbitration are left free to choose the members of the tribunal, to define the dispute, and, if they so agree, to lay down in advance the rules, principles or legal system that shall be applied. A party may withdraw from an arbitration at any stage, even during the course of the hearings, unless there is a treaty obligation to a contrary effect.

Arbitral tribunal

The person or persons appointed to arbitrate are required to perform a judicial function, and this quite irrespective of the means chosen to arrive at their award (*see* below: Law to be applied). The rules of natural justice apply, that is to say that both parties must be given an adequate, and equal, opportunity to present their case. The arbitrator must decide impartially "on the basis of respect for law" (Article 37 of The Hague Convention No. I). This phrase should not be taken to mean "on the basis of law" but on the basis of respect for law, or, more accurately, respect for the judicial nature of the arbitral process.

An arbitrator fulfils the role of a judge, and it is for this reason that the institution is known as an arbitral "tribunal" (as distinct, for example, from a conciliation "commission"). Moreover, it is only on this basis that the parties agree to accept the award as binding (*see* below: Nullity of the award).

The tribunal may consist of: a sole arbitrator, as, for example, Judge Huber in the *Palmas Island Arbitration* (1928) — one of the most celebrated judicial pronouncements in international law; a mixed commission, constituted on a basis of parity, with provision for reference to an umpire in the event of disagreement (the arbitrations under the Jay Treaty between the United Kingdom and the United States are the earliest modern arbitrations); or a collegiate body, with the parties each naming one or more members and other friendly states nominating other members (e.g. the *Alabama Arbitration* of 1872, perhaps the most important arbitration ever to take place).

The obligation to go to arbitration

By customary international law "no state can . . . be compelled to submit its disputes with other States to mediation or to arbitration, or to any other kind of pacific settlement." This statement in the *Eastern Carelia Case* (P.C.I.J., 1923) is still valid. However, a state may undertake to submit to arbitration by treaty. The obligation may apply to existing or to future disputes; to specific cases or to general categories.

"Compromis"

States undertake to submit existing disputes to arbitration by means of a "special agreement", generally referred to as a *"compromis"*. Moreover, a substantial proportion of the numerous bilateral treaties providing for the submission of future disputes to arbitration condition this obligation upon the conclusion of a *compromis* once a dispute has arisen between them. In this way states preserve their freedom of action to fashion the arbitration to the exact shape found suitable to the dispute which has materialised. As stated above, this is one of the essential respects in which arbitration is distinguishable from judicial settlement.

Law to be applied

The only rule is that the tribunal applies whatever it is instructed to apply in the *compromis*. Only if there is no instruction will it apply public international law. In the *Alabama Arbitration* (1872) the parties set out in the *compromis* the three rules of warfare at sea in relation to neutral vessels in the light of which the tribunal was to give its award.

Arbitral procedures

The Hague rules (*see* below) provide that the arbitration is to take place on the basis of a *compromis* in which the parties define the object of the litigation, the mode of nomination of the arbitrators, any special powers and generally any conditions as to which the parties may be agreed. For the rest, the rules do not materially differ from those applicable to a case of judicial settlement, except that the deliberations of the tribunal take place in private. Decisions are taken by a majority of the members.

The award

The award decides the matter in issue "finally and without appeal". It is binding on the parties to the dispute, but on no one else.

Revision of the award

As the object of the arbitration is to settle disputes, no appeal is allowed from the award of the arbitrator. On the other hand,

> "the parties can reserve in the *compromis* the right to demand the revision of the award. In this case, and unless there be a stipulation to the contrary, the demand must be addressed to the tribunal which pronounced the award. It can only be made on the ground of the discovery of some new fact calculated to exercise a decisive influence upon the award and which was unknown to the tribunal and to the party which demanded the revision at the time the discussion was closed" (Article 83 of the 1907 text).

An example of revision occurred in the *Schreck Case* (United States–Mexico Mixed Claims Commission, 1874), in the first hearing of which the umpire acted on the mistaken belief that Mexican nationality law was based on the *jus soli*. Since questions of municipal law before international tribunals are treated as questions of fact, the award was revised after a rehearing by the umpire.

Nullity of the award
The rule that an arbitral award "settles the dispute definitely and without appeal" (Article 81 of the 1907 text) rests on three assumptions: that the instructions in the *compromis* are carried out; that the arbitrators exercise a properly judicial function; and that the award gives the reasons on which it is based. An unreasoned award is a nullity: so is one where fraud, corruption or partiality is proved in the umpire or in one of the arbitrators; so too is an award which decides a question not submitted or decides the questions submitted but not in the way the umpire was asked to decide them. An example of the last type of nullity is provided by the *Orinoco Steamship Company Case* (United States–Venezuela Mixed Claims Commission, 1903). In 1903, umpire Barge decided a claim made by the United States against Venezuela. The umpire granted $28,000 to the United States out of the sum of $1,400,000 claimed. In 1909, a treaty between the two states made provision for a new arbitration which "shall first decide whether the decision of umpire Barge in this case, in view of all the circumstances and under the principles of international law, is not void." The tribunal decided that "in view of the express provision of the [*compromis* of 1903] that the Umpire was to decide according to absolute equity and without regard to objections of a technical nature or the provisions of local jurisdiction, Umpire Barge exceeded his jurisdiction in rejecting . . . certain of the claims . . . for technical reasons." The tribunal said "excessive exercise of power may consist not only in deciding a question not submitted to the arbitrators, but also in misinterpreting the express provisions of the [*compromis*] in respect of the way in which they are to reach their decisions."

Suitability of arbitration for the settlement of disputes which have already arisen
State practice and the history of arbitral awards make it clear that arbitration is most suitably used in relation to existing disputes: obligations in regard to future disputes are most suitably directed towards judicial settlement. It is significant that the earliest, and the most recent, examples of the use of arbitration were in respect of claims, or whole series of claims, based on facts and events which

had already taken place. The two major attempts by treaty to stimulate arbitration for the settlement of future disputes arose before the institution of a permanent international court (the Permanent Court of International Justice was established in 1932) and have in practice ceased to operate with the advent of such a court. A brief description will, however, be given of these attempts since both treaties are still in force.

The Hague Convention No. I (1899 and 1907). Part IV of this convention is devoted to international arbitration. It is divided into chapters concerned with arbitral justice, the Permanent Court of Arbitration, arbitral procedure and, in the 1907 text, summary arbitral procedure. Of the first chapter, the following provisions are worth setting out since they describe and reflect the law of arbitration in general.

> "The object of international arbitration is the settlement of disputes between states by judges of their choice and on the basis of respect for law."
> "Recourse to arbitration implies the undertaking to submit in good faith to the award."

Permanent Court of Arbitration. The First Peace Conference of 1899 agreed to set up a permanent court of arbitration (the P.C.A.) which would be competent with respect to all cases of arbitration not submitted by special agreement between the parties to any other judicial body. The "court" was in fact merely a panel of persons, each contracting party naming four. From this panel the parties to a dispute could each choose two arbitrators, who would themselves choose the fifth, the whole comprising a "tribunal" for the settlement of the dispute. A permanent international bureau was established at the Hague to serve the court and for general administrative purposes, and the whole was to be supervised by an administrative council consisting of the ambassadors accredited to the Netherlands under the presidency of the Dutch Minister of Foreign Affairs. The court gave its first award in 1902 and its last (the twentieth) in 1932. The complete list is given in *Oppenheim's International Law*, seventh edition, Vol. 2 at p. 40.

By the time the Second Peace Conference had amended The Hague Convention No. I, in 1907, the P.C.A. was already functioning. Experience had shown the need to make provision for a summary arbitral procedure. Moreover, the rules for arbitral procedure were expanded to fill no less than thirty-four articles. They were to apply to all cases of arbitration unless the parties agreed otherwise.

In the General Act of 1928 (and in the European Convention for the Peaceful Settlement of Disputes of 1957) a quite different role was given to arbitration.

The General Act (1928). This convention set out rules to apply both to arbitration and to judicial settlement. The parties were expected to have recourse to the latter in the case of "disputes as to their respective rights", one of the better formulations of the concept of so-called "legal disputes". Only in relation to other disputes, presumably "disputes as to their respective interests", were they recommended to have recourse to arbitration. Since, clearly, one cannot ask an arbitral tribunal to apply law of any sort to settle a conflict of interests which are not grounded in rights, the plenipotentiaries instructed the arbitrators to decide cases *ex aequo et bono*. These provisions have never been acted upon.

JUDICIAL SETTLEMENT

In the context of international disputes "judicial settlement" differs from arbitration in two principal respects: it requires submission of the dispute to an existing court of justice, the judges of which are elected and known in advance; and it requires the application to the dispute of international law. So far as the second of these propositions is concerned, Article 38 of the Statute of the International Court of Justice poses something of a dilemma, for although paragraph 1 appears to confirm it ("The court, whose function is to decide in accordance with international law such disputes as are submitted to it . . ."), paragraph 2 does not, for it reads as follows: "This provision [i.e. paragraph 1] shall not prejudice the power of the court to decide a case *ex aequo et bono*, if the parties agree thereto."

It has been said of this provision (*Oppenheim's International Law*, seventh edition, Vol. 2, p. 69) that the International Court of Justice "while predominantly a Court of Justice . . . [is] not precluded from acting in a less rigid capacity if the parties choose so to authorise it." For the overriding function of the court is to settle disputes between states rather than to serve as a vehicle for the application of international law. In fact, to date, the court has had no occasion to decide a case *ex aequo et bono*.

Establishment of the International Court of Justice

A so-called "Permanent Court of International Justice" was set up, after approval by the Assembly by the League of Nations, in 1920. The statute became binding on members only as the result of ratification of the protocol of signature of the statute, of 16th December 1920. The court was dissolved in April 1946. In its place was established the "International Court of Justice", which is one of the six "principal organs" of the United Nations and is "the principal judicial organ". The statute of the court, annexed to the Charter, is, according to Article 92, "an integral part" thereof.

Accordingly all members of the United Nations are *ipso facto* parties to the statute (Article 93(1)). In addition, "States which are not members of the United Nations may become a party to the Statute . . . on conditions to be determined . . . by the General Assembly." The principal condition is acceptance of the obligations in Article 94, of which paragraph 1 requires the giving of an undertaking "to comply with the decision of the International Court of Justice in any case to which it is a party"; and paragraph 2, that should any party fail to do so "the other party may have recourse to the Security Council, which may, if it deems necessary, . . . decide upon measures . . . to give effect to the judgment."

Access to the International Court of Justice
"Only states may be parties in cases before the court" (Article 34(1) of the statute). The court is "open to the states parties to the . . . statute" (Article 35(1)).

Jurisdiction
To be a party to the statute is not sufficient to endow the court with jurisdiction over a specific dispute, for the jurisdiction of the court comprises only the "cases which the parties refer to it and all matters specially provided for . . . in treaties and conventions in force" (Article 36(1)). By Article 37, the latter phrase is deemed to include treaties and conventions conferring jurisdiction upon the Permanent Court of International Justice.

However, by a separate and additional declaration states may also declare that they recognise *ipso facto* and without special agreement, in relation to any other state accepting the same obligation, the jurisdiction of the court in all or any of the following classes of legal disputes:

(a) the interpretation of a treaty;

(b) any question of international law;

(c) the existence of any fact which, if established, would constitute a breach of an international obligation; or

(d) the nature and extent of the reparation to be made for the breach of an international obligation.

Acceptance of this "Optional Clause" is therefore on a basis of complete reciprocity. It follows that where the declaration of acceptance is made with reservations, the other party may enforce that reservation against the party making it.

Compulsory jurisdiction
In practice the states which have made the declaration have hedged it around with such strict reservations as to have reduced to a minimum the potentiality offered to the international community by

this provision. The most infamous is the so-called "Connally" reservation which forms part of the current declaration of the United States, and which excludes "disputes with regard to matters which are essentially within the domestic jurisdiction of the United States of America as determined by the United States of America."

Advisory opinions

The court may also give advisory opinions on any legal question. The bodies authorised to request an advisory opinion are the Security Council and the General Assembly at any time and on "any legal question" (Article 96(1) of the Charter), and other organs of the United Nations and the specialised agencies when authorised by the General Assembly, in relation to legal questions arising within the scope of their activities (Article 96(2)). Any state entitled to appear before the court, or any "international organisation considered . . . as likely to be able to furnish information on the question," may submit written and oral pleadings (Article 66(2) of the statute).

The power of the court to decide whether it has jurisdiction

By Article 36(6) of the statute: "In the event of a dispute as to whether the Court has jurisdiction, the matter shall be settled by the decision of the Court." To judge by the case-law, this provision is in practice the most important part of the jurisdiction of the court. Few if any contentious cases start without consideration of the arguments of one of the parties that the International Court of Justice has no jurisdiction in the case in issue. An analysis of this case-law (or "jurisprudence" as it is often called) demonstrates that:

(a) the court will only assume jurisdiction once it is convinced that the parties consent thereto;

(b) it is sufficient if this consent was established as from the time of commencement of proceedings, although it may also be established by the conduct of the respondent thereafter (*see* below);

(c) the court will assume jurisdiction with respect to the respondent on one of three bases: where its competence arose before, at the time of, or after the submission of the case to the court.

Competence established before submission of the case to the court. This refers to cases where the respondent state has, *vis-à-vis* the applicant, a treaty obligation under which it has agreed to submit certain disputes to the jurisdiction of the International Court of Justice (or the Permanent Court of International Justice) and the dispute in issue is one such.

Competence established at the time of submission of the case to the court. This occures where the parties agree to submit the dispute to the International Court of Justice by virtue of a special agreement or *"compromis"*. Unlike the *compromis* in a case of arbitration, submission to the International Court of Justice obliges the parties to participate in the entire hearing of the case up to judgment, and to comply with the judgment.

Competence established after submission of the case to the court of the applicant (forum prorogatum). While the governing principle in the exercise of jurisdiction by the court has always been the "consent of the parties", it is one of the very conceptions of justice that consent may be as much implied from actions, as expressed in words. Where a state, designated as "respondent" by an "applicant" state, first pleads to the substance of the charge and only subsequently alleges that the court lacks jurisdiction, the court may nevertheless imply consent from its conduct and assume jurisdiction. It is, however, significant that in the one case, the *Corfu Channel (Preliminary Objection) Case* (I.C.J., 1949), in which this occurred, the respondent (Albania) refused, and refuses to this day, to comply with the judgment.

Procedure before the court

The principal difference between arbitral and judicial procedure is that in the former the parties may withdraw at any time, while in the latter they are obliged to remain subject to the power of the court until it has given final judgment. As a general rule, hearings before the court are given in public, those before an arbitral tribunal in private. The procedure is in both cases *contradictoire* (the evidence of one party is given in the presence of the other party, and may be contradicted). While the "decision of the Court has no binding force except between the parties and in respect of that particular case" (Article 59 of the statute), the jurisprudence of the court has shown an admirable consistency. In this respect, the Permanent Court of International Justice and the International Court of Justice may be considered as one World Court.

Index